ESCHATOLOGICAL OPTIMISM

Daria Platonova Dugina

Translated by Jafe Arnold

Edited by John Stachelski

2023

PRAV Publishing
www.pravpublishing.com
prav@pravpublishing.com

Translation copyright © 2023 PRAV Publishing

All rights reserved. No part of this book may be reproduced or distributed in any form or by any means, electronic or mechanical, including photocopying, recording, or by any information storage and retrieval, without permission in writing from the publisher.

Cover images:
Front: Son/Videnie (2023) by Makar Bogdanov
Back: Die Toteninsel (1883) by Arnold Böcklin

ISBN 978-1-952671-78-4 (Paperback)
ISBN 978-1-952671-77-7 (Hardcover)
ISBN 978-1-952671-79-1 (Ebook)

TABLE OF CONTENTS

FROM THE TRANSLATOR AND PUBLISHER	**9**
FROM THE EDITOR: ON AND FOR DASHA	**13**
FOREWORD - THE MAIDEN SLAIN BY THE RAY OF THE LOGOS	**17**
PART I: ESCHATOLOGICAL OPTIMISM	**35**
Eschatological Optimism: Sources, Development, and Main Directions	37
Eschatological Optimism and the Metaphysics of War	73
Athos, the Feminine Principle, Apophaticism, and Eschatological Optimism	115
PART II: THE FEMININE PRINCIPLE AND THE PROBLEM OF THE SUBJECT	**121**
Woman and Tradition	123
The War of the Sexes	131
Homo Hierarchicus: Tripartite Anthropology and the Experience of Hierarchical Society	139
The Man of Light in Iranian Sufism	177
The Sublime and the Aesthetics of Great Pan	181
The Poor Subject	183
The Russian Kitezhian, Oleg Fomin-Shakhov	185
Andrei Bely's Petersburg and Infernal Russia	187
The Political Subject of Populism and the Problem of "Unhappy Consciousness"	195

PART III: NEOPLATONISM AND THE IDEAL *POLIS*   203

    The Political Philosophy of Proclus Diadochus   205

    The Political Platonism of Emperor Julian   259

    Julianism   269

    Emperor Julian, Empire, and Neoplatonism   277

    The Apophatic Moment   281

    Apophatic Tradition in the Theology of Dionysius
    the Areopagite   289

PART IV: PHILOSOPHICAL FRAGMENTS AND THE INVOLUTION OF MODERNITY   295

    The Voluptuous Universe of Lucretius Carus   297

    Wolffian Theology and Gogol's Insight into Decay   303

    Bergson and Popper's "Open Society": A Traditionalist View   315

    Dark Deleuze: A Postmodern Reading of Leibniz's Monadology   331

AFTERWORD - DARIA DUGINA: PHILOSOPHY AS DESTINY   341

ESCHATOLOGICAL OPTIMISM

Daria Alexandrovna 'Platonova' Dugina
(1992-2022)

From the Translator and Publisher

The book you are holding in your hands cannot open without acknowledging the shocking, painful fact that determined its existence. This book has come to be because of the early, tragic death of its author. On the night of 20 August 2022, four months before her 30th birthday, Daria Alexandrovna 'Platonova'[1] Dugina was killed in an act of terrorism. Daria's life was cut short by a bomb detonated in her car while she was on her way back to Moscow from the Tradition Festival of Literature and Music in Zakharovo, where she spoke alongside her father, the premier Russian philosopher and geopolitician, Alexander Dugin. Daria's death — her murder, her assassination — immediately became an event of international significance. We can find some redemptive solace in the fact that in the year that has passed since her ascension, Daria Platonova Dugina's name and legacy have resounded around the world. The mentions paid to her by world leaders and figures, including presidents, ministers, and even the Pope, the honors awarded to her posthumously, the works of art and monuments raised to embody her as a symbol and as an idea, the streets and squares named in her honor, and diverse other initiatives dedicated to her — all of these and other instances of Daria Platonova Dugina's entry into the historical record have already reached such a scale that their enumeration would require a separate text.

This book is yet another testimony to Daria, but one of a special, unique, even singular sort: it is an invitation and window into Daria's own thinking, a mosaic exhibit of her spiritual activity, a glimpse into the landscapes and dynamics

---

1 "Platonova" was the pen name under which the majority of Daria Dugina's works — including television appearances, journalistic and philosophical texts, conference presentations, lectures, etc. — appeared in her lifetime. She adopted the name out of her deep spiritual and intellectual attachment to the founding father of philosophy, Plato. That being said, whoever endeavors to further research the origins, history, and associations of this name in Russia will also encounter cases of martyrdom and renowned authorship.

of her worldview, an opportunity to read and hear her words on diverse occasions. Above all else, this book affords the unique possibility which many people around the world had, yet still many did not: the opportunity to think with Daria Platonova Dugina as she truly was, i.e., as a philosopher, a contemplator, a person for whom ideas are a matter of life (and death).

Although the lines and thoughts that compose this book are hers, and indeed the very title of this book, *Eschatological Optimism*, is the name of the foremost intuition which Daria was pursuing on the eve of her death, the publication of this book is something she could not have foreseen any more than she could have foretold her own sudden martyrdom. However, there is a glaring, mysterious connection between the thoughts which preoccupied Daria and which appear in this book and their resonance with her death. We dare not say any more on this; instead, we leave this intuition to readers' own experiences, discernments, and interpretations. What we can say decisively is that *Eschatological Optimism* is the definitive philosophical testimony of Daria Platonova Dugina. Opened with a foreword by her father, Alexander Dugin, and closed with an afterword by her mother, Natalia Melentyeva, this book consists of a collection of Daria's lectures, talks, conference and seminar presentations, essays, articles, academic treatises[2], and notes, including those published in her lifetime and those hitherto unpublished, which have been compiled and edited by her family, friends, colleagues, and admirers. In Russia, this volume is being published alongside an edition of her diary and poetry, *The Depths and Heights of My Heart* (*Topi i vysi moego serdtsa*, Moscow: ACT, 2023).

Many things could be said, have already been said, and will still be said about Daria by many people around the world, by

---

2   It is unfortunate for the world that Daria did not have the time to complete her doctoral dissertation at Moscow State University on Neoplatonic political philosophy. Fortunately, some of Daria's works anticipating her dissertation, such as her MA thesis and papers on the same topic, can be found here under the third section, "Neoplatonism and the Ideal *Polis*."

those who knew her personally[3] as well as those who experienced her intellect and personality from afar. It is a testimony not only to the lingering rawness of her death, but just as much to her personality and character, that it remains difficult to write about her in the impersonal, "official," "historical" way as Platonova or Dugina. Hopefully, the publication of *Eschatological Optimism* will alleviate this for readers and future writers by showing that Daria's name indicates an historic trajectory of thought, a philosophical life, and that her fate bears similarities to at least two major figures of the ancient philosophy which she loved, lived, and breathed. The first is Socrates, who wrote no texts before his political execution and whose thinking was therefore bequeathed to be carried on and immortalized by those who had heard his words and thought alongside him, all the while knowing that their records and interpretations could never adequately capture and convey the original experience of the inceptual thinker. The second is Hypatia, one of the first and most renowned female philosophers. Hypatia represented the school that was Daria's foremost interest and academic engagement, Neoplatonism, and she was likewise murdered for her views and political counsel. Thankfully, unlike Socrates, Daria did commit many of her thoughts and observations to writing, and unlike Hypatia's, these writings survive. *Eschatological Optimism* is at once an intensive and extensive exhibit of Daria's oeuvre which has been elected to be brought forth to the world.

Daria Platonova Dugina was fluent in — which is to say that she thought, felt, read, wrote, and expressed herself in — Russian, French, and English, and she was well-studied in Church Slavonic and Ancient Greek. In translating this volume into English, I have attempted to balance between these languages relevant to Daria's intellect, soul, and person, i.e.,

---

3   My own words for Daria have hitherto taken on the form of the text "Memento Mori, In Memoriam — Daria Platonova Dugina", *Continental-Conscious* (8/10/2022) [https://continentalconscious.com/2022/10/08/memento-mori-in-memoriam-daria-platonova-dugina/] and a social media post republished by Katehon / Tsargrad Institute as "Eschatological Optimism of Darya Dugina" (4/3/2023) [https://katehon.com/en/article/eschatological-optimism-darya-dugina].

between upholding her primordial Russian tone and structure, following the flow and abruptions of the French that she loved, and juggling between Daria's own manner of speaking English, the existing English translations of sources which she cites and discusses, and the spirit of authentic English that might convey both the archaic and contemporary resonances of her philosophizing. In other words, my translation is based on my hearing and interpretation of Daria's own translations and of the possibilities of translating her multi-lingual interpretations. When it comes to the authors and texts with which Daria dealt, especially the ancient Greek sources, this has been no easy feat. Hence, let the qualification be voiced that, on the one hand, one should always return to the source, as Daria did, and on the other, that these texts showcase dynamic thinking and interpreting rather than stringent philologism, in keeping with what she felt was most important.

It is a tremendous honor and pledge that Daria Platonova Dugina's Eschatological Optimism is being brought to the world by PRAV Publishing. In fact, when PRAV Publishing was still a nascent vision, idea, and plan for the future, Daria was one of the first of less than a handful of individuals across the world to know of it and to offer thoughts on its potential realization. It also happened to be the case that my last exchange with Daria regarded the final PRAV publication she lived to receive. It is both my hope and PRAV's that Daria will receive and bless this volume as well, and that it will inspire countless readers to embark upon the path of thinking in a time and world in which the βιος θεωρητικος and φιλοσοφία can turn out to mean a real eruption and illumination of possibilities.

- Jafe Arnold
PRAV Publishing
1 June 2023

From the Editor: On and For Dasha

The nations will be addled, the seas will all wilt,
but the dawns will be embroidered with lustrous silks,
And our girls, in remembrance of the end of an age,
will detach and spread over the paradisal lay.

- Nikolai Kluev

Had we of sacred cause come together in some momentary omniscience to elect a perfect martyr, I suspect we would lack the strength to make a truly consummate choice. We are therefore blessed to be the subjects of a God merciful enough to spare us from tasks like that once asked of Abraham, whose faith was so faultless he willingly raised an axe over his own child. If called to make such a choice, would we falter in our adoration, and thus fail to be true eschatological optimists? We have been spared many of these overwhelming decisions: despite our weaknesses, doubts and fears, we have been chosen to experience a time of supreme heroism, and God has exalted our lives and this moment by welcoming the only martyr adequate to the scale of what is emerging.

No one knew the day nor the hour - Lord, how those torpid years shifted without warning into spasms of violence and bedlam, how those once cryptic prophecies in their mordant irony so abruptly began to unveil the advent of apocalypse and loss. With our arms outstretched like quivering whiskers, we were thrust into the aphotic fog of war, unsteadily inching forward until the density of sorrow and confusion began to fully envelop us, until we began to feel an unyielding panic, as though we were desperately struggling to claw our way out of a tight black sack... And the moment we began to accept that we would soon be engulfed and devoured by these naked days, the light of a martyr's *auto-da-fé* illuminated our path, freeing us from the bestial fear of death's invincibility. Daria Dugina leads us.

To me, she was Dasha, a beloved friend and my godmother, tasked with guiding me through the mystery of an eschatological religion at a time of apocalypse, helping me "move ever closer toward the Russian Dasein," as she once described it. To this end, she gifted me, at the very beginning of my journey, a copy of the Gospel of John, the last and most final of the Gospels. Ironically, the most critical wisdom she shared with me was that not all of us are called to risk our lives in battle, that those of us who have received 'the Call' have other means of answering it. At the height of my own rage and zeal, she encouraged me to remain at my position on the noetic front; my most earnest hope is that this book and these words honor that wish.

In her philosophy, Dasha reflected on a painful consensus among some of the greatest thinkers of the past few centuries: that the brutality of war has the unique property of revealing elements of the truth and purpose of man. "War", she writes, "is a key point and moment in the strategy of resisting the world of illusion. It is a challenge to the world, a revolt against it, a desire to subordinate it to sacred will, to saddle it like a force, a stream, and to carry out a *coup d'état* in the name of higher values." Philosophers such as Hegel, Heidegger, and Dostoevsky are first among those who also understood war as something more than "politics by other means." Moral or immoral, justified or belligerent, the existential ramifications of war unearth deeply rooted truths hidden within the fractaling mazes of discourse *das Man* erects to protect itself from the horror of its own authenticity and mortality.

This is precisely why, despite the West's century-long love affair with Russian literature, it was inevitable that history would extinguish attempts to turn the deeply patriotic, conservative and Orthodox Dostoevsky into another cosmopolitan "Existentialist" of world literature. It was inevitable that the powerful spiritual truths of his, and other national texts, would become too stark a challenge to our global unipolar order as its cracking foundations began to induce defensive belligerence. Peace is a labyrinth. In peace-time, ideas are so easily warped and stretched grotesquely - but the seeds of truth in great writing grow again wherever buried. Dostoevsky wrote that "War develops in [man] love of his fellow men and brings nations together by teaching them esteem for each other. War rejuvenates men," a quotation now repeated ad nauseam as 'proof' of Russian culture's eternal ethical implication in the 'crime' of its own statehood (though ironically, things are so dire that even the pacifist Tolstoy is now threatened with excommunication from the canon). However, the vitriolic renegotiation of Russia's place in world literature and culture is ultimately a testament to the complex truth of Dostoevsky's statement: few on either side of the current geopolitical conflict would argue that recent events haven't resulted in new, unexpected and deep national alignments. Things, in fact, are rarely quite so clear: truth often swims so deeply that we can't even see the ripples at the surface. But war, like philosophy, plumbs those depths.

And what do we make of Dostoevsky's invocation here of "love," that ineffable idea at the center of the human experience with its proverbial proximity to war? It is there we find the center of the Orthodox and Russian *Weltanschauung* that Dasha championed throughout her too short life: an attentiveness to contradictions that defy rational categorization, truths one can arrive at only through the paradoxical combination of affirmation and negation, and the central importance of the intersection of life and death as represented in the cross. Anyone who knew Dasha will attest to the fact that she embodied this book's titular optimism in her politics and faith, and I will add that in her thoughts and actions, I have rarely met someone so clearly and deeply guided by love.

As prophesied, this moment in history is characterized by the collision of contradictions and the unwinding of a chaotic reversal of signs: war and peace, empire and liberator, philosopher and combatant - it is therefore perfect that Daria's prescription of eschatological optimism was born of reading Emil Cioran's profound ontological pessimism. Daria's martyrdom is the last and ultimate reversal of the stranded human type explored in her philosophy, a final tug which unties the knots and unfastens the encumbering layers: it is the same one once promised in Christ's triumph over death. While there are certainly those for whom death is the end, for whom one's demise is tantamount to defeat, this book attests to the fact that others do indeed find transcendence, and that in her dormition, this book's author has achieved the supreme victory she yearned for in her life and thought - and that perhaps there is hope for us yet.

- John Stachelski
11 July 2023

- FOREWORD -

The Maiden Slain by the Ray of the Logos

The Moment of *Sophia*

It is very difficult for me to write about Daria, because, especially in recent times, she had become everything to me: a friend, a thinker, a joy to be cherished, a partner in dialogue, a source of inspiration, and a pillar of support. The pain from losing her doesn't dare subside; on the contrary, all of it persistently flares up with ever renewed force. Nevertheless, I understand that it is necessary to open her book, *Eschatological Optimism*, with words that she herself would have liked to hear and which might be useful to the reader.

Daria Dugina was a thinker, a philosopher. She was such organically and wholeheartedly. Yes, she was at the very beginning of her philosophical path, and some thoughts and ideas require a long time, sometimes many years (and others many centuries), to be thought through, but that is another matter. Something fundamental is decided before all else: whether you are a philosopher or not. Daria was a philosopher. This means that, whatever her path through the worlds of philosophy could have been, the beginning of her path is already valuable, important, and deserving of attention. The most difficult thing of all is to get into the territory of philosophy, to find an entrance into the closed palace of the king. One can besiege its walls for as long as one likes, yet still remain outside of it. To break through and find oneself in this most securely guarded palace depends on the vocation, the Call, that the genuine thinker hears in their depths. Daria heard this call.

Aristotle distinguished between two kinds of systematic thinking involved in philosophy. The first is the moment of *sophia* (σοφία), the sudden and instantaneous flash of the mind, the illuminating insight of the Logos. Such a flash might occur in one's youth, adulthood, or old age. It might not happen at all. According to legend, Heraclitus claimed that up to a certain moment he knew nothing, and then he knew everything all at once. This is the moment of *sophia*. For Heraclitus, as for Aristotle, the Logos is one and indivisible. If someone has been granted the honor of experiencing its presence, they henceforth become a different kind of human: a philosopher. Henceforth, whatever this person thinks, wherever they turn their gaze, they now act and live in the rays of the Logos, in communion with its unity. This is what happens when one is initiated into philosophy. In Plato's *Republic*, this is called *noesis* (νόησις), the capacity to raise individual intellectual conclusions up to the primordial and supreme world of eternal ideas. Daria Dugina bore this mark. She passed through the moment of *sophia*, and it was irreversible.

Her *Phronesis*

There is yet another, second kind of thinking. Aristotle called it *phronesis* (φρόνησῖς), and Heraclitus pejoratively called it "polymathy," that is "having much knowledge" (which, in his opinion, "does not teach the mind"). In Plato, this corresponds to *dianoia* (διάνοια), or that rational thinking which does not collect everything together into one, but divides everything into parts, classes, and categories. If *sophia* comes instantly (or never), then *phronesis* necessarily requires time, experience, study, reading, observation, exercise, and diligence. *Phronesis* is also important. The crux lies in this: if the experience of *sophia* has taken place, then further exercise of the mind is always built around the immutable axis of the Logos. If it has not, then *phronesis* becomes something like common, mundane wisdom, which is, of course, valuable, useful, and deserving of all sorts of praise, but has nothing to do with philosophy. No matter how much phronetic people may exercise reading, analysis, and rational operations, if they have not previously entered the closed palace of philosophy, then their activity — no matter how stubborn and intensive — remains like wandering around the outskirts. This might be technically useful, but it nonetheless remains something completely exterior and, in some sense, profane.

It is in this sense that Daria's *phronesis* stood only at the very beginning of a great philosophical path. She was just beginning to master philosophy on the fundamental level, to deepen her knowledge of theories and systems, to become fully acquainted with the history of thought, theology, and the infinite field of culture.

Here, perhaps, is the most important point of this book, *Eschatological Optimism*. This is a book of living thought. What is important here is not the scale, depth, or sheer volume of the theories, names, and authors cited in it. What is important is how a genuine philosopher reveals, lives, and embodies what they think in their very being. What is important is that they think philosophically, in the light of Sophia. Herein lies the novelty and freshness of this book. In the end, Daria writes and speaks not in order to move outwards to meet diverging lines of interpretations and observations of details, but to invite those to whom it speaks to make their journey inward, to live philosophy, to commit to a "turn" (ἐπιστροφή), as the Neoplatonists called it, and which Daria reiterates by no coincidence. This turn is key to her. Having experienced *Sophia*, she wanted to help others — readers, listeners, all of us — to experience the same illuminating insight by the Logos. Her book consists of multifaceted and widely differing approaches to the closed court of the king — in one place there is an imperceptible breach in the wall, in another there is an underground passage, in another there is a low-lying fence. Whoever has been inside knows how to enter, how to exit, and how to return.

Therefore, Daria Dugina's book is initiatic and dedicatory. For someone who has the gift, the calling, the will to philosophy, this book might become a revelation. For phronetic people, it might be a useful and concise encyclopedia of Platonism. For aesthetes, it might be a model of graceful thinking. For those seeking the mystery of Russia, this book might be a humble milestone along such a difficult and noble path.

Daria as a Sign

Daria Dugina's book is also a sign. Martin Heidegger complained that people who are deaf to the true call of the Logos tend to take the sign, the icon, or something pointing to something else to be self-sufficient. In this lies philosophical idolatry. The meaning, significance, and predestined purpose of a sign is that it points not to itself, but towards something else. Its appeal is such: look not at me, but at what I point to, for in this is I myself, my mission, my nature, my calling; I am not the answer, but I know the way to the answer and I am bringing you to know it; I am not the content, but only the map, which by following you might leave the realm of omnipresent, all-encompassing superficiality and move into the depths and up to the heights of living, meaningful being. It is no coincidence that Daria Dugin's second book is called *The Depths and Heights of My Heart* (*Topi i vysi moego serdtsa*, Moscow: ACT, 2023).

Daria always thought of herself as a sign and her philosophical works as a compiled guide. She did not pretend or claim that this sign would be the final and conclusive one, or that her map was complete and displayed all of the most important nodes and objects in the world of ideas. She was a modest thinker, she knew what philosophical tact is, what a boundary is, and what happens when you go beyond such a boundary. Hence why she was so attentive to the topic of the Frontier (to which another work by Daria is devoted). In her texts, talks, and presentations, she pointed only to those segments of the philosophical path that she knew or which she had not yet passed, but which drew her towards them, promising revelations, encounters, comprehensions, and maybe even bitter disappointments. But such is the philosophical life. Any and all of her experiences of this life are invaluable.

The Philosophical Hero

Daria is a philosopher furthermore because her whole life, from her birth to her tragic death, proceeded in complete harmony with the primal element of philosophy. The main point of orientation in our family is Tradition, and this means that philosophy is conceived primarily as religious, vertical, oriented towards God and heaven, where the beginnings and principles of thought must be sought. The absolute truth conveyed to us in the Gospel of John, "In the beginning was the Logos" ('Εν ἀρχῇ ἦν ὁ λόγος), is the guiding star. Daria Dugina was killed by the enemy when we were returning from the Tradition Festival. Tradition is the beginning and the end, the alpha and the omega. In her philosophical fate, Daria's omega, the point of end, was pierced by the same ray, the ray of the Logos.

Daria Dugina became a philosophical heroine. She descended into the world along the ray of the Logos and ascended back up along it into heaven. The seal of martyrdom was placed onto her thought, her mission, her intellectual life. Such is worth — and costs — a lot.

The ancient Greeks could not accept that a true thinker might leave forever, die, and disappear. They were sure that a devotee of the Logos, loyal to the very end, to the omega, does not die, but becomes a new star in the eternal, celestial horizon of ideas, or even becomes a god. Socrates and Plato were revered by entire generations of followers who were sensitive to philosophy as incarnations of Apollo, and the Neoplatonist Plotinus was seen as the figure of Rhadamanthus, the eternal judge who came into the world to remind people submerged in time of the unchanging radiance of eternity.

Christianity left such pagan notions behind, yet it raised the feat to an even higher, previously unthinkable pedestal. Now God himself, the Logos itself, came into the corporeal world, became a man, suffered, was killed, resurrected, and ascended to heaven, to the eternal throne due to him. After Jesus Christ, this path was followed by a whole host of Christian saints and martyrs. They set off to follow the Logos, suffered for Him, died in Him, were resurrected in Him, and ascended to heaven. In Christianity, moreover, no one merely disappears without a trace. Those who have given their lives for their friends, for Christ, the Son of God, for the Logos, and for luminous, vertical thought, are all the more alive and shall shine from the eternal heavens for those of us who remain here.

One must not only be born and live as a philosopher, but die as a philosopher. And to do so in full accordance with one's spirit, one's faith, with the sign pointing upwards to the heavens is the essence of the true thinker. A genuine philosopher cannot but be a hero. The tragic seal imprinted on the philosopher's life is the highest recognition. Only that which grows out of suffering is genuine and worthy. Such is the lot of those in the world who carry within themselves something that is not of this world. This is the source of the philosophical grief that Daria lived so penetratingly, and which she pursued not as a girl, not as a child, but gallantly and courageously.

Eschatological Optimism: Towards Theory

The main topic of this book, which consists of Daria Dugina's philosophical essays, is "eschatological optimism," as is thematized in the title. It is best to follow Daria herself here, as she tries to define this notion not in strictly rational terms, but empirically and phenomenologically, sharing her experience of living and experiencing this idea and inviting those who are drawn to this experience. In some sense, Daria authored the concept of "eschatological optimism" as such. It is of no importance whether we find it among her favorite authors (Cioran, Evola, Jünger) or imagine it to be something original and the first in a line that would lead us to read philosophical and cultural theories from an altogether specific angle. The point is not in words, but in how certain terms, expressions, or phrases become a method, a means of deciphering, a basis for interpreting.

"Eschatological optimism" is a paradox. It is a combination of doomed fatalism and the triumph of free will, an acute experience of the world's collapse and faith in the victory of the spirit, a faith which is rendered only more ardent by the fact that it has no confirmation. The eschatological optimist is capable of synthesizing and experiencing at once and to the extreme the highest degree of despair as well as an all-consuming, joyful hope. The end of the former is the beginning of the latter. The pain of the end is the joy of another beginning. But we, as humans belonging to two worlds at the same time, should not avoid suffering the doom of this world. Our calling is to suffer along with it, alongside its collapse, its imperfection, and its perversions and slide into the abyss. The human being is a suffering creature. This is not to be avoided. After all, such is our destiny, our fate. Otherwise, why would our God have suffered on the cross? He suffered, and that means that we should do the same. This world is already the end of a world, and this pain permeates all of its structures, all of its layers, all of its levels. If we are attentive, then we will read on these pages how being suffers, how the universe cries. Its tears are our souls, our thoughts, our laborious dreams.

But there is yet another side of things. Eternal heaven is so far away, so inaccessible, so unattainable, yet it is within us. To be more precise, if we are to be extremely keen to experiencing that which is not inside us, if we are to build our lives around this ontological perforation, this black hole, then one day a new star will be born within — the star of the hidden realm, the "un-evening" [*nevechernii*] light of resurrection. Then, at some turning point of grief, nearly imperceptibly to the eschatological optimist themself, the darkness will turn into light. Heaven will be at arm's length. Unexpectedly and abruptly. Like an explosion.

Platonism and Christianity

Daria Dugina was a Platonic philosopher, a Platonist. To this we should add: she was an Orthodox Christian Platonic philosopher. Brought up since her childhood on the ideas of the Traditionalists (René Guénon, Julius Evola, Mircea Eliade, and their followers) as well as Orthodox Christian culture (Daria, like us, her parents, belonged to *Edinoverie* and to the Old Believers' Rite of the Russian Orthodox Church tradition), Daria discovered Plato and the Platonists at the very beginning of her studies at the Faculty of Philosophy at Moscow State University. It all started with Dionysius the Areopagite, the pinnacle of Christian Platonism. Areopagitism became her guiding star allowing her to connect Orthodox Christian theology with the Platonic universe. The deeper she went in her studies in Platonism, the further she discovered an organic connection with Orthodoxy and with Traditionalism. The Traditionalist philosophers themselves mentioned Plato only in passing without focusing much attention on him. In Christianity, following the hasty and intellectually controversial judgments passed on Origen in the Justinian era, a steady distrust of Plato's teachings took hold. The very fact that the foundation of Christian theology itself — Orthodoxy — in its terminology, conceptualization, structure, meaning, orientation, etc., was developed by the Alexandrian school and its direct successors, the Cappadocian Fathers (the most vibrant representatives of Christian Platonism), led to it finding itself in the shadow of sharp anti-Platonic attacks. Of course, this affair was aggravated by the Monophysites, the Monothelites, and later by the obviously unsuccessful theological seeking of the disciples of Michael Psellos and John Italus. Finally, in the Palamite polemic, the opponents of St. Gregory Palamas, Barlaam and Akindynos, tried to substantiate the criticism of hesychasm with reference to Plato. However, if we look deeper and we abstract from these historical vicissitudes, in which the cultural and even political context played a large role that was not directly connected to the world of ideas, then the unity of the attunement, verticality, and the unconditional devotion to heaven, eternity, and higher horizons of being brings Platonism close to Christianity beyond any doubt. The first Christian apologists were well aware of this, and the Cappadocian St. Basil the Great, the supreme authority of Christian Orthodoxy (and, in fact, a follower of Origen, whose texts he compiled into the first volumes of the *Philokalia* alongside his associates St. Gregory the Theologian and Gregory of Nysa), urged Christians to acquaint themselves with the works of the Hellenic teachers. Finally, if we turn to the Greek originals, then the Areopagitic texts are at times simply indistinguishable from the works of Proclus and his school.

When Daria discovered this, she was completely seized by Platonism, and in many ways she inspired those close and beloved to her — naturally, philosophers — to commit to indepth studies in Platonism.

Moreover, Daria took note of the astonishing closeness between Plato, the Neoplatonists, and the European Traditionalists, between whom she discovered a complete unity of ontologies: the Traditionalists had described an ontology that is approximately and polemically opposite to that of the fragmentary and distorted ontologies of Modernity, and the Platonists had an extremely developed, detailed, and fully expounded ontology, one no worse than the Hindu Advaita-Vedanta. Daria thereby discovered the possibility of essentially expanding the language of Traditionalism, insofar as we can fully incorporate Platonism as a thoroughly correct version of traditional metaphysics into Traditionalist philosophy. For those who understand the meaning of language, this is simply an incredibly significant discovery.

In condensed form, all of these considerations are contained in this book, *Eschatological Optimism*, in which Platonism is treated and referenced in a whole section as well as throughout the various texts and discourses compiled into this volume.

Daria's thought harmoniously and subtly synthesizes Orthodox Christianity, Traditionalism, and Platonism, strengthening and reinforcing what is paradigmatically common among them instead of putting them into contradiction and conflict. Daria even treats Julian the Apostate in the context of political Platonism and the metaphysics of Empire — the basis of the Emperor's Katechontic mission in the pure Christian understanding — rather than in the sense of a polytheistic restoration. This is a bold move, but it is grounded in the whole structure of her philosophical worldview. It is not an attempt at revising Orthodox Christian tradition, which for Daria was to the very end the highest and only truth, but rather a drawing of attention to the paradigmatic likeness of the structure — and that is an altogether different matter.

The Poor Little Subject

Daria Dugina devoted much attention to the problem of the subject. Even in her early youth, she noticed, quite naively but with astonishing accuracy, that a weak subject predominates in Russian culture, in our society and people. She called such the "poor subject" or even the "poor little subject." To be honest, we even teased her about this. After all, despite all the correctness of such a discernment, we thought it was not worth dwelling on. But this idea fascinated Daria, and she repeatedly returned to this formulation. In a womanly way, she felt sorry for this "poor Russian subject" that was so tender, helpless, and clumsy, yet so dear, kindred, and beloved. Daria could sympathize with and share the pain of another person. Even when there was nobody nearby who deserved care and compassion, she would manage to find someone. The concept of the "poor subject" became the expression of this deep feeling of her soul. She pitied not some person or creature, but a concept, an idea. Hers was a deep, spiritual, philosophical pity.

This concept conditioned her path in many ways. On the one hand, she felt that in none other than the "poor subject" lies some kind of truth that is difficult to formulate, some hidden revelation, some kind of difficult, tragic, painful truth. Pushkin's protagonists were piercingly clear to her, especially

Samson Vyrin from *The Stationmaster*, or Evgeny in *The Bronze Horseman*, the mad Akaky Akakievich in Gogol's *Overcoat*, or the drunken Marmeladov in *Crime and Punishment*. Behind the feebleness of ordinary, weak Russians incapable of defending themselves, Daria erased their banality and divined their hidden greatness, their heroic fidelity to some hidden, unspoken truth and a secret, mysterious Russian message to the world. Sure, Russians are weak, feeble, and mad, but there is something else inside them, and this something else piercingly and acutely resounds to those whose ears are attuned to the Russian wave. Daria loved the "poor subject," because only a woman, in her boundless, inexhaustible, pitying tenderness, in the infinity of her compassion, in her sacrificing, in her purely feminine majesty, so inaccessible to the other sex, can love such a subject.

At the same time, Daria carried within herself the will for a strong, steadfast, courageous, heroic subject. Russian weakness and poverty gave rise within her to an unbridled desire to make up for and seize such with her own strength. A powerful, strong-willed, deep, and active subject should be born not against, but out of such weakness. What is of foremost importance is to not become like the cold intellectualism of the West, which knows neither compassion nor pity, is deaf to feebleness and poverty, and is haughty and individualistic. This is not what Russian strength is about; this is not how the Russian subject is supposed to be built. The Russian subject is to be strong in sacrifice, courageous in serving the whole — the people, the state, the Church — and deep and wise not for the sake of boasting, but in order to pass on the light seen at the heights of contemplation to others, to the unfortunate prisoners at the bottom of the cave. A strong subject, a Russian hero, is first and foremost a sacrifice. This sacrificial victim knows that his fate is tragic, that his path is one of suffering, but he consciously chooses this path and wishes for no other path for himself.

Daria cultivated will, intellect, and deep, steadfast, powerful, and heroic subjectivity. This was her conscious choice. But this power that she accumulated and compelled herself to cultivate within was originally not for herself alone. By virtue of some kind of astonishing fatality, she knew that she was fated to become a hero, to sacrifice for the sake of the people and the Russian Idea. Her strong, powerful subjectivity was deliberately oriented towards surrendering itself to weakness, to igniting by its own fire the corruption of the weak little subjects of a semi-living society, so that they would be kindled and filled with her power which would become their own.

Who could have known that this fire would be the flame of a young philosopher's car blown up by enemies when she was returning from the peaceful Tradition Festival at Pushkin's Zakharovo estate. Even talking about this is horrific, but she and no other saw the path of the hero that she always wanted to become.

Daria Dugina's Feminism

For Daria, the question of sex and gender was of great importance. Following the philosophy of Traditionalism and above all Julius Evola's *Metaphysics of Sex*, she was raised on the fact that man and woman represent two metaphysical worlds. No direct analogies between them are reliable. Every detail, not to mention something more, carries a different meaning, a different purpose, a different form, and different substance in the world of man and in the world of woman. Daria saw in this the richness of being. It is enough to accept this, and instead of one universe, two open up before us. The relation between them is not at all reducible to the flat logic of power/subordination, completeness/lack, directness/curvature, presence/absence, etc. Everything is much more complicated, for each world has its own dimension, its own topology, its own semantic structures, its own languages and dialects. Daria seriously posed to herself the question of the language of women. After all, even when they are amongst themselves, women continue to speak the language of men. Only in rare moments — and above all when they are alone with infants — do women's deeply concealed sounds and syllables break out. They are relics of a forgotten, lost, primordial mother tongue submerged in the depths of the unconscious.

Daria took an interest in feminism, and one of the sections of *Eschatological Optimism* is dedicated to this topic. Here Daria finds herself before a dilemma. Women's desire to uphold their sovereignty in the face of toxic masculinity is understandable. There is something justified in it. After all, a woman is not a thing, not a slave, not property, not a second-class creature, and not an incorrigible fool — such is a male view that is, in fact, characteristic of a lower type of rude, carnal, primitive men. The higher the man, the more attentive he is to the feminine and the more delicate and subtle. But the fair posing of the question of women's dignity is almost never or extremely rarely brought to the fore in modern feminism. Feminists most often slip into one of three extremes: they demand complete equality with men (and by taking the values of the male world to be criteria for the norm, they thereby abolish their own sex and simply become "men"); they establish matriarchy, which only parodies the brutal domination of men; or they call for the abolition of sex altogether as something deliberately bearing inequality and stand in favor of asexual cyborgs.

Daria believes that this is not right. There must be another way out. She finds it in the standpoint of a feminism which insists on the autonomy of the two worlds, male and female, masculine and feminine. There should be no prescriptions for the feminine world. A woman true to her nature can choose and most likely will choose service to God in monasticism, service to family, children, to a wonderful and heroic man, to an idea, to a cause, to the affirmation of higher values. In so doing, she does not betray her sex, but allows the infinite wealth inherent in her sexual nature to reveal itself. The highest destiny of a woman, as well as a man, as Daria's beloved Plato said, is being a philosopher. Sure, woman is weaker and burdened with many worries, but this only means that she must work on herself more, keep up with everything and become even stronger, stronger than her weaknesses, and then her weaknesses will become her strengths, her surface will become her depth (as Nietzsche believed). This is a completely different feminism — Daria Dugina's feminism, which is quite compatible with Orthodoxy, patriotism, and reverence for the family.

Postmodernism on the Attack

Daria Dugina was interested in contemporary philosophy, especially Postmodernity and Postmodernism. Of course, her truth was elsewhere — in Tradition, Orthodoxy, and Platonism — but some aspects of Postmodernity fascinated her. Daria fairly deeply studied Lacan, Deleuze, and object-oriented ontology. A whole section of *Eschatological Optimism* is devoted to these studies.

Daria was fascinated by Postmodernity's entangled topos that has turned philosophical discourse into an ironic charade which, as it has unraveled, has not seen meanings cleared up and accumulated, but made more obscure, extinguished, flickering out on the farthest periphery, plunged into utter corporeal meaningless. For Daria Dugina, Postmodern philosophy and object-oriented ontology are the domain of philosophical demonology, analogous to the medieval legends of sorcerers' and heresiarchs' black miracles, a kind of *Hammer of Witches* which tells of what should not be done or uttered under any circumstances, but which some are nevertheless saying and doing. This is how a scout plunges into the completely alien and deeply disgusting identity of the enemy in order to peer into its final grounds. This is how Daria's strategy in her research into Postmodernism can be interpreted. Her experience was one of metaphysical reconnaissance carried out in enemy territory with the aim of studying their structures, communications, their operations and supply systems. In order to fight an enemy, it is first and foremost necessary to understand him, and to not succumb to his hypnosis and propaganda (as, alas, the vast majority of the Russian philosophical community does), but also to not plug one's ears and pretend that nothing is happening. It is happening. Armed with their own epistemological strategies, Postmodernity and object-oriented ontology are attacking the poor Russian subject and, taking advantage of the latter's weakness, are immersing themselves into the corrupted networks of moderated and controlled perversion.

Postmodernists and the advocates of speculative realism are good in that they openly declare their intentions. Deleuze called for turning the human being into a schizophrenic (schizomass) which, in his option, will, upon escaping reason, no longer be subject to "capitalist exploitation," and object-oriented ontologists call for abolishing the human being altogether and finally extinguishing even the residually smoldering subjectivity in man to make way for the triumph of Artificial Intelligence, neural networks, cyborgs, or some kind of deep ecology.

Daria was convinced that the Orthodox Christian thinker and Traditionalist philosopher is simply obliged to delve into figuring all of this out so that the exotic rhetoric does not take them by surprise and leave them defenseless. This is what she sorted out. And she generously shared the results of her quest with anyone interested.

Yet, Daria was only beginning to develop her studies on this front, and the most important, fundamental process of her systematic deconstruction of Postmodernity was abruptly cut short by her death. But it cannot end there. Daria Dugina persistently developed the philosophy of Traditionalism and drew upon her authorities and great predecessors. Her philosophical feat must be continued by those who take her place in the ranks. To this end, it is of principal importance to understand what she was heading towards. Upon dealing with the principles of her critique of Postmodernity and object-oriented ontology — with all the subtle ambiguity of her interpretations which partially played along with Postmodernist irony, turning it against those who imagined that the monopoly on the laughter that collapses structures belongs to them alone — her cause of deconstructing the pseudo-philosophy of modern and contemporary times can and must be continued. This is a testament for her unborn children, to all those who will take her place in the unbroken lineage of philosophers who have for centuries dwelled in the fields of the great Plato.

We are One in the Logos

To conclude this foreword, I would like to say the following. Those who only observe from the outside and do not plunge into the essence of thought might say to me: You as a philosopher are only attributing your own thoughts to your tragically killed daughter, and you won't find or hear them in her own texts and speeches, because she was completely different, she was her own individual with her own worldview and her own convictions. Of course, Daria was completely independent and original in her views. However, like myself, like my family, like my teachers and my followers, her deep individuality did not consist of a reduction of intellect to private, individual reasoning. Heraclitus's words — διὸ δεῖ ἕπεσθαι τῶι κοινῶι· ξυνὸς γὰρ ὁ κοινός. τοῦ λόγου δ' ἐόντος ξυνοῦ ζώουσιν οἱ πολλοὶ ὡς ἰδίαν ἔχοντες φρόνησιν, "it is necessary to follow the common, but although reason [*logos*] is common and universal, the majority live as if they had their own individual reason" — were for Daria (and for all of us and for all of "our own") the purest expression of the ultimate truth. The Logos cannot be the property of an individual. On the contrary, a person should belong to the Logos, follow it, honor it, and, if this following is true and correct, then we shall draw near to it as one, even while some differences remain. With Daria, we are one with the Logos, one in Christ and in His truth. We have been, are, and shall be.

Dasha is no more. But this is impossible. It just can't be. I believe that there is no me and no us without her. No one can convince me of her absence. No arguments can serve to do so. On the contrary, this book, *Eschatological Optimism*, convinces us that she is still here. These are not merely her notes, but the pulses of her mind, her spirit, her soul. This is the concept of her philosophical life. This life had a beginning, but it has no end.

— Alexander Dugin

***

PART I:
ESCHATOLOGICAL OPTIMISM

ESCHATOLOGICAL OPTIMISM: SOURCES, DEVELOPMENT, AND MAIN DIRECTIONS

I. Eschatological Optimism as an Idea and Life Standpoint

Eschatological Optimism as a Philosophical Interpretation and Life Strategy[4]

Today, I would like to give a lecture that is in a sense interactive, because all of the theses and hypotheses that I will voice still seem quite hazy to me. They are more like contours of thought, outlines of a project for beginning to think of the history of philosophy as a process. Therefore, I welcome questions during the lecture.

The topic of eschatological optimism is rather dangerous and complex. It is dangerous because it has yet to be developed until now, and is fraught with many traps and unexpected twists. While preparing for today's lecture, I realized that despite the fact that the hypothesis of "eschatological optimism" can explain many historical-philosophical processes, lend them additional dimensions, and open up new contexts with a certain depth, there nevertheless still remain a number of blank spots. My preparation was based on constantly questioning myself, searching for open problems and identifying inconsistencies. And yet, I think that I have every right to bring forward this hypothesis for discussion, as doctrines where things appear perfectly aligned are always actually imperfect and, even worse, boring.

Jean Baudrillard wrote that when one leaves this world, they must leave it no less complex than it was before. Therefore, I think

---

4   The present text is an edited transcript of a lecture delivered online to the Moscow-based Signum Open Lecture Forum on 6 November 2020.

that the presence of some contradictions and inconsistencies — for example, different readings of eschatology in antiquity and in the Christian context — complicate the study of eschatological optimism on the one hand, while preserving on the other the living principle of the process of thinking over the course of our open study of the topic.

To begin, I would like to note that eschatological optimism can be viewed from two angles. Firstly, it can be interpreted as a hypothesis for getting to know the historical-philosophical process, in which we can examine various thinkers as eschatological optimists and distinguish two main tendencies within their works: an acknowledgement of the catastrophic finitude and ephemeral nature of the world given to us (which we shall call "the finitude of illusion"), and, at the same time, a peculiar acceptance of this world as something that is deceptive and illusory, while maintaining an attitude of positive will towards this illusion. We could say that eschatological optimism is not simply an awareness that the end is near, of possible death, but also the acceptance of this death into one's life along with the decisive will to resist it, that is, to live. This means taking the side of pure transcendence and proclaiming a radical "No!" to this world while at the same time declaring a radical "Yes!" to the world that is to be found beyond this illusion.

In other words, we propose to interpret eschatological optimism as a certain way of reading a philosophical text which reveals how different thinkers exhibit a paradoxical combination of dwelling in a world that is finite and an illusion, a simulacrum, while at the same time having a positive, volitional approach to the end of this illusion. Many philosophers' texts can be read in this way, but today I will dwell especially on Platonism, Neoplatonism, the Hegelian system, Nietzscheanism, and especially on the works of the Romanian thinker Emil Cioran. This list alone is already intimidating, because an adequate treatment of such a corpus of texts, such an amplitude of the philosophical tradition, seems impossible, given that each philosopher and current deserves at least a separate lecture or even a whole course. Nevertheless, today we will try to get at least a little closer to this subject within the time allotted.

Secondly, eschatological optimism can be understood not only as an interpretive grid, not only as a code for deciphering one or another text, but also as a philosophical strategy for life. In fact, all of the thinkers I've just mentioned and brought into focus, were, in my opinion, eschatological optimists. They accepted the finitude of the world, but also adopted a will to live. You might recall that one of Guénon's books, *The Reign of Quantity and the Signs of the Times*, concludes with the formulation: *"La fin d'un monde n'est jamais et ne peut jamais être autre chose que la fin d'une illusion"* — "The end of a world never is and can never be anything but the end of an illusion."[5]

So, in addition to being a code for some of the philosophical currents that we'll be talking about today, eschatological optimism can also be a philosophical strategy for life as such. We are likely living in the era of the end of the world — this can be seen in the pandemic, in the various natural disasters that have become more frequent, and in the fundamental shifts in politics, geopolitics, and philosophy. After all, what is the point of things like the de-territorialized thinking of Postmodernity or object-oriented ontology!? This is the real end of philosophy, or at least of human philosophy. In such circumstances, we are in need of the life strategy of eschatological optimism. How are you supposed to live when you understand that some mythical substance called "coronavirus" is rhizomatically spreading around you? I myself am now self-isolating because of this phenomenon, the details of which are not entirely clear. In circumstances like these, eschatological optimism can be a starting point for life, for understanding the meaning of what is happening, for seeking strategies and the motivation to exist. It provides grounds to live with an orientation towards something other than the illusory given reality of the disintegrating and fragmenting world around us.

---

5   René Guénon, *The Reign of Quantity and the Signs of the Times*, trans. Lord Northbourne (Hillsdale: Sophia Perennis, 2004), 279.

Philosophical Unhappiness

I want to start with Platonism and think through two philosophical events: the experience of breaking with the horizon of immanence and the experience of the philosopher who has ascended to contemplate pure ideas and then makes a political return to the cave (I have in mind Plato's Cave, in which people lead a mechanical existence, blind and fixated only on vague shadows, deprived of the opportunity to contemplate true things, i.e., the ideas). In Plato's works, such as the *Republic*, I've been struck by the theme of "philosophical unhappiness," that is the unhappy misfortune of needing to dwell within an illusory reality. You might recall that in the beginning of the fourth book of Plato's *Republic*, there is a chain of reasoning that leads to the idea that the ruling estate of philosopher-guardians ought to seek happiness first and foremost for the whole, not for themselves. One of the participants in the dialogue, Adeimantus, points out to Socrates that such selfless service would make the philosopher-guardians themselves unhappy. He says:

> How would you defend yourself, Socrates, if someone told you that you aren't making these men very happy and that it's their own fault? The city really belongs to them, yet they derive no good from it. Others own land, build fine big houses, acquire furnishings to go along with them, make their own private sacrifices to the gods, entertain guests, and also, of course, possess what you were talking about just now, gold and silver and all the things that are thought to belong to people who are blessedly happy.[6]

Socrates then poses the question: "With this in mind, we should consider whether in setting up our guardians we are aiming to give them the greatest happiness, or whether... our aim is to see that the city as a whole has the greatest happiness."[7] He then arrives at a conclusion: let the philosopher not be happy, let him even be unhappy, but at the same time, he must protect the

---

6   Plato, *Republic* 419. [Throughout this volume, all translations and quotations of Plato are from the edition Plato, *Complete Works*, eds. John M. Cooper and D.S. Hutchinson, multiple translators (Indianapolis: Hackett Publishing Company, 1997) — Trans.]

7   Ibid., 421b.

entire *polis* as the guarantor of the happiness of all other estates. The philosopher-ruler will have happiness not for himself, but for his estate of contemplators. It is far more pleasant for the philosopher to remain in pure contemplation of the Supreme, but he is devoted to justice, and this compels him to think not only about himself, but about others, about the citizens of the state entrusted to him. In this case, his happiness will directly lie in personally being unhappy while the *polis* as a whole will be harmonious and observant of the balance needed for justice to reign.

This should catch our attention. The philosopher-ruler is to be unhappy? This is somewhat unexpected. Yes, he will be unhappy, but this is by virtue of the fact that the happiness of the lower estates and the values by which they live all belong to the sphere of illusion. Such is an illusory happiness. Moreover, all happiness is illusory. Everything is illusory except for the highest justice. The philosopher-ruler chooses "unhappiness" in the ordinary sense in order to reach the truth. Only self-sacrifice, sacrificing the personal for the sake of the common, makes the thinker truly happy.

Justice Above All

The second point that is extremely important for analyzing the role of the philosopher-ruler in Plato's *Republic* is the famous "myth of the cave" from the seventh book. I don't think I need to retell the myth in detail, as I believe my audience is already sufficiently versed in Platonism. I'll only very briefly recall the main moments of the myth.

The philosopher is the one who, unlike the rest of the prisoners chained at the bottom of the cave, is not content with watching the shadows on the wall, and so frees himself from his shackles and sets off to exit the cave in search of the source of the true light. He ascends along the path leading upwards, where he sees a religious procession carrying statues that cast the shadows on the wall which the prisoners take to be reality, although it is only an illusion. Further, the philosopher goes even higher to the fire burning at the entrance, and finally out into the light. He sees the true world — the sky, the earth, the stars, and the sun. Here a mystical experience takes place: what really is, what genuinely exists, is revealed to him. From here on, he can always distinguish true being from simulacra, fabrications, and shadows. This is an experience of total rupture with reality, or rather, with what he had previously accepted as reality up to the moment of exiting the cave. The reality he left behind turns out to be illusory. Here the philosopher is happy, but he is not just. Justice consists in his obligation to return after contemplating the true world, the pure Good, the Idea.

The thinker's personal happiness comes into conflict with the demand of justice. This is how it is presented in Plato. Socrates explains:

> It is our task as founders, then, to compel the best natures to reach the study we said before is the most important, namely, to make the ascent and see the good. But when they've made it and looked sufficiently, we mustn't allow them to do what they're allowed to do today.[8]

Socrates' further dialogue with Glaucon discloses his train of thought:

> [Glaucon:] What's that [that they're allowed to do today]?
>
> [Socrates:] To stay there and refuse to go down again to the prisoners in the cave and share their labors and honors, whether they are of less worth or of greater.
>
> [Glaucon:] Then are we to do them an injustice by making them live a worse life when they could live a better one?
>
> [Socrates:] You are forgetting again that it isn't the law's concern to make any one class in the city outstandingly happy but to contrive to spread happiness throughout the city by bringing the citizens into harmony with each other through persuasion or compulsion and by making them share with each other the benefits that each class can confer on the community. The law produces such people in the city, not in order to allow them to turn in whatever direction they want, but to make use of them to bind the city together.

---

8   Plato, *Republic* 519d.

[Glaucon:] That's true, I had forgotten.

[Socrates:] Observe, then, Glaucon, that we won't be doing an injustice to those who've become philosophers in our city and that what we'll say to them, when we compel them to guard and care for the others, will be just. We'll say: "When people like you come to be in other cities, they're justified in not sharing in their city's labors, for they've grown there spontaneously, against the will of the constitution. And what grows of its own accord and owes no debt for its upbringing has justice on its side when it isn't keen to pay anyone for that upbringing. But we've made you kings in our city and leaders of the swarm, as it were, both for yourselves and for the rest of the city. You're better and more completely educated than the others and are better able to share in both types of life. Therefore each of you in turn must go down to live in the common dwelling place of the others and grow accustomed to seeing in the dark. When you are used to it, you'll see vastly better than the people there. And because you've seen the truth about fine, just, and good things, you'll know each image for what it is and also that of which it is the image. Thus, for you and for us, the city will be governed, not like the majority of cities nowadays, by people who fight over shadows and struggle against one another in order to rule — as if that were a great good — but by people who are awake rather than dreaming, for the truth is surely this: A city whose prospective rulers are least eager to rule must out of necessity be most free from civil war, whereas a city with the opposite kind of rulers is governed in the opposite way."

[Glaucon:] Absolutely.

[Socrates:] Then do you think that those we've nurtured will disobey us and refuse to share the labors of the city, each in turn, while living the greater part of their time with one another in the pure realm [of being]?

[Glaucon:] It isn't possible, for we'll be giving just orders to just people. Each of them will certainly go to rule as to something compulsory, however, which is exactly the opposite of what's done by those who now rule in each city.[9]

This passage describes the return to illusion, slumber, and dreaming by the one who has awakened and come to know true reality. This return takes place not for the sake of creating one's own happiness within this illusion, but in order to make

---

9   Plato, *Republic* 519d-520e.

others happy — this is the point of eschatological optimism. While knowing that the space at the bottom of the cave is that of illusion, the realm of slumber and dreaming, one must still return and try to open the prisoners' eyes and remove their fetters. This is what I call "eschatological optimism."

One might notice that the concept of eschatological optimism has a kind of mythopoetic character. I do not claim that this is a strictly philosophical concept. This is more of a metaphorical image, one which allows us to understand what paradigmatic points are present in fundamental philosophy. This is philosophical myth. Eschatological optimism is a formula that describes the sad and even unfortunate descent of the awakened philosopher into the world of dark illusions and heavy nightmares.

The Return to the Apophatic

Let us move on to a no less interesting topic, one that is even sharper and more mystical: cataphatic and apophatic theology in Platonism. Apophaticism posits that God, or the Platonists' 'One', is ineffable and unknowable in principle. We can positively contemplate only the realm of the given, the manifest, the cataphatic, and accordingly we can fully think about and discuss in rational terms only this realm. I view cataphaticism and apophaticism through the prism of the Neoplatonic tradition, primarily through Proclus and his analysis in the sixth book of his commentary on Plato's *Parmenides*.[10] Proclus notes that cataphatic theology speaks of the predicates of the One, raising each predicate to the supreme degree — for example, "the most beautiful," "the most intelligent." Apophatic theology, meanwhile, speaks of the One as that which is beyond everything (ἐπέκεινα τῆς οὐσίας), beyond our world and beyond the cave, sleep, illusoriness, language, and all possible descriptions. It is absolutely transcendent.

---

10 Proclus, *Commentary on Plato's Parmenides*, trans. Glenn R. Morrow and John M. Dillon (Princeton: Princeton University Press, 1987).

When we consider the philosopher's return to the cave along with his inner orientation towards the pure One, we obtain a theology that is simultaneously cataphatic and apophatic. This synthesis is tied to the situation of being submerged in an inferior world while preserving the inner experience of the transcendent. This is the essence of eschatological optimism. Optimism in this case will manifest itself in the recognition of the possibility of communicating about the One, i.e., through cataphaticism. We admit that the One can be something positive, some quality raised to its superlative. For example, the Good is the most beautiful, the most intelligent, the supreme, the most honest. But, at the same time, we also retain the apophatic axis, which confirms to us that, amidst all of its supreme attributes, the Good is unknowable. There is an element of eschatology in this. We are approaching a limit, an end (ἔσχατος). The cataphatic region is finite. We are only capable of understanding the One, the Good, to a limited extent; any further, and our mind is useless. The One both is and isn't understood. Insofar as it is understood, the world exists, but when we approach this border, it ends. We are entering the realm of great un-knowing.

Three Phases of Platonism

In the history of philosophy, Neoplatonism represents the era of *"epistrophe"* (ἐπιστροφή), the experience of return. Yuri Shichalin, an historian of ancient philosophy, presents a model that divides ancient philosophy into three stages corresponding to the three phases of Neoplatonic philosophy, i.e., to the triad of "abiding" (μονή), "procession" or "emanation" (πρόοδος), and "return" (ἐπιστροφή). μονή is the One abiding within itself. πρόοδος is the descent of the One into the world, that is, the creation of the world. The divine chalice, the chalice of the One, overflows and its substance flows outwards. This is how the world is created. From the One first appears the Intellect, and then the Intellect-Soul, and from it the corporeal cosmos. This manifestation unfolds until it reaches its limit. Here begins ἐπιστροφή, the process of return. The soul proceeds back from matter and returns to its source by embarking on the path of reverse ascent.

Yuri Shichalin applies this Neoplatonic triad to the history of philosophy. Plato himself is the realm of μονή that contains everything all at once — all interpretations of Platonic doctrine, all possible outcomes of thought, all possible readings. When we read Plato, we might notice that there are theses inlaid in his texts which can at times contradict each other. For example, we can find both the acknowledgement and the refutation of the One in the *Parmenides*. Practically everything can be deduced from Plato — sumptuous Neoplatonism as well as object-oriented ontologies which contradict him in everything. If we carefully look at the second part of the *Parmenides* dialogue, where the One is denied and there is only the Many, we can easily recognize atomism, the materialism of Modernity (New Time), Postmodernism, and even speculative realism. The ninth hypothesis which considers the many not to correlate with any other many is already a rejection of correlationism[11], and this is a point with which the contemporary speculative realists Quentin Meillassoux[12] and Graham Harman[13] concur. Accordingly, Plato himself represents an immense, fundamental philosophical platform synchronously encompassing numerous implicit currents.

The descending emanation, the "procession," πρόοδος, is interpreted by Shichalin in terms of the historical-philosophical process to have been the fragmentation of Platonism, i.e.,

---

11 Correlationism, from "correlation" (Latin *correlatio*) refers to a contemporary line of questioning in the philosophy of Object-Oriented Ontology which holds that classical philosophy built all of its models of knowledge on correlations — between idea and copy (Plato), subject and object (Descartes), life and body (Deleuze), etc. Object-oriented ontologists put forth an alternative system that rejects any correlationism, and instead holds that a thing is revealed in itself in complete separation from every other thing.

12 See Quentin Meillassoux, *After Finitude: An Essay on the Necessity of Contingency*, trans. Ray Brassier (London: Continuum, 2008).

13 See Graham Harman, *The Quadruple Object* (Winchester: Zero Books, 2011); idem., *Weird Realism: Lovecraft and Philosophy* (Winchester: Zero Books, 2012).

the derivation of new, separate disciplines out of his corpus, particular conceptions associated with rhetoric, logic, ethics, etc. Here one can also find something consonant with the skepticism of Pyrrho and others. On the whole, this is fragmentation. This spans up to Middle Platonism, up to Numenius or Philo of Alexandria, where elements of ἐπιστροφή are already noticeable.

Accordingly, the third stage in the development of the history of philosophy per Shichalin is the fully-fledged ἐπιστροφή of the Neoplatonists. The Neoplatonists play a special role in this model. The fragmentation ends with them, as they turn in the opposite direction and undertake to return to the origins again, directing their gaze to the supreme and striving to return to the One through mystical experience. Accordingly, the Neoplatonists are the highest phase of the development of the Platonic tradition. Unlike Plato himself, Neoplatonism has a clear hierarchy and structure. When we encounter the works of Proclus Diadochus, we see a rather rigorous, analytical mindset. Here everything begins with the highest, purely transcendent, apophatic Principle, the One, the Good, which is beyond everything (ἐπέκεινα τῆς οὐσίας). Then, step by step, altogether rationally, a gigantic, systematic model of the cosmos — noetic and physical — unfolds, one that descends from the transcendent to the immanent levels.

The experience of reading Proclus is exciting and extremely interesting. Try to read, for instance, Ludwig Wittgenstein first, and then from him go to Proclus, and you'll see that the structure of their analytical thinking is quite similar. In Wittgenstein, the dominant thesis is "Whereof one cannot speak, thereof one must be silent," whereas in Proclus an analogous thesis figures in the context of apophatic theology. Nothing can be said about the One, but the silence on the One in Proclus is not empty like in Wittgenstein, but rather the most substantive silence one can imagine. Heidegger called this "sigetic philosophy" or "the philosophy of silence."

The Return

So, the Neoplatonists were the masters of systematizing Platonic discourse. And here we find the extremely important experience of a strange, somewhat paradoxical acceptance of the immanent world. Plotinus once expressed to his students that he is very ashamed of his body; for him, the very fact of possessing a body was extremely painful, a cause of acute pain. At the same time, however, if we carefully analyze his works, Plotinus did not reject manifestation in the corporeal world. He believed such to be necessary, first and foremost, in order to begin one's ascent. To some extent, Plotinus was an eschatological optimist. The "I" is manifest here, and this "here" is, of course, destroyable, perishable, has a predisposition toward death, and has the tendency to pull down, to sink and destroy. And this "here" is temporary. By the path of ἐπιστροφή, by returning and climbing up the ladder of virtues, the sciences, rites, prayers and offerings to the gods, the "I" returns to its origins along the levels of being to its source, to the world to which it organically and primordially belongs.[14]

Plotinus' faith in ascent is constant — and this is eschatological optimism. We are thrown into the world, but we also take up this thrownness as a chance. Liberation is needed, as is the experience of mystically going beyond the contours of one's own finitude — such is the experience of theurgy, the experience of breaking with the individual and passing into the realm beyond. We find ourselves at the bottom so that we might move upwards.

There were various schools within Neoplatonic philosophy, some more rationalistic and some more mystical. For example, the Pergamon school, to which Emperor Julian belonged, was associated with regular mystical experiences inspired by the works of the Eastern theurgists, the *Chaldean Oracles*, Hermes

---

14 In late Neoplatonism, and this is markedly different from the case in Plotinus, there is a clear distinction and attribution of different deities to each level - the Henads, the Intellect, the Soul, the cosmos, etc.

Trismegistus and the *Corpus Hermeticum*. The experience of mystical rupture, of one's finitude colliding with something unknown, something infinite, is extremely important in Neoplatonism.

The Figure of the Master in Hegel

For the next important phase in the study of eschatological optimism, I would like to focus on Hegel. Today we won't examine the entirety of the complex array of Neoplatonic influence on the ensuing history of philosophy, nor will we pay particular attention to apophatic theology in the Christian doctrine of Dionysius the Areopagite. In principle, I think that questions around Christian mysticism demand a separate lecture. I will therefore move straight to Hegel and establish what I have determined to be eschatological optimism within the Hegelian system.

At the center of my consideration is the famous dialectic of Slave and Master along with Hegel's formulation that "life is a way of enduring death."[15] According to Hegel, there exist two types of consciousness: the consciousness of the Slave and the consciousness of the Master. The Master differs from the Slave in that he takes the risk of facing death, while the Slave surrenders his freedom to the Master, so that only the Master has the experience of a brush with death. In Hegel, eschatological optimism is directly connected to the concept of death: one's attitude and relation to it. The Slave is not an eschatological optimist; he is its opposite. You might recall Martin Heidegger's interesting formulation which goes something like: "the absence of eschatological thinking is a pure form of nihilism." The Slave whom Hegel describes has no such eschatological thinking. He does not believe in finitude, he refuses to face his finitude, he refuses to cross paths with death. He gives his freedom to the

---

15 G.W.F. Hegel, *Phenomenology of Spirit*, trans. A.V. Miller (Oxford: Oxford University Press, 1977); Alexandre Kojève, *Introduction to the Reading of Hegel: Lectures on the "Phenomenology of Spirit"*, trans. James H. Nichols, Jr. (Ithaca: Cornell University Press, 1980).

Master so that he will come to terms with death in his stead. This is reminiscent of modern man, who is more or less ready to fully trust the mediasphere, to open up to it and allow it to constitute his perspective. "If people are dying from the coronavirus, then I could die too." Everything is as it says. "If people are not dying from it, then I won't die either." This process of delegating one's relationship to death to someone exterior, to a would-be "Master," can be highlighted both in the mediasphere as well as in the field of contemporary philosophy. Passively accepting the element of materiality and matter, the path of subordination to it, is another way of turning away from death. Object-oriented ontology is inextricably tied to slave consciousness. This is not a proclamation of doomed will in the face of inevitable death, present everywhere and always, but a striving to elude and avoid it at any cost. Let matter itself face death and thereby free consciousness from the direct experience of finitude. In other terms, the Hegelian formula "life is a way of enduring death" substantiates the position of eschatological optimism, and in Hegel's system, it spills over into the figure of the Master. The Master is an eschatological optimist.

Nietzsche

Let us move on to Nietzsche's philosophy, to the nihilism that Nietzsche exposed and to his understanding of the human being as an "arrow of longing for the other shore." In Nietzscheanism, it seems to me, what is clearest and most desperately manifest is the final cry of illusion, the cry of the last man who is categorically unready to confront death.

After an inspired speech by Zarathustra on the exhaustion of man and the need to overcome him, the crowd shouts: "We have heard enough already about the tightrope walker, now let us see him too!"[16] Nietzsche then describes the last humans in even more scathing terms: "Then the earth has become small,

---

16   Friedrich Nietzsche, *Thus Spoke Zarathustra*, trans. Adrian del Caro (Cambridge: Cambridge University Press, 2006), 7.

and on it hops the last human being, who makes everything small. His kind is ineradicable, like the flea beetle; the last human being lives longest. 'We invented happiness' – say the last human beings, blinking."[17] This is the Hegelian Slave once again, the antithesis of the eschatological optimist.

Nietzsche's *Übermensch*, on the other hand, becomes such by an act of will which, starting from the shore of illusoriness, directs its volitional gesture, its intention, towards the other shore, a shore of which it knows nothing. In fact, in this volitional decision, in Nietzsche's singling out of the volitional need to overcome the human, is inlaid in apophatic optimism: wherever this arrow is shot, wherever it flies, wherever it turns, there is no certainty and no guarantees whatsoever. It is a desperate cast, a gesture towards nothingness, aimed thither where there are no poles. One of Evgeny Golovin's songs begins with the words "Where there are no parallels and no poles..."

Accordingly, eschatological optimism is to be found in Nietzsche's recognition of the illusory nature of the surrounding world, in his cold ascertainment of the worthlessness of the last man who blinks, and, at the same time, it is to be found in what appears to be the absolutely groundless act of calling for a departing, for casting the arrow to the opposite shore. No one knows what lies on the "shore across," hence it can only be a free act of will to overcome the finitude of any illusion. This is Nietzschean apophaticism. The worthless nothingness of nihilism is to be overcome only by will directed toward the primordial One.

Cioran: The Optimistic Reflex of the Dying

Next, I would like to move on to a wonderful Romanian philosopher whom I really appreciate: Emil Cioran. He was close to Eugène Ionesco, Mircea Eliade, Lucian Blaga, later Paul Celan, Samuel Beckett, and Henri Michaux. When I read an entry on him today, I noted that he is generally regarded

---
17 Ibid., 10.

to have been heavily influenced by the culture of European pessimism. This is how Schopenhauer, Nietzsche, and Klages are categorized in one philosophical encyclopedia. I quite liked the expression "cultural pessimism." Accordingly, Emil Cioran's works are distinguished by their extreme hopelessness.

I became acquainted with Cioran's works while in France. Until recently, many of his works were not translated into Russian. Emil Cioran was a consistent Romanian nihilist, an extremely pained one. The majority of his works are in the form of aphorisms. All of them are quite melancholic. I'll read you now verbatim one quote used in the announcement of my lecture: "On a gangrened planet, we should abstain from making plans, but we make them still, optimism being, as we know, a dying man's reflex."[18]

Cioran had quite an interesting life. He was brought up in a religious environment, and at first undertook religious studies. His life then took a turn and he ended up being influenced by Schopenhauer, Nietzsche, and Klages. He gradually became a kind of "nihilist." His experience of the First World War was brutal. From his pen appeared such works as *A Short History of Decay*, *Syllogisms of Bitterness* [known in English as *All Gall Is Divided*], *The Trouble with Being Born*, *Anathemas and Admirations*, *The Evil Demiurge* [known in English as *The New Gods*], etc.[19] All of these are written in aphoristic style, consisting of heavy and painful fragments that are somewhat like the dark fragments of Vasily Rozanov.

There are two components in Cioran's eschatological optimism. On the one hand, he recognizes the illusoriness of this world, its finitude, and how it is absolutely, impenetrably

---

18   Emil Cioran, *Anathemas and Admirations*, trans. Richard Howard (New York: Arcade Publishing, 2012), 195.

19   E.M. Cioran, *A Short History of Decay*, trans. Richard Howard (New York: Penguin Books, 2010); idem., *All Gall Is Divided: The Aphorisms of a Legendary Iconoclast*, trans. Richard Howard (New York: Arcade Publishing, 1999); idem., *The Trouble with Being Born*, trans. Richard Howard (New York: Arcade Publishing, 2012); idem., *The New Gods*, trans. Richard Howard (Chicago: University of Chicago Press, 2013).

closed, with no way out. Cioran writes that he finds himself in a world that is condemned, that we are all obviously doomed, cursed victims of this condemnation. We have no way out in any direction — no way, up or down, because "we are condemned and crucified on the cross of interpretation." Elsewhere, Cioran wrote: "We are born already crucified." And elsewhere: "The soul is already a crucifixion."

At the same time, Cioran says that "optimism is the reflex of the dying." But even this convulsive reflex is necessary in order to somehow maintain the status of the universe, for optimism constitutes the world (in the same way that a spasm characterizes a dying person). Oddly enough, this is a healthy reaction to the meaninglessness of this world into which we are thrown. Despite the fact that Cioran's works bear no religious element and no salvational doctrine that might change a person's fate by opening up the call to leave this universe and take a leap of will towards the Absolute, which is to say that there is no positive transcendence, he nevertheless accurately captures the most important condition of this world: its illusory nature, the absolute meaninglessness permeating its exhaustion. This starting point of human existence constitutes the basis of optimism as the spasmodic reflex of the dying.

Therefore, in my view, Cioran is extremely important for understanding eschatological optimism. In fact, the very notion of "eschatological optimism" came to my mind after I read Cioran for the first time, in 2013 or 2012. That is when I started finding this hopelessness of the immanent world, the tragic experience of its finitude, in other works by other authors and schools, as well as, in spite of everything, a consciousness of the need to have an optimistic, volitional attitude towards it.

Jünger: Turning the Ship into the Forest

One important author whom I recently discovered to be a bearer of eschatological optimism is Ernst Jünger. Jünger's life and works had many stages, but I have in mind first and foremost his work *The Forest Passage*. It was recently released in Russia by Ad Marginem with brilliant commentary by Alexander Mikhailovsky. In this text from 1951, Jünger speaks of "passing into the forest." At some point, the time will come when a person has to break with the given reality of the hopelessness of the surrounding world. Jünger calls for resistance, for joining the fight against this world and for rising above the illusory reality to whose very illusoriness we testify through the very act of our abruption. In Jünger's work, we find an interesting formulation which I will now quote:

> The forest rebel is that individual who, isolated and uprooted from his homeland by the great process, sees himself finally delivered up for destruction. This could be the fate of many, indeed of all — another factor must therefore be added to the definition: this is the forest rebel's determination to resist, and his intention to fight the battle, however hopeless.[20]

Jünger speaks of modern man being thrown into a space in which technology and matter essentially destroy him, in which he loses his axis of rebellion and sovereignty in the face of materiality and illusoriness. He writes of the necessity of committing to revolt against the modern world, saddling its reality, subduing it, and passing into the forest. What Jünger means by "forest" is very important. He does not mean departing into a physical forest, nor guerrilla struggle against the system— he also does not mean slipping away into a space where there are no more illusions, because illusion is everywhere. The illusion is in the illusion itself. The forest is none other than something differentiated, something distinguished, something greater. The point is that, in the very center of this illusoriness, in the center of the deceptive, finite reality that devours man through technology, through *Machenschaft* as Martin Heidegger called it, man ought to cultivate a vertical axis within himself, a verticality which will be absolutely different from the surrounding illusion and the world as a whole. This axis of rebellion is what is meant by the "forest passage."

---

20 Ernst Jünger, *The Forest Passage*, trans. Thomas Friese (Candor: Telos Press Publishing, 2013), 25.

Jünger chose the image of a ship to articulate the situation of the one who passes into the forest, an obvious reference to Dionysus. When Dionysus faced his enemies on the ship, the matter at hand was essentially a clash between two elements: the forest, the wooden, the ship-like, and the aquatic. The indomitable god causes the ship to become entangled in lush vegetation. The deck, masts, sides, and rigging are overwhelmed with wild ivy. The ship is turned into a forest. Dionysus thus vanquishes his enemies by way of a miracle. This metaphor serves Jünger as an illustration of the need to remain within the reality in which he found himself, in which he was manifest, into which he was born, while at the same time constituting some kind of transcendent volitional principle from the inside, within the immanent, something that will cut and break through the illusion until it collapses.

Evola: Differentiated Man's Rupture of Levels

We encounter similar concepts among the Traditionalists. First and foremost, there is Julius Evola and his concepts of "riding the tiger" and the "differentiated man."[21] This is one and the same idea. According to Evola, modern man finds himself under the destructive influence of matter, under the clichés of the consumer society, under the proliferating pressure of technology, which represses him and dictates to him the need to follow its intrusive, alienating algorithms. The majority surrender, shrug their shoulders, and merge with Modernity and its laws.

But, in spite of everything, there are certain individuals — "differentiated men" — who accomplish superhuman efforts to break this illusoriness, to subordinate it to their will, to overcome it, and to subject it to an act of radical transcendence. The differentiated man continues to remain within the world, but, at the same time, his most important standpoint in his

---

21 Julius Evola, *Ride the Tiger: A Survival Manual for Aristocrats of the Soul*, trans. Joscelyn Godwin and Constance Fontana (Rochester: Inner Traditions, 2003).

perception of this world is his piercing awareness of its finitude, its illusory nature, and the steadfast conviction that this illusion lacks an ontological status. Such a volitional tension results in the gesture of a sharp break, an experience of rupture. Evola calls this *"la rottura del livello,"* "rupture of level," a puncture made in this illusion.

Summary

In the works of the philosophers I've spoken of today, we encounter indications of the experience of eschatological optimism. I would now like to summarize what I mean by eschatological optimism. We have considered various concepts and figures ranging from Plato to Julius Evola. Of course, each of these elements demands a separate lecture, but let us try to identify the basic criteria that can be traced throughout all these doctrines.

Firstly, eschatological optimism is the consciousness and recognition that the material world, the given world which we presently take to be pure reality, is illusory: it is an illusion that is about to dissipate and end. We are extremely, sharply conscious of its finitude. But, at the same time, we maintain a certain optimism; we do not put up with it, we talk about the need to overcome it.

Across different teachings, this finitude can be overcome in different ways. In theological Platonism, it can be overcome on the path of turning to the One that is to be found ἐπέκεινα τῆς οὐσίας, "beyond being," and through the path of apophatic mystery. This optimism is also manifest in political Platonism, when the philosopher returns to the finite world not to serve the finite, but the infinite.

In Neoplatonism, the experience of eschatological optimism means gradually ascending up the hierarchy of virtues and along the ladder of the elements of the soul, through the soul's self-improvement from the lower to the higher virtues. Once the higher levels are reached, the Neoplatonist's path leads even higher, as he tries to escape the finitude of this world through the theurgical, mystical act. In the political philosophy of Neoplatonism, which is, by the way, implicit in the late Platonists and more explicit in the early Neoplatonists (in Plotinus, for instance), this ascent is also associated with political virtues. In general, it is difficult to separate metaphysics from politics in Platonism. Take, for example, Plotinus' project for a Platonopolis. This is something incredibly interesting: despite the fact that Plotinus seems to be repelled by the earthly world, he does not give up trying to build the ideal kingdom of philosophers. Proclus, despite all of his abstraction from the material world, participated in the political life of his native Athens, from which he was expelled for a while. Thus, in Neoplatonism, eschatological optimism can also manifest itself through political efforts, through the experience of political service.

In Hegel's system, the experience of eschatological optimism is embodied in the Master and the Slave's relations to death. The Master is an eschatological optimist; he becomes one as soon as he says a radical "No!" to death and takes upon himself the burden of confronting it face-to-face. The Slave's consciousness is the opposite: he absolutizes corporeal life and sacrifices everything in order to avoid death. The absence of eschatological optimism is what makes the Slave the Slave. This position could be called "non-eschatological pessimism," and it is a formula for spiritual bondage.

In Nietzsche, eschatological optimism is manifest in volitional ecstasy, an ecstasy by which one goes beyond oneself and leaves this illusory reality.

In Cioran, eschatological optimism is found in despair, but at the same time, it still exists, albeit as a "reflex of the dying." This is the most pessimistic variant, but it is still within the framework of optimism as the paradoxical optimism of despair (which is largely Gnostic, hence Cioran's references to the "evil demiurge").

In Evolian doctrine, eschatological optimism manifests itself through the experience of the rupture of levels, through subjugating matter to one's own will, through *"cavalcare la tigre"* — "riding the tiger." Immanent finitude is subordinated to a subject who relies upon a pure act of will.

In his *Forest Passage*, Ernst Jünger also speaks of subjugating the "here and now," that is, of finding oneself within the world, not leaving it. The Forest does not cancel out the Ship, but rather transforms the Ship into the Forest in a Dionysian way.

I would like to conclude my lecture by repeating the quote from Guénon: *"La fin d'un monde n'est jamais et ne peut jamais être autre chose que la fin d'une illusion"* — "The end of a world never is and can never be anything but the end of an illusion."

II. Eschatological Optimism in Questions and Answers

Question: In what sense do you use the word *"polis"*?

Daria Dugina: *"Polis"* (πόλις) is the Greek name for the state or city-state. In a more general sense, the term πολιτεία was used, which we translate as "Republic" (or "State," as in Russian) in the title of Plato's dialogue.

Question: Is a direct political reading of eschatological optimism possible?

Daria Dugina: Yes, undoubtedly. One example of such eschatological optimism in power is Julian the Apostate, who did not aspire for power at all. In fact, he even complained that he had to take the throne. After he became Emperor, he spent all of his nights writing philosophical works and was very indignant whenever he had to deal with any political affairs. As a Neoplatonist, Julian was an eschatological optimist. Eschatological optimism is also the gesture of recognizing that all elections or other political rituals are fake, and yet still participating in the system. It means that you understand that it won't be possible to influence the results of a vote, but you still go to vote and still express your position. This is a kind of heroism of despair. I'm talking more about the American elections now. In general, the American electoral system is rather insane and quite archaic. But eschatological optimism is when you understand that your decision will not greatly affect the outcome, the illusion, yet you still go to face it out of recognition of the need to cultivate political virtues within yourself. You understand that it is likely useless, but you continue anyway. Even knowing that your cause has no tomorrow, you remain faithful to it to the very end. But, of course, such a cause, even if it is political, should be motivated by higher orientations, by a transcendent horizon.

Question: Can we speak of eschatological optimism within the framework of Gilbert Durand's terminology? Isn't eschatological optimism a manifestation of the radical diurne in the conditions of the totality and irreversibility of death? It would follow that eschatological pessimism is the position of the mystical nocturne.

Daria Dugina: That is a very precise definition. Yes, indeed. That is what I have in mind. It's been mentioned that the Radical Subject and eschatological optimism are very close to each other. If we recall the concept of the Radical Subject, then there is certainly the element of the radical diurne. Eschatological optimism is the radical diurne. The models I've mentioned today, perhaps with the exception of Cioran, pertain to the mode of the radical diurne. This is the Platonic rise, or Apollonianism towards a given reality, the Neoplatonic ascent of the diurne as an experience of rupture. This is Hegel with his Master's confrontation with death. This is Nietzscheanism as the Apollonian arrow thrown beyond. This is Evola, who was a defender of Apollo, an apologist for the radical, solar, transcendent diurne. This is Ernst Jünger, who also held to such a heroic standpoint — in the very least, his book The

Forest Passage seemed to me precisely such a manifesto of the unwavering diurne.

Question: Would the Christian approach to death be a anifestation of slave mentality?

Daria Dugina: No, of course not. Christianity is inextricably bound to Neoplatonic doctrine, and the experience of apophatic theology is fully developed in the Neoplatonic vein. In his *Theologia Mystica*, Dionysius the Areopagite writes of the need to go beyond positive (cataphatic) characterizations of God and switch to apophatic contemplation. Of course, Christianity can be interpreted in various ways. But, in fact, the Christian attitude towards death can in no way be an example of slave mentality. Christianity as a whole is to some extent an eschatological optimism. Here we can see a certain acceptance of the end of the world, the recognition that everything extant is not genuine, and that what is genuine is the spiritual world, paradise, from which we have been expelled and have forgotten. At the same time, Christianity affirms the need for a positive, volitional attitude towards the end of illusion, towards death. It seems to me that the ideal formula is that of the monks of Athos. Silouan the Athonite said: "Keep your mind in hell and do not despair." This is a state in which you are conscious of death, hell, and the horror of the material world, its doom, decay, and finitude, but you still don't despair. Through this act of "non-despair," a person tries to save their soul, to pray for it. This means that a person does not reconcile with death, does not shift the decision of their death onto someone else. This means that a person accepts this death within themself, keeps their mind in hell, and does not despair.

Question: Isn't breaking with the illusion of the world and leaping into the unknown fraught with fear and despair rather than optimism?

Daria Dugina: It is, indeed. In this lies the peculiarity of eschatological optimism. On the one hand, it is desperate; on the other hand, it nevertheless retains some hope for salvation. In essence, the leap is the decision to cast oneself forth with the hope that there is still something else, while at the same time being conscious of the fact that there might not be something else out there, or that you might very well turn out to be unworthy for it. The leap into the unknown, accompanied with fear and despair, is most accurately described by Cioran. In the Platonists, the Neoplatonists, and Hegel, this leap is not fearful, but optimistic. These are different versions of eschatological optimism.

Question: In your opinion, is eschatological optimism inherent in the Russian Symbolist poets? You spoke about Jünger's understanding of technology's power over man. In Fyodor Sologub's poem "Devil's Swing," all of life is "in the shadow of a ragged spruce."

Daria Dugina: It seems to me that there is some eschatological optimism in the Russian Symbolist poets. I once gave a talk about the influence of Neoplatonic doctrine on the Russian Symbolists. I mentioned that the Russian Silver Age authors are imbued with a sense of loss of true reality, of higher reality, and that they dreamed of such. You know, for some reason, I am now reminded of Andrei Bely. He also had some elements of eschatological optimism. On the one hand, he was thrown into the world, while on the other, he cultivated the hope that it is possible to get out of it, that this world must be fought and even conquered. But I don't think he prevailed. In his novel *Petersburg*, despair — the dark, mystical, Cybelean, matriarchal space of the simulacral city — wins out.

Question: In his novel *Julian the Apostate*, did Merezhkovsky accurately portray the Emperor as an eschatological optimist?

Daria Dugina: I think so. He is the archetype of the eschatological optimist as such. He was desperate, unhappy, and one who, in fact, became a victim of the new world that replaced the beautiful, already fading world of Antiquity.

Question: Is Berdyaev an eschatological optimist? Here is a quote from his book: "This world is not a cosmos; it is a non-cosmic state of disunity and enmity, the atomization and disintegration of the living monads of cosmic hierarchy. The true path is the path of spiritual liberation from the world, of liberating the human spirit from the captivity of necessity. This ghastly world is the offspring of our sin."

Daria Dugina: To some extent, yes, he could also be called an eschatological optimist.

Question: Is Lev Shestov an eschatological optimist?

Daria Dugina: I don't know Lev Shestov very well, but from what I remember... No, I cannot say right away. It seems to me that eschatological optimism is a very subtle definition. There might be elements of eschatological optimism in someone's works, but this doesn't mean that they are an eschatological optimist. Like in Cioran, there are elements of eschatological optimism, but at times he cannot be called as such; instead, he should be called an eschatological pessimist.

Question: As I understand it, eschatological optimism implies the necessary presence of a reality which exists parallel to the material world. Is eschatological optimism possible outside of the systems of Plato and Hegel, for instance rejecting God and treating reality as an illusion? The axis of Jünger's "forest passage" implies that a person cultivates the so-called "second world" themself. What should optimism be for an atheist?

Daria Dugina: I'm not entirely sure about Jünger on this point. In *The Forest Passage*, he writes that religion can aspire to create a different reality for a person. For myself, eschatological optimism is impossible if one rejects God or the One or any principle beyond, any transcendent Absolute. This apophatic principle can be called different things in different contexts. From my point of view, I would say that any system that loses the Absolute, that loses the transcendent essence, collapses and turns not into eschatological optimism, but into nihilism, into "non-eschatological pessimism." For eschatological optimism there must be another reality, another world connected with God, with the apophatic One, with the Other, with some higher principle. Jünger, by the way, does not dismiss this.

Question: Can you please say where in life, in the surrounding world, we can encounter eschatological optimism?

Daria Dugina: Within ourselves. When we live in the midst of a pandemic, we understand that we might die at any moment, but at the same time we build up an inner, existential defense against this pandemic. I count myself among those who believe in Covid, who accept Covid as it is. I even interpret it from the point of view of an existential challenge, a call for change, a chance for awakening humankind. It seems to me that if we properly read the works I talked about today, if we properly think about our finitude, if we acknowledge death, if we cultivate in ourselves a sense of the finitude and illusoriness of our body, and if we think about what is beyond, then we'll discover eschatological optimism within ourselves.

Question: Daria Alexandrovna, is eschatological optimism for you primarily an encounter with the sacred or with the profane? Is this poetic-philosophical doctrine aimed at overcoming the material and heading towards the absolute?

Daria Dugina: For me, eschatological optimism is a kind of departure from the profane in the direction of the sacred, which does not necessarily involve encountering the sacred itself. That is, you can take a strong-willed leap into the beyond, but you still might not have a genuine mystical experience. You might never go beyond your own boundary, yet you must do everything to go beyond it. The eschatological optimist inevitably dwells in the profane, in the given reality, and in illusion, but they are oriented towards sacrality. Whether they can reach sacrality or not remains unknown. They head towards the beyond and decide to go beyond without knowing whether or not they will succeed. This is the peculiarity of eschatological optimism and its closeness to the notion of the Radical Subject. Sure, it is a difficult state — I am here, I am in this reality, it is profane, and I am heading away from it, towards something which might not accept me. Everything is at my own risk. But this is much more interesting than being a "non-eschatological pessimist."

Question: So, is it necessary for the eschatological optimist to wait for an exterior call?

Daria Dugina: No, no. The eschatological optimist never waits for an exterior call. They begin their path from the call from within. This is what Heidegger called the "call of being" or the "call of conscience" (*der Ruf des Gewissens*). Or this might be an existential call when a person confronts death and faces finitude. It might be an inner call when a person faces tragedy, a pandemic, the coronavirus. For example, when loved ones die. Or when a person is confronted with a sharp awareness of the finitude of the surrounding world. This is a sharp call. The call must grow from within. It will never be exterior, outside somewhere, and if it is, then you'll hear it only once you have already heard the call from within. It is like a prophecy. You'll be able to decipher it only once you are innerly ready to decipher it. Otherwise, it will remain an unintelligible abstraction. By the way, it is still a mystery to me how laws are even possible in Plato's *Republic*, because in the fourth book Plato writes that these laws will be Apollo's laws, yet Apollo's laws are the laws of the Pythia, which is to say that they are koan-like utterances, prophecies yet to be deciphered. This has always been a mystery for me. If you have the call within, if you cultivate it within yourself, then you'll hear the call from outside. But one cannot be passive in this regard. You should try to invoke this call through various practices, whether religious, existential, or through the experience of being attentive to the world. If you have no such call, then simply read books, read everyone I've listed today — the Platonists, Neoplatonists, Hegel, Nietzsche, Cioran, Heidegger, Evola. The call will come to you through reading these books. Even if it's altogether fleeting, it might linger on within you. It is wonderful if it lingers on. Then everything begins.

Question: Can the system that Eliade expounded in *The Myth of the Eternal Return* be called eschatological optimism?

Daria Dugina: Yes, quite so, I think.

Question: How do these words from Nietzsche's *Thus Spoke Zarathustra* fit into the concept of eschatological optimism?: "There are preachers of death, and the earth is full of people to whom departure from life must be preached. The earth is full of the superfluous, life is spoiled by the too many. May they be lured from this life with the 'eternal life!'... There are the terrible ones, who carry the predator about in themselves and have no choice but lust or self-laceration. And even their lusting is self-laceration. They have not even become human beings, these terrible ones: may they preach departure from life and pass away themselves! There are the consumptive of the soul: scarcely are they born when they begin to die and long for the teachings of weariness and resignation."[22]

Daria Dugina: When I was talking about eschatological optimism, I mentioned two types of people: those who ask to see the tightrope dancer and those who take the path of overcoming the illusion by taking the leap. Nietzsche should be read dramatically. He might have internal contradictions, but this is good, it means that his thinking is alive.

Question: Nietzsche put forward the idea of the "eternal recurrence" — how is this compatible with eschatology?

Daria Dugina: I would like to unpack this question in more detail, because it arose in my mind today while I was preparing for the lecture. I understand eschatology not as the temporal finitude of the world, but as its finitude in the sense of its fundamental limitedness, its irresistible illusoriness. The world given to us is not eternal, which means that it has already ended.

---

[22] Nietzsche, *Thus Spoke Zarathustra*, 31.

Eternal is the world of the One, the world of the Good, the world of the Divine, the other world. My will is directed towards the latter. As for finitude, here it is to be understood not as the finitude of the world as such, but as the finitude of the profane world, as the end of an illusion.

Question: Is Arthur Schopenhauer's idea of "world will" connected to eschatological optimism? If yes, then how so?

Daria Dugina: I was reading Schopenhauer just before our seminar today. Schopenhauer recognizes that the surrounding world is meaningless and that only the act of will constitutes space. As a matter of fact, it seems to me that Schopenhauer, especially in his treatise "On the Insignificance and Sorrows of Life," comes to the conclusion that there is absolutely no meaning to the surrounding reality, that it is impossible to speak of any other reality or describe it, but one can speak of a rigid concentration on will. Yes, this is certainly an eschatologically-optimistic perspective.

Question: How does Dasein correlate with eschatological optimism?

Daria Dugina: This is a difficult question. When Dasein exists authentically, it finds itself in the position of eschatological optimism. Death (*Sein-zum-Tode*) is disclosed to it. Thus, it encounters Being itself. It recognizes the finitude of the world. In this moment, authentically existing Dasein becomes an eschatological optimist. Consciousness of the profaneness of the world around us (as the field of *das Man*) and an aspiration for a transcendent way out of it constitutes the essence of Dasein's authentic existence.

Question: Is Edgar Allen Poe an eschatological optimist? His last book, *Eureka*, is about our tragic universe and how its finitude is tantamount to a revelation harbored in misfortune.

Daria Dugina: Thank you. I haven't thought about this. I will definitely reread it in this context.

Question: What can you say about Baudelaire in the context of his *Flowers of Evil*?

Daria Dugina: For me, Baudelaire is also a kind of eschatological optimist. At eye level on my bookshelf stands a volume of Baudelaire gifted to me by Alain de Benoist, *My Naked Heart*. It seems to me that eschatological optimism is very much felt within the French decadent milieu. So, yes, indeed, Baudelaire — namely Baudelaire — can be considered a representative of eschatological optimism.

Question: What place does the Radical Subject occupy in the concept of eschatological optimism?

Daria Dugina: The Radical Subject is essentially the bearer of eschatological optimism, just like Evola's "differentiated man." The Radical Subject is precisely that person who, in the absence of Tradition, becomes a bearer of Tradition, who in a time when there are no stars in the sky, says in spite of everything "Arise, o Soul!" "*Auf! O Seele!*" — to quote the baroque poet Christian Hoffmann von Hoffmannswaldau. Therefore, you have a very accurate understanding. Eschatological optimism is connected to the concept of the Radical Subject. That is something I wanted to talk about, but I restrained myself, and you have guessed it correctly.

Question: How do you relate to eschatological pessimists who fanatically serve the forces of evil, darkness itself, through dirty, vile deeds on earth? Are they your enemies, or how do you philosophically relate to them?

Daria Dugina: I respect them, because if a person chooses their strategy of will, if they recognize the finitude of this illusion, then even if they consciously set out to destroy this illusion, then I perceive this to be an act of will, and this is undoubtedly valuable to me. But, of course, it is another matter that I prefer to be in the space of eschatological optimism, to carry out a positive volitional decision to try to get out of this illusion in the direction of the ineffable Supreme, the unknowable abyss above. This concept is much more appealing to me. Evil is easy to find and easy to see. In order to see evil, one must go up, not down. Evil is frightening, and what frightens can best be found at the top. I'm saying this from the point of view of Christian mysticism. Remember: demons come to monks and to clergymen more than anyone else. They are the ones who experience the most terrible torments when they acknowledge the power of their sin and the depth of the sinful fall. They are the ones called to keep their mind in hell. Imagine holy men who are tormented by demons — they are the ones who know real evil, not some petty debauchees. When you ascend, moving in the direction of the Absolute, only then do you begin to understand how scary what lies ahead truly is, and how many imperfections within yourself you can find along the way… You do not need to seek evil out. Firstly, there is enough of it; secondly, the true volume of evil is revealed only when one nears the pure Good.

Question: Are the Gnostic systems more eschatologically pessimistic or optimistic?

Daria Dugina: It's complex and difficult when it comes to the Gnostics. I initially wanted to talk about them, but then I realized that I simply can't cover everything. There are different Gnostic systems. Nevertheless, it seems to me that Gnostics are eschatological pessimists, even while they might still have some kind of eschatological-optimistic dimension. Here we would need to look into exactly whom you have in mind. Right now only the Gnostic Valentinus comes to my mind. Although there are other, much more pessimistic systems and authors, it seems to me that Valentinus was quite a Gnostic eschatological optimist. But Gnosticism, without a doubt, requires a separate study. In this lecture, I've focused more on Platonism. Therefore, I think that if I develop the doctrine of eschatological optimism further, I will pay special attention to Gnosticism.

Question: What is your attitude towards the philosophy of fantasy? Is it worth looking for deeper meanings in *Warhammer* and *Game of Thrones*?

Daria Dugina: Oh! I haven't thought about eschatological optimism in *Game of Thrones*. However, deeper meaning must be sought everywhere and always in everything that surrounds us, even in cinema. What you see on the screen and what is supposedly done for the needs of the unenlightened, narrow-minded public is none other than the result of 300 years of the history of philosophy, if not 400. The reality that we take to be genuine is in fact the work and construct of Modernity. If ancient philosophers could have seen any element of our reality, they would have perceived it in a completely different way than we do. They would have perceived it as only a *doxa*, an opinion, not as that which really exists. Therefore, I think that it is necessary to look for the deep dimension in everything — even in fantasy, in *Game of Thrones*. In *Game of Thrones*, I mostly like tracing the issues of geopolitical confrontation between North and South, between two civilizational models — the culturological civilization of Cybele and the civilization of Apollo. I don't know anything about *Warhammer*, I've never played computer games.

Question: Another question: Please, tell us a bit more about eschatological pessimism — is it completely opposite to optimism?

Daria Dugina: No, it is not completely opposite, because it is also eschatological. It implies a world that is finite, perishable, and profane, yet it believes that it is necessary to refrain from any action insofar as everything is pointless. Such eschatological pessimism is nihilism in its worst manifestation. In fact, it leads to a passive acceptance of this profane world. This is essentially like a cooling down of the body. It is a sad and passive position based on the understanding that everything is finite and everything is over. Cioran, in fact, is torn between this eschatological pessimism and eschatological optimism. In some of his works, there is a direct call for rebellion. It's as if he's saying "Everything is meaningless, so I must cultivate opposition to this meaninglessness within myself. Why? I myself don't know. Yes, it will be just as meaningless, but, all the same, I must cultivate this element in myself, I must cultivate opposition." He is thus thrown from deep eschatological pessimism into eschatological optimism.

Question: So, it turns out that, in the conditions of the end times, there are two opposite positions: eschatological optimism as a radical rejection of death and darkness, and eschatological pessimism as a passive acceptance of death and conciliation with a dissolution into nothingness, and these are somehow combined and have similar proportions. At first glance, it is difficult to distinguish between them, which resembles the problem of the Radical Subject and its double. What do you think about this?

Daria Dugina: A genius question! It is very, very subtle. Yes, it really does look like the Radical Subject and its double. It seems to be a simultaneous acceptance of the profaneness of the world and its finitude. But in one case, one adopts the strong-willed decision to overcome it, while on the other hand, there is a refusal to take any action. This is a very interesting topic, indeed.

Question: Is Camus' *Myth of Sisyphus* a testimony of eschatological pessimism?

Daria Dugina: Yes, this is exactly the point when we are dealing with real eschatological pessimism.

Question: Does this mean that, at the peak of achieving a certain spiritual state of ascent and transcending oneself as a human being, the line between eschatological optimists and pessimists is erased, and both merge with nothingness in finitude and in the face of the infinite?

Daria Dugina: I wouldn't say so. The state of going beyond, of transgressing, can in principle be quite similar. But, at the same time, the eschatological optimist's experience of going beyond will still represent some unity with the Divine, with the world beyond, with the Absolute, whereas the eschatological pessimist's experience will be one of facing nothingness. And, in my opinion, here we are talking about different nothings: a nothing above and a nothing below. It is somewhat uncomfortable or inappropriate to discuss such questions, because we're already entering the horizons of mysticism — nothing above, nothing below. But I would respond to you with the following words: the eschatological optimist has the aim of reaching the abyss from above, while the eschatological pessimist has only the prospect and perspective of falling into the abyss below.

Question: Can Kierkegaard's "leap of faith" be considered a sign of eschatological optimism?

Daria Dugina: Yes, it is possible that there are quite a few elements of eschatological optimism in Kierkegaard. There is Abraham's despair accompanying the sacrifice of Isaac. This awareness of the need to face death might also be a sign of eschatological optimism.

Question: Is Georges Bataille an optimist or pessimist?

Daria Dugina: I think he is an eschatological pessimist; he turns his gaze to the nothing below and moves into the abyss below. I really like Bataille, especially his works on the "inner experience," where he dissects mysticism and transgression, as well as his prose. Nevertheless, he is an eschatological pessimist.

Question: Are accelerationists eschatological optimists?

Daria Dugina: I don't think so. They do not associate matter with finitude and perishability. They accept matter, live according to its laws, try to follow and imitate it. They accept the inevitability of this profane matter's movement, completely.

Question: How do you distinguish the higher nothing from the lower nothing in the conditions of the absolute end — are these two abysses ultimately one?

Daria Dugina: I think this question is a rhetorical one. I'm afraid to take on the role of answering it, of saying "What do you mean, the higher nothing is fundamentally different from the one below. The higher nothing should be determined by such and such characteristics, and the lower by others" — one could proceed in this way, but doing so would be a false approach. The question of how to distinguish between the abyss above and the abyss below is a question which, it seems to me, has troubled very many deeper thinkers, philosophers, and writers. And I think that few of them, even the most ingenious, have found an answer to this question. So, let's leave this question open.

***

ESCHATOLOGICAL OPTIMISM
AND THE METAPHYSICS OF WAR

He who has tasted the things above easily despises what is below.
He who has not tasted the things above is like
cattle relishing in the fields below.

   - John Climacus, *The Ladder of Divine Ascent*

I. The Unhappiness of Being: Romanian Pessimism

Greetings, friends and colleagues! Today, I would like to speak on the topic of eschatological optimism.[23] The topic sounds catchy, striking, and beautiful, but what I'm going to voice today is merely a hypothesis, a sketch of a philosophical approach. While working on the texts of Cioran, Evola, Jünger, and other thinkers, I have wanted to unify their teachings into one group and designate them with one name. For a long time, I couldn't find a framework to categorize them together. It was obvious that doing so would have to be connected with the sharp apocalyptic feeling of an approaching end, but at the same time with a volitional orientation towards partaking in battle, in revolt. The term "Traditionalism" fits for a number of authors — for Cioran and Jünger to a lesser extent than for Evola — but nevertheless does not adequately describe the essence of what has attracted me to their theories.

Today, we will try to analyze three main concepts:

- Emil Cioran's philosophy in the broader context of 20th-century Romanian metaphysics;
- Julias Evola's concepts, primarily his views on war, types of heroism, revolting against the modern world, and his thesis on "riding the tiger";

---

[23] The present text is an edited transcript of a lecture delivered at the bookstore Listva in Moscow on 21 March 2021.

- Ernst Jünger's works, first and foremost his rather well-known, revolutionary and vivid manifesto, The *Forest Passage*, with which many of you here today should be familiar.

Eschatological optimism is not a readymade, finished concept, it is not a generally recognized category in the philosophical-historical tradition. It is only a hypothesis, a proposal for reading and interpreting texts. It is a complex array of views based on the recognition that the material world is a kind of illusion, along with the decision to resist this illusion.

There are two standpoints which need to be taken into account. The first is that the world surrounding us, that which is directly given, is an illusion. Remember the important words of René Guénon: "*La fin d'un monde n'est jamais et ne peut jamais être autre chose que la fin d'une illusion*" — "The end of a world never is and can never be anything but the end of an illusion."[24] The second is that the surrounding world is completely meaningless, it no longer has any point, it is the victim of regress, it is "in decay," to draw from Apollinaire. "*Les dentelles s'abolissent*" is one of my favorite phrases — it speaks of the "decay of the fabric of meaning." This feeling of being absolutely lost that is found in various philosophical contexts could be called "god-forsakenness," "lack of meaning," or the Kali-Yuga. We will have more to say about the Kali-Yuga today. I'll immediately note that the etymology of "Kali-Yuga" does not come from the name of the goddess Kālī ("black"), but from the name of the demon Kali, whose name means "mixing," "shaking," "violence." There is also a third semantic node: the Sanskrit term *kāla* ("time" and also "time of death"). All of these concepts in Hinduism are strictly distinct from one another. This was an interesting revelation for me while I was preparing for this lecture. In Hindu eschatology, the final battle that completes the end times is the battle between the goddess Kali (the good) and the demon Kali (the Asura) or against the Kali-Yuga itself

---

24 René Guénon, *The Reign of Quantity and the Signs of the Times*, trans. Lord Northbourne (Hillsdale: Sophia Perennis, 2004), 279.

as the era of the reign of the Asura Kali. At the same time, the goddess Kali is a hypostasis of Shiva, the god of eternity. It could be said that Kali-eternity is in struggle with and prevails over Kali-time. Then will come the tenth avatar, Kalki. This is how many meanings we have at once in the term Kali-Yuga.

Accordingly, war is a key point and moment in the strategy of resisting the world of illusion. It is a challenge to the world, a revolt against it, a desire to subordinate it to sacred will, to saddle it like a force, a stream, and to carry out a coup d'état in the name of higher values. What values? We still stop here for now, because we must move consistently so as to not slide into banality.

For the authors we will be examining today, the question of "for the sake of what" or "for what purpose" the metaphysical war is waged is not entirely obvious. At times it is a big question mark for them. The authors whom we will be considering practically always speak of the need for war and revolt, but the "why?" of this war, this revolt, this revolution, is not often named directly or is taken as a default. There is something apophatic in this, just like how in the time of the apostles in the Athenian Areopagus there was an altar to an "unknown god." These authors were afraid to say what or who will be beyond illusion, whether or not it will be God, or something Supreme. They prefer to leave this point empty. We will not fill in this point — that is not our aim. Our aim is to understand how, given the illusoriness of the world, one can oppose it, why this is necessary, and what motivations there are for such a coup, revolt, and struggle.

Principles of Eschatological Optimism: The Experience of Rupture

Let us note the main positions that seem to us to be the most important in eschatological optimism.

Firstly, the eschatological optimism of the authors whom we are considering today, as well as those we are not examining but will examine in the future, operates via an experience of rupture.

Julius Evola formulates this experience as: *"la rottura del livello."* This is a break with illusoriness and a passage to something Other, a break with the inertness of matter and the ties that bind us to it, it means separating oneself from a world that is at once given and an illusion.

Secondly, we have the element of hierarchy. Eschatological optimism believes that in the world there is a higher and lower, there is that (the other) and this (the given). This confrontation constitutes war. The war waged in eschatological optimism is a war between illusoriness, i.e., what is lower and given, against what is on the other side beyond, what is superior to us and transcends our own boundaries. This is what the Neoplatonists called "ἐπέκεινα τῆς οὐσίας," "beyond being." They used this formula to speak about the apophatic One, about the highest principle.

The Unhappiness of "Being In-Between" and Overcoming Time

One of the most important characteristics of eschatological optimism is unhappiness. A person who challenges the given, opts for revolt, proclaims a categorical "No!" and expresses total disagreement with everything surrounding them — such a person is unhappy. After all, they renounce the state in which Nietzsche found the last humans: "'We invented happiness' – say the last human beings, blinking."[25] This person rejects spectacles, entertainment, and refuses to behold the tightrope dancer. They want something else, they challenge the given, and they take a risk, they challenge themselves by directing their will and striking out from within.

Trying to go beyond the boundaries of self, the eschatological optimist, the "metaphysical frontiersman," abides in a sphere of at once holding on to the given and casting out towards that which is not, on the border of this world and the one beyond. Such is the structure of the rift — this person's hands are

---

25 Friedrich Nietzsche, *Thus Spoke Zarathustra*, trans. Adrian del Caro (Cambridge: Cambridge University Press, 2006), 17.

outstretched in both directions: one holds the sky, while one grabs the earth and tries to push off from it.

Another important characteristic of eschatological optimism is the necessity of overcoming time. Time, according to Plato, is a moving likeness of eternity. But this likeness is somehow defective. It must be overcome in order to return to eternity.

We encounter an extremely skeptical discourse on time in Cioran, especially pronounced in his works devoted to history, wherein Cioran radically criticizes history as such and says that it is necessary to break through to the bottom of time and break out into eternity. We also encounter this in Jünger when he says that whoever passes into the forest puts themself in the territory of eternity. Such a person does not operate on the plane of time and is not subject to progress or regression. They are transformed, for they no longer partake in the trappings of temporality.

There are numerous expressions of the inevitability of existing 'in-between'. One representation of this seen in many traditional images is a human with one arm raised and the other lowered[26] — this gesture indicates the position of thrownness in the domain located between the 'here' and the 'there'. What now comes to mind are the images of Egyptian deities floating in the intermediate space without touching anything. They are found in-between — between the apophatic here and the apophatic there. Thus does the figure of the metaphysical frontiersman gradually emerge — the eschatological optimist, the human who exists in the rift, on the edge between two worlds.

The Forerunners of Eschatological Optimism

When I started analyzing the question of eschatological optimism and did my first introductory lecture for the Sigma project, I started with Plato. I said then that Platonism is an

---

26 This is how Gustav Meyrink in *The Golem* interpreted the hierogram of the Hebrew letter *aleph*.

experience of eschatological optimism. Then, having spent some time working on this topic, I came to understand that this was an anachronistic attempt to see in Plato what actually appears only in the era of nihilism. Therefore, an amendment to my first lecture would be to see eschatological optimism as a process that manifested in the late 19th and early 20th centuries. The forerunners of eschatological optimism were the eschatological pessimists — those who exposed the nihilistic essence of Modernity, saw nothing in New Time and its culture, and faced this nothing at once desperately and passively.

Friedrich Nietzsche was a forerunner of eschatological optimism. Some of his works and fragments can be read from the point of view of eschatological optimism, especially those passages on overcoming the "lion stage" and "infant phase" in the transformations of the spirit and those about the "playful god" Dionysus. Nevertheless, Nietzsche's philosophy is to be found at the end of the old beginning. It is the border zone between the old beginning and the new. Here I am referring to Martin Heidegger's characterization. In his analysis of Nietzsche's formula "God is dead," Heidegger describes Nietzsche as the spokesman of the final stage of European metaphysics, i.e., the final stage of the old beginning.[27]

Lucian Blaga: The Great Anonymous, Transcendental Censorship, and Ontological Mutants

Now let us move straight on to eschatological optimism. Here is where everything most interesting begins. For me, for a long time, the perfect example of eschatological pessimism was Emil Cioran. I had never encountered a more depressing and tragic thinker. Every time I had an attack of melancholy, I turned to him. Cioran became for me the equivalent of a "Gloomy Sunday" or Diamanda Galás' music. His work is like

---

[27] See Martin Heidegger, *Nietzsche*, 4 vols., trans. David Farrell Krell (San Francisco: Harper Collins, 1991). On Heidegger's understanding of the "new beginning of philosophy," see Alexander Dugin, *Martin Heidegger: The Philosophy of Another Beginning*, trans. Nina Kouprianova (Arlington: Radix / Washington Summit Publishers, 2014).

an outcry of despair, a stylistically impeccable expression of the painful perception of reality. I would likely have considered Cioran to be a totally unique, lone genius had I never become acquainted with the works of Lucian Blaga and subsequently placed Emil Cioran within the context of deeply tragic 20th-century Romanian philosophical thought.

We'll begin our introduction to Emil Cioran by way of this other key figure in Romanian philosophy, Lucian Blaga (1895-1961). Blaga was a philosopher and theoretician of culture. His most famous work is *The Trilogy of Culture*.[28] I read it in French, I am not sure if there is a Russian translation. I recently began studying it and I immediately realized that here was a great and severely overlooked figure. Blaga authored an incredible ontological theory which holds that the world was created by the Great Anonymous (*le Grande Anonyme*).[29] He is a Gnostic, but with a very strange twist. This is not straightforward Gnosticism. There is something very Russian about it, very fractured, very Dionysian, very mixed, and mad. Blaga says that man is thrown into the world created by the Great Anonymous by way of subtraction, not addition.

Who is the Great Anonymous? According to Blaga, at first there exists the Absolute. The Absolute is powerful, great, and endowed with all supreme characteristics. But, being Absolute, it cannot create an equally absolute world. If the highest God, this Great Anonymous, directly created a world as absolute as himself, then this world would be identical to him. This is to say that he would have created himself, just as perfect, powerful, and fully-fledged as himself. Then, instead of one Absolute, there would be two. This cannot possibly be, because if there are two Absolutes, then the first Absolute ceases to be absolute and loses its superiority, power, and perfection.

---

28 Lucian Blaga, *La trilogie de la culture* (Paris: Librairie du savoir, 1995). See Lucian Blaga, *Selected Philosophical Extracts*, trans./eds. Angela Botez, R.T. Allen, and Henrieta Anisoara Serban (Malaga: Vernon, 2018).

29 Lucian Blaga, *Les différentielles divines* (Paris: Librairie du savoir, 1990).

Then Blaga says that the Great Anonymous engages in creation in a limited way, employing transcendental censorship. This means that he deliberately creates a world that is not good enough; he deliberately depreciates the quality of this world so that it would never coincide with and be identical to him as the one and only Absolute. Therefore, our world and the humans thrown into it were produced by this Great Anonymous in a somewhat incomplete fashion. This means that the universe is a kind of error, a "glitch," the product of intentional censorship and the withholding of certain ontological components. And just as the created world is imperfect and incomplete, so are we incomplete and imperfect. This is a dangerous situation, because we are deprived of genuine knowledge, as the Great Anonymous hides himself from us. He makes himself unknowable, he remains hidden and concealed from us. While this resembles apophatic theology, I wouldn't rush to make such a claim, as there are too many Gnostic influences present here, as well as a Gnostic style of thinking.

The person who begins their great awakening, i.e., the philosopher, strives for knowledge, for the highest and ultimate truth. They climb the ladder of contemplation until they reach a certain horizon. Blaga calls this the "horizon of mystery." In geometrical terms, this could be represented as a trapezoid, that is, a triangle with a truncated top. A person climbs up the hierarchical steps thinking that they lead directly to the One, to where all the rays converge. But if this were the case then the world itself would be absolute, whereas it is actually manifested by the power of "transcendental censorship." This means that the vertex of the triangle is cut off (censored). Where the last step, the highest segment of the triangle should be, there is nothing. There is a plateau, a plane. Man cannot know what the Great Anonymous is. Moving along the steps of positive knowledge, he can reach only the horizon of mystery. The human attempt to reach, to see, to know the Great Anonymous ends here. The condemned state of man in such a world as Blaga describes — which is our world and is only one among others — consists in the fact that we are always limited by this horizon of mystery. It is impassable.

At the same time, however, there is a difference between ordinary people who are content with their place in being, and philosophers who ascend to the horizon of mystery. When a person turns their gaze from the lower, from the given, from illusion, to the higher, an important change takes place within them — an "ontological mutation" in Blaga's words. The structure of this person's consciousness changes. The philosopher becomes an ontological mutant. Blaga thought that culture is precisely the pact which man makes with the Great Anonymous upon reaching the horizon of mystery. When the pact is concluded, the Great Anonymous gives some portion of knowledge to the ontological mutant, i.e., to the awakened human. But not directly; rather, this knowledge is granted in an apophatic way, through absence. Culture is the link between the Great Anonymous, between ultimate, supreme, absolute truths, and the human being. The mystery of culture is the central topic explored in detail in Blaga's *Trilogy of Culture*.

Two Types of Consciousness: Luciferian and Paradisiac

Blaga speaks of two types of people and two types of consciousness. There is Luciferian consciousness and there is Paradisiac consciousness. How are they different? Luciferian consciousness is that of the awakened human who turns to the Great Anonymous, or more accurately to the horizon of mystery, which is unknowable and can only be intuited, which one can only approach from a distance to the extent that culture allows. At the same time, this Luciferian mind is an ontological mutant. Plus, it is unhappy, because it cannot fully understand the Great Anonymous. Such a Luciferian person feels condemned, cursed by virtue of the fact that the possibility of being one with God has been cut off.

The Luciferian type understands that they have been deceived, they are aware of the punitive function of transcendental censorship, yet they still feel and understand that the Great Anonymous exists, that it cannot but exist. Finding themselves within this middle position as a metaphysical frontiersman, an ontological mutant, they lead a life that is torn by the contradiction between the will to absolute knowledge and the impossibility of achieving it.

Here Lucian Blaga manifests a perspective which is close to eschatological optimism. Condemned Luciferian man is thrown into the world. At the same time, there is the possibility of the horizon of mystery. This possibility is small and depends on the culture into which a person is born. For example, Romanian culture was of great importance to Blaga. He provided a poignant description of the Romanian landscape which he called Mioritic, one that is immersed in death and decay.[30] Its striking future is exemplified by the decayed fences of Romanian peasants, cultural objects placed within the primal element of decay. We also have such fences in Russia. I sometimes still encounter them even in the center of Moscow.

What exactly is this kind of "collapsing fence"? It is a direct consequence of transcendental censorship, from which follows a lack of the right to replicate the divine order. It is a piercing sense of futility, the feeling that the human being is thrown, that they are an ontological mutant who is incapable by nature and essence of reproducing the highest geometric order of forms. Thus, human fences are always dilapidated and run down.

In his characterization of Romanian society, Blaga says that this piercing sense of futility, the Mioritic landscape permeated with death, must be accepted. He also characterizes different societies and says: look, in English society the fences are straight, but who appears behind them? Cars drive out from beyond them with gentlemen dressed in tailcoats, or, at worst, their tidy servants. And in Romanian society, where the fences are crooked, who comes out of them? Blaga says: because

---

30   Lucian Blaga's term "Mioritic" is based on the tragic Romanian folk song "*Miorita*," the protagonist of which celebrates death as the mystery of solar union.

of the skewed, barely hinged gates, spirits come out. In Russian lands as well, where the fences are run down and the gates are skewed, spirits also come out from time to time. I myself can bear witness to this: I've seen them. They are very strange, perhaps we simply take them to be people who have had a little too much to drink. But I think that things are actually much more serious. Something powerful and disturbing is concealed in them, perhaps a deep ontological mutation.

Paradisiac consciousness (from the word "paradise") is the consciousness of the ordinary citizen, the layperson who does not notice anything of this sort, who wouldn't even be able to guess that some horizon of mystery exists. Everything seems to match up and they make ends meet only because they have never really tried to make sense of them.

Cioran: Enthusiasm as a Form of Love

The ontological mutation to which Blaga devotes attention is the highest reward for the human being in contrast to other animals. Blaga (like Spengler) distinguishes between the notions of culture and civilization. Higher types of animals can organize civilization, but they cannot organize culture. Thus, we come to Emil Cioran.

Only quite recently while preparing for this lecture, I figured out that Cioran is an absolute ontological optimism — this was quite a revelation for me.

Cioran was born in 1911 and died in 1995 in Paris. As Professor Marinescu, an enemy of Eliade's, recounted, Cioran died alone, suffering from Alzheimer's disease and abandoned by everyone. No one visited him, and he died in horrendous poverty. He had come to France after the war and essentially divorced the Romanian language, writing nothing more in Romanian, only French. It is interesting that he was the son of an Orthodox priest who had graduated from the Faculty of Philology and Philosophy in Bucharest. But let's not dwell on his biography in detail.

Throughout Cioran's works, we are always faced with his disappointment in the illusoriness of the world. He constantly talks about the decline and end of mankind. He is convinced that human civilization has exhausted and ruined itself. Cioran has been called the prophet of the age of nihilism. Dictionaries and encyclopedias associate him with the culture of pessimism. But this is superficial knowledge about Emil Cioran.

In order to understand who he really was, we must turn to his text entitled "Enthusiasm as a Form of Love" from the collection *On the Heights of Despair*.[31] This is one of his early texts from 1934, written when Cioran was 23. A translation of this text by Alexander Bovdunov, a specialist in Romanian philosophy and culture (I highly recommend looking into his works on Blaga, the Great Anonymous, and his other work), has been published on the Center for Conservative Studies' websites.

What is enthusiasm? Cioran says that it is the determination, the readiness, to act no matter what, and he emphasizes that such an act might not have any result. Enthusiasm means that the duality and imperfection of the world should not be taken into account whatsoever. It is an attempt to overcome the artificial dualism of any given thing, and reach the horizon of mystery. It is a strategy of refusal. What is important is that Emil Cioran describes enthusiasm as a form of love. He says that true love does not think of itself in any dualist terms such as myself/the other and is not directed towards anything. This is love of the highest order. This love floods everything, a love that is absolutely vertical, not horizontal.

Intrinsic to the inner nature of every enthusiast is a cosmic, universal receptivity, the ability to accept everything and to direct oneself in any direction out of an overabundance of impulses from within without losing anything in the interim, to participate in any act with an inexhaustible vitality that is spent on the pleasure of realization, on the passion of embodiment and effectiveness. For the enthusiast, there are no criteria and

---

31 E.M. Cioran, *On the Heights of Despair*, trans. Ilinca Zarifopol-Johnston (Chicago: University of Chicago Press, 1992).

no prospects, there is only the refusal, the anxiety of giving, the joy of fulfillment, and the ecstasy of the result. This is what is of foremost importance for the person for whom life is a toss, an eagerness, in which the only thing of value is the fluidity of the life process, the immaterial impulse that raises life to the height at which destructive forces lose their intensity and negative impact.

The enthusiast does not know defeat, and he does not know the goals of his own war, but he nevertheless rises up and revolts. He revolts by renouncing the illusoriness, he revolts against the banal pleasure imposed by modern civilization. He leaves the consumer society. He is, Cioran says, the only one who feels alive when everyone else is dead. The enthusiast feels himself to be eternal.

Cioran describes enthusiasm as a love which lacks an object for love, an overflowing love. Moreover, this description of love is close to the one given in Plato's *Phaedrus*: love not for an object, not for science, and not even for an idea, but love in and of itself. This is the highest form of love.

This text of Cioran's is a unique testimony of eschatological optimism. If you get to know Cioran on the whole, you will be struck by his deep pessimism, his cursing of being. His text *Anathemas and Admirations* is indeed worth reading on a "gloomy Sunday."[32] But, amidst all of this, Cioran has nothing to do with pessimism and nihilism. He is a true eschatological optimist.

The enthusiast overcomes dualism. Dualism is poison to the enthusiast. He is beyond duality and schism.

The Evil Demiurge

Now let us take a look at Cioran's Gnostic views. In his text "Discord,"[33] he speaks of two truths. He begins his exposition

---

32　Emil Cioran, *Anathemas and Admirations*, trans. Richard Howard (New York: Arcade Publishing, 2012), 195

33　See Emil Cioran, *Drawn and Quartered*, trans. Richard Howard (New York: Arcade Publishing, 2012).

with his understanding of history. From Cioran's point of view, history is a lie. History is made for people who, to invoke Lucian Blaga's metaphysical picture, are prisoners of non-Luciferian (Paradisiac) consciousness. They are the captives in Plato's cave. They are objects, uncritical receivers, consumers of the illusion surrounding them. Accordingly, history is a punishment, a curse.

In the text "Two Truths," Cioran resorts to a metaphysical model composed of three instances.[34] This model is very close to Lucian Blaga's. There is the "good God," also called the "sleeping god," who is beyond everything. This God is good. He cannot create the world, because he is incapable of transcendental censorship. Committing an act of deceit is abhorrent to him. He is truly and integrally good. He has no cunning. He is omnipotently good. This good God cannot create, and so He is outside the world. Cioran even scolds Him, saying that He is "too soft a god." Cioran has a strange metaphor for this figure which is interpreted in a qualitatively different way than the apophatic God of fully-fledged theology who is simply beyond. This good God has no irony, whereas the territory of our world is deeply ironic. The realm where the sleeping god is found is ἐπέκεινα τῆς οὐσία.

Meanwhile, our world is created by a different, evil god who is less refined and inactive. This evil god has a copyright on defects. This evil god creates us, creates the world, introduces transcendental censorship, and administers it. He creates an inauthentic, un-absolute world. This god is in fact an evil god, an evil demiurge. Here we are faced with a Gnostic theory. On this point, it would be fully appropriate to recall Lucian Blaga's Great Anonymous. Here it is, the central topic of the Romanian Logos! It penetrates Cioran, Blaga, and other Romanian geniuses. They are synced in their thought that this evil god is the source of all vices and shortcomings in the universe. This evil god is the devil. Cioran's description of the devil is marvelous. The devil acts like a modern person, like a manager. He is simply an administrator pinned with the function of directing history.

---

34   [Russian edition:] Emil Cioran, *Posle kontsa istorii* (Moscow: Simpozium, 2003).

He is the manager of this world. According to Cioran (and this is where his eschatological optimism is manifested), man's first imperative is to revolt against the devil and to reject temptation and illusoriness.

Secondly (and this is already a higher type), when you have cultivated the ontological mutation within yourself, you move to the second level and enter into battle with the "evil demiurge." This is where the problem arises: after all, you find yourself within the historical process, the Kali-Yuga, and the people around you abide in this phase of the deep oblivion of being. In such a situation, in such a phase, how can you escape the historical process and go beyond its limits? Here Emil Cioran speaks of something terrifying, about the need to break through and out of the fabric of history, to hurl yourself out of history, to take yourself out of it and to take it out of yourself; to knock at the door of eternity from below. This means going to the very bottom, knocking oneself down, and entering the territory of hell. Cioran characterizes this special operation as a mystical experience grounded in a radical break with the human as such. It is the experience of rejecting one's very self as a product of transcendental censorship. It is an absolute "No!" to this censored self, and at the same time, an absolute "Yes!" to ontological mutation, whereby this "Yes!" indicates insanity and severance. When we break through history and go out of time, it means that we have gone beyond the boundary of ourselves. This is where mystical experience begins. Eschatological optimism is a call to overcome and overrun the boundary, to go through it, to shoot an arrow towards the other shore and decide to cross over. This ontological challenge is what Emil Cioran's eschatological optimism poses. This is the deepest, riskiest spiritual experience, and no one knows how it will end. It is also a state of being condemned to something: after all, there are no promises, no guarantees that you will find bliss or a contemplative life upon leaving the historical process and taking yourself out of time. You will never see any encouragement from among eschatological optimists. You will struggle when there are no stars, as Christian Hoffmann von Hoffmannswaldau said:

Auf, o Seele, du mußt lernen,   Up, o Soul, you must learn
Ohne Sternen,   Without stars
Wenn das Wetter tobt und bricht,   When the weather rages and breaks
Wenn der Nächte schwarze Decken   When the black covers of night
Uns erschrecken,   Frighten us,
Dir zu sein dein eigen Licht.   To be your own Light for yourself

Living on the Edge

Cioran tells us: you are doomed, you do not know how successful your ontological mutation or your decision to break with everything would be; it is entirely possible that you will completely fail, and that your efforts will have been meaningless.

Wouldn't it be much more fun to stand and blink and say, like Nietzsche's last people, that "we've invented happiness?" Cioran says that, all the same, it is necessary to get rid of this petty-bourgeois, philistine dream. He experiences a deep hatred and deep dissatisfaction with the most basic conditions of human existence, with the fact of what has been given to man and who man is. He speaks of absolute unhappiness, of ontological deception. He categorically disdains this deception.

If we read Cioran through the prism of Gnosticism, then, on the one hand, we will find in front of us a deeply unhappy person who has been thrown into a meaningless world; yet, on the other hand, this person still has hope that in the very gesture of enthusiasm, in the pure act of going beyond his own boundaries, in the act of ontological mutation, he might attain something higher, something more worthy. Although he might not attain anything, this act in and of itself is happiness — the happiness of the process of rising up and revolting not as a finale, but as an arrow thrown towards the other shore, rather than at a target which it might (or might not) hit.

Late Cioran was more skeptical, strict, harsh, and depressed. Yes, he was melancholic. If you open *Anathemas and Admirations*, you will see an eschatological pessimist. He proclaims that the end of the world is coming and that it will be proven that everything is cursed, that humanity is doomed to terrible torment. But the whole point is that Cioran does not simply state this inevitability — he does not coincide with it, he is not satisfied with it. He is in-between, balancing between despair and hope — after all, it is typical of Romanian culture to flounce around like this.

I'll read a fragment from his notebooks (1957-1972): "I cannot live in any other way, only at the limit of emptiness or fullness, only extremes."[35] This is an important metaphor. Cioran lives in the territory of ontological mutation, always on the edge.

In Cioran we encounter the term "melancholy," which he constantly repeats, as he is obsessed with melancholy and nostalgia. For Cioran, the term "nostalgia" designates remembrance of a world that once was, but which we have since lost. It is an attempt to remember what we once had, but do not have now, and will never have in the future. Melancholy, according to Cioran, is the longing for another world, yet he remarks that he has never known what kind of world. This is unlike the man of Tradition, who remembers in spite of everything and is sure that "truth will win in the end" (as Guénon said[36]) and that the true proportions of ontology will be restored after the end of the illusion.

Eschatological optimism is a phenomenon peculiar to the 20th-century's nihilistic tradition. In Tradition and mainstream Traditionalism, eschatological optimism is impossible, even in the Kali-Yuga when the true world that was and will be is remembered or still present despite the density of the illusion. In eschatological optimism, we find ourselves thrown into a world that is already hopelessly rotten.

---

35 E.M. Cioran, *Notebooks*, trans. Richard Howard (New York: Arcade Publishing, 2007).

36 René Guénon, *The Crisis of the Modern World* trans. Marco Pallis, Arthur Osborne, and Richard C. Nicholson (Hillsdale, NY: Sophia Perennis, 2004).

The Partisan: Breaking into Eternity from Below

Further on, we find something in Cioran that is similar to Ernst Jünger's "theory of the partisan." Cioran calls for abolishing the public and argues that one must learn to navigate without interlocutors, without relying on anybody, and by absorbing the whole world into oneself while accepting the tragic challenge of fate and getting used to living with the state of doom. While analyzing German grammar in his diary, Jünger wrote that the verb he hates the most is *besitzen*, "to possess," while the most remarkable word is the neologism *entwerden*, literally meaning "to cease to be."

When you read Cioran and encounter these metaphysical pitfalls, please try to work your way through them and correctly interpret them with reference to Romanian culture and the paradoxical Gnostic theme connected to eschatological optimism. From there you will be able to build a full picture of Cioran's disturbing, profound thought. For me, turning to the Romanian context was a revelation. It is thanks to Lucian Blaga that all of this was revealed in full. For me, Cioran was originally an absolutely doomed thinker. I read his *After the End of History* in which he discusses the Apocalypse and in which, in general, everything seems quite clear, and I interpreted this nostalgia to be a black despair, horror in the face of having been completely forsaken by God and left in hell. But it is important to remember that, alongside this black ontology, Cioran still proposes escaping time and breaking through to eternity, even if it is from below.

Cioran's Significance for Russian Philosophy

Now let us talk about Cioran's place in Russian culture. Why are we talking about him here in Russia? Why do we need these Romanian fences and this ontological mutation? What's the point of the dark poetics of this unknown Romanian Dionysianism? Cioran himself says that Russia is the country, the space, in which the realization of eschatological optimism is possible. He does not have the formula for "eschatological optimism," but what he describes corresponds to it. I'll read a passage of his about Russia:

> With its 10 centuries of horrors, twilights, and promises, Russia has proved more capable than anyone of harmonizing with the night side of the historic moment that we are experiencing. The apocalypse suits her wonderfully, she has a knack and penchant for it, and, because the rhythm of her movement has changed, she is exercising it today more so than ever in the past.[37]

This is Cioran's thesis on Russia. An altogether similar note can be heard in Jünger's *Forest Passage*, where he talks about the roles of Russia and Germany. Martin Heidegger also paid considerable attention to this relation. In the Fourfold, *das Geviert*, the Sky corresponds to Germany and the Earth to Russia. We Russians are touched by Cioranism and eschatological optimism, and we have nowhere else to go. We are doomed to this ontological *Differenz*[38], to this ontological mutation. We might or might not follow it. We might abandon the strategy of desperate metaphysical battle and become happy like the last people. But that is not what this talk is about.

II. The Metaphysics of War

The Sicilian Baron Julius Evola

Now let us discuss Julius Evola. Here we come to a more solar, more diurnal type. If we take Gilbert Durand's modes of the imagination, then the Romanian type of consciousness corresponds to the nocturnal.[39] If we apply the strategy

---

37 Quoted in [Russian edition:] Jean Baudrillard and Emil Cioran, *Matritsa Apokalipsisa. Poslednii zakat Evropy* (Moscow: Algoritm, 2019).

38 The ontological difference is a fundamental notion in Martin Heidegger's philosophy which means the ability to distinguish between Being (*Sein*) and beings (*Seiende*). See Martin Heidegger, *Being and Time*, trans. Joan Stambaugh (Albany: State University of New York Press, 2010).

39 See Alexander Dugin, *Voobrazhenie. Filosofiia, sotsiologiia, struktury* (Moscow: Academic Project, 2015).

of Noomakhian analysis, then the Romanian Logos is the Logos of Dionysus, although we can find many variations within it.[40]

Baron Julius Evola was born in Sicily. According to legend, the gates to hell can be found in Sicily. It has an interesting atmosphere. Whoever has been there likely remembers the scorching sun, 45 degrees Celsius, the shadowy mafia, the atmosphere of vague existential anxiety — very vivid impressions. If everyone is getting married with eternal weddings being held in mainland Italy, then in Sicily one can feel the presence of death and hell — someone is always being buried, death is everywhere, the women walk around in black headscarves. I went in to see a Catholic mass there, and noticed that everyone was wearing black shawls.

The Sicilian Baron Julius Evola was born on this sunny island. His thought is permeated with aporias, oppositions. By now, many works have been written about him and many of his own books have been published. As an introduction, I recommend the special program *Finis Mundi* — I think everyone here has at least heard of it at some point or another.[41]

Julius Evola was a man at the very epicenter of metaphysical war. He constantly said that only war makes a man. When asked why it is necessary to fight, he responded: because it constitutes the human being. If, however, one objected that what is needed is not war, but peace, he would respond: peace is the product of war, peace is impossible without war.

Julius Evola was an eschatological optimist, because he recognized the illusoriness of the world. He affirmed that everything around us is a by-product of the Kali-Yuga, the result of the deep degradation of mankind, the cosmic environment, and being itself. He begins his book *Revolt Against the Modern World* with an important formula: there are two worlds, the

---

40 See Alexander Dugin, *Noomakhia. Neslavianskie gorizonty Vostochnoi Evropy: Pesn' upyria i golos glubin* (Moscow: Academic Project, 2018).

41 Alexander Dugin, "Julius Evola: Magicheskii put' intensivnosti", *Finis Mundi* [https://paideuma.tv/video/yulius-evola-magickeskiy-put-intensivnosti-aleksandr-dugin-finis-mundi#/?playlistId=0&videoId=0].

immanent and the transcendent, this one and that one.⁴² There are also two orders: the order of the given reality of material, temporal existence, and the order of eternal being. This is the basic structure of the metaphysical difference (*metaphysische Differenz*) Julius Evola constructs.

I went through Cioran's works in search of some eschatological optimism in him, from the early works (most of which have still not been translated), particularly *Enthusiasm* from 1931, to his later ones, and things were not so simple and unambiguous. But with Julius Evola, things are quite different. Everything is vividly clear and obvious in Evola — you can open up to any page in his books *Pagan Imperialism*, *The Metaphysics of War*, and *Men Among the Ruins*, and you'll find yourself in the midst of ontological rupture and absolute war.⁴³

Profane War and Sacred War

What are the West and Western civilization from Evola's point of view? They are that against which one needs to wage an inner war. The ontological mutant must declare a revolt against Western civilization. The West is not horizontal, nor hierarchical: it is the absence of a strict, caste-based order. But, for Julius Evola, the absence of a caste-based order does not imply mere void, but rather an inversion of true proportions: an inverted, reversed hierarchy. Instead of aristocrats, who he sees as the best in all senses — political, philosophical, existential — the West is ruled by the lower estate. At the same time, Evola argues that the West's degeneration has reached such a point that even the ruling merchant estate, the bourgeoisie, no longer remotely resembles the merchants of ancient times. They are greedy, ignorant, cruel, and stupid degenerates, veritable non-humans. Their outlook is pathologically inorganic, and their will

---

42 Julius Evola, *Revolt Against the Modern World*, trans. Guido Stucco (Vermont: Inner Traditions International, 1995).

43 Julius Evola, *Pagan Imperialism*, trans. Cologero Salvo (Gornahoor Press, 2017); idem., *Metaphysics of War: Battle, Victory and Death in the World of Tradition* (London: Arktos, 2011); idem., *Men Among the Ruins: Postwar Reflections of a Radical Traditionalist*, trans. Guido Stucco (Vermont: Inner Traditions, 2002).

to material wealth is immeasurable. The West no longer knows what the state is, it does not know what nature is. It boasts of having subordinated nature to its mercantile interests. In fact, it has committed savage violence against nature by trying to extract its wealth in a consumerist manner. Modern Western man does not understand nature, he destroys it.

Modern Western man no longer knows what war is. He deceptively calls for peace and exclaims "if only there were no war!" But in practice, he cynically provokes the most terrible and bloody wars of all time. In these wars, the human soul is completely annihilated, because when a person fights only out of compulsion, by coercion or for money, they lose the highest meaning of sacred war and become a banal, blind puppet. Man no longer knows why he goes to war. He deliberately becomes a purely quantitative unit, an "unknown soldier." He goes to die without any understanding of the reason he is fighting, such as the American soldiers who went to die in Iraq or Afghanistan. Americans' relationship to these senseless predatory wars is depicted quite well in the series *Homeland*. Having no inner core and totally ignorant of holy war, American soldiers quickly break down. They are all, en masse, "unknown soldiers" who die without reason.

Evola criticizes this profane, mercantile relation to war. He argues that war is always being waged, but when it is waged by democratic regimes, it denigrates and destroys a person rather than elevating them. The soldier who dies in a sacred war goes to Valhalla, while the soldier who dies in a war waged by a democratic regime gains nothing; oftentimes their family doesn't even receive compensation.

Evola had a very poor opinion of the democratic understanding of war. The modern West does not know genuine war, genuine death, genuine life, genuine existence. It does not know the taste of true being, and it does not know true hierarchy. This is the most terrible curse there could ever be. Evola speaks of hierarchy not simply as something necessary, but as an expression of the cosmic order and universal harmony itself. All order is hierarchical, leading the many to the One and making the relationships between individual parts harmonious and meaningfully conceivable. Evola calls for restoring hierarchy by all means. Hierarchy is also needed within a person. There is a kind of caste structure in the soul, a necessary vertical element, a hierarchy of principles. The highest principle is the contemplative principle, reason. The second is the martial. The third is the carnal, the bodily. These three principles are taken from the classical Indo-European model of societal organization which we also encounter in Platonism. In the *Phaedrus*, Plato describes the structure of the soul as a chariot with a charioteer and two horses, white and black. The orderly, educated, disciplined person on the one hand, and the political system on the other, should be based on this trifunctional system.

These principles should be operative both within a person and within the state as a whole. Evola says that if a hierarchy is built only within the self and this self is not built into the state, it is useless. We must fight with ourselves and with the outside world, and in this struggle eschatological optimism is manifest. Despite the fact that we see degenerate democracy around us, despite the West and its senseless civilization forsaken by God, the highest Light, we must still go out into this world and fight in the name of a higher ideal, for the sake of how things should be.

In Plato's myth of the cave, the ascent from the bottom of the cave into the light does not happen without a subsequent descent from the light back into the darkness in order to illuminate it. Many scholars do not notice this or lose sight of it, instead paying attention only to the ascent, to how one frees themself from the shackles of the cave, ceases to be a prisoner, etc. But in Plato, in Proclus, or in the example of the life of Julian the Apostate, we see the need for war and for descending into this lower world in order to put it into order, to transform it, for without such action no order is possible within. In this lies the metaphysics of war: being a warrior of Light, one descends into the darkness in order to battle it and prevail over it, to turn it into Light. This is the fundamental thesis of Platonism.

Julius Evola examines the notion of "holy war" and takes into consideration the Islamic context of "lesser" and "greater" *jihad*. In Islam, there is both "exterior" ("lesser jihad") and "inner" ("greater jihad") holy war. The inner war is much more important than the exterior. Nevertheless, Evola insists that they must coexist and be harmonized. The feat of the warrior and the feat of the intellectual are inseparable. The intellectual must always be armed, even if he will never use a weapon in practice. The intellectual must first cultivate a readiness to go forth, to step out from the masses and declare a resolute "No!" to modern civilization.

According to Evola, the differentiated man is he who, in the ultimate, thick, dark illusion, in the extreme conditions of the end times, in the minute of cosmic midnight, decides to revolt against the modern world and to build an inner, transcendent axis — in spite of everything, no matter what. Sure, he might be alone. But, according to Evola, even the desperate revolt of the loner is already meaningful. According to Cioran, such a revolt might not make any sense or have any point, but it is valuable in and of itself. After all, a noble being cannot reconcile themself with the conditions of the Kali-Yuga, globalism, and liberal democracy. In any situation, they spontaneously rise up and revolt, even if they do not have the slightest chance of victory. For Evola, such a revolt is inherently charged with meaning. It is work for the sake of a higher principle, for the sake of the higher, absolute "I," and this higher "I" is the divine element concealed in the very depths of man. This is heroic work done in the name of Tradition, and is therefore never meaningless. Hierarchies are a duty. Empires are commands.

It follows that Empire represents the sacred organization of politics. But it is also something more than politics. Empire is what elevates earth to the heavens. It is first and foremost a spiritual notion. Therefore, it is necessary to cultivate Empire within oneself and to exert every effort to build it in the exterior world.

Now we will move straight to my favorite topic: the metaphysics of war. During the New Year's holidays, I was ill with coronavirus and found Evola's book *The Metaphysics of War* in my apartment. In this book, Evola describes the different types of heroism. We have already mentioned that there is no peace without war. Wars are waged by authoritarian regimes as well as democratic ones. It is impossible to imagine an era in which there would be no war at all. In one form or another, war always exists. In any situation we can possibly think of, there is always opposition, division, and hence potentially hostility, confrontation, and conflict.

For Julius Evola, and here I'll quote his Metaphysics of War, "War offers man the opportunity to awaken the hero who sleeps within him." War should not in any case be taken to be a challenge, a call to some kind of direct action, to go and kill or deal with someone. This must be a war of a different character. When I, following Evola, pronounce the word "war," I have in mind a domain of deep metaphysical revelation. We are talking about war against the dark element, war against the Kali-Yuga, against the devil. Evola does not use the term "devil," as he prefers to speak about revolting against the "tiger" of modern civilization, but the meaning is one and the same. We Christians call it the devil and his satanic order.

I want to quote Evola once more: "A warrior tradition and a pure military tradition do not have hatred as the basis of war." This is very important: true martial tradition does not know hatred. Warriors are genuine peacemakers, people who are filled with love above all else. This is a paradox, and it might seem that this is not the case at all, but if we attentively examine Julius Evola's description of the metaphysics of war, this formula will become much clearer to us.

Three Types of War: Spiritual, Aristocratic, Mercantile

Evola emphasizes that there are different types of heroism and different types of war. This has become key to my understanding of various political, geopolitical, and even cultural processes.

From Evola's point of view, war in its highest dimension is war of the spirit. It is the affair of the highest caste. The meaning of this type of war comes from its role as a path to supernatural accomplishments, to the hero's achievement of immortality. This is the sacred dimension of war, the "greater jihad" that transcends the immanent and its laws. The second type of war is typical of the military aristocracy. This type of war is waged for glory and power. Its participants decorate their names with glory (if they fight admirably), found states, and their descendants receive the status of nobility from their ancestors' feats. It is these spiritual and heroic wars that are characteristic of traditional civilization.

But there is a third type of war. Here, instead of the mystic, ascetic, and heroic, instead of the fully-fledged spiritual human being, we encounter the ordinary soldier, that is, the citizen who fights to protect his own well-being or someone else's. This type of war is purely material, devoid of the metaphysical and heroic dimensions. It is fought not by the warrior, but by a soldier following orders, under the sway of material compulsion or for the sake of some kind of benefit. Sometimes, such a soldier might fight for no reason at all. In Jünger, this archetype is manifest in the figure of the "unknown soldier" who is knowingly doomed. Such a soldier no longer understands why they need war, since they are not waging an inner war and have no heroic principle. The existential drama of a soldier to whom war is a completely foreign element is manifest in the figure of the deserter, perhaps most vividly of all in Céline's *Journey to the End of the Night*. There is still a fourth type: the war of slaves. War of this type is waged by those who are generally devoid of any subjectivity and essentially represent automatons, and is conducted by purely technical means.

In accordance with these types of wars, different types of heroism take shape in Julius Evola's work. The highest heroism is the subordination of matter to spiritual principles, which leads a person to a higher existence, a higher being. This is the royal path. The second heroism is the calling of the Kshatriya caste of warriors. It reflects the tragedy of the warrior. A hero is a tragedy. He does not see the light clearly, the higher world remains distant and inaccessible to him, but he fights against this world no matter what. It is this great despair that compels him to fight. The third type of heroism is connected with the degeneration of the martial principle. Although soldiers called to war might behave admirably on the front by throwing themselves at the embrasures, saving comrades, going on the attack, such important deeds alone are not enough to elevate a hero to a new metaphysical level. These are merely virtues of peaceful life put into an extreme context.

Mercenaries

Julius Evola also singles out mercenaries for discussion. I think that the phenomenon of mercenarism should be a topic for a separate lecture. This phenomenon is diverse and multifarious. There are different points of view regarding what "mercenarism" means. Historically, the Swiss have been the classical landsknechts. It is no coincidence that Céline puts words from the song of the Swiss Guard in the preface to Journey to the *End of the Night*:

Notre vie est un voyage	Our life is a journey
dans l'hiver et dans la nuit.	In winter and in night.
Nous cherchons notre passage	We seek our path
dans le ciel où rien ne luit.	In the sky where nothing shines.

There are American private military companies (like Blackwater), there are Middle Eastern ones, and there is the private army of the Saudi prince which probably adheres to some kind of religious-ideological guidelines. There is also the Turkish PMC SADAT, which is interesting because it interprets modern geopolitical processes through an eschatological, religious optic. Its members profess a special cult devoted to Recep Erdogan, whom they hold to be the Mahdi promised to the peoples of Islam. This PMC interprets its seizure and control over territories in the Middle East as an eschatological mission to create the Great Caliphate in the fight against the devil, Dajjal. Russian PMC's have also appeared, but this requires a separate study. The mercenary phenomenon is ambiguous — there are different styles and types, and each of these manifestations demands special attention.

True War is Always Meaningful

Julius Evola stands on the side of metaphysical war, something most clearly present in higher forms of spiritual and martial heroism. In the conditions of the modern world, any stubborn and desperate resistance to this world, any uncompromising struggle against liberalism, globalism, and Satanism, is heroism.

By virtue of his Gnosticism, Cioran instead belongs to a type of tragic, decadent heroism; Evola has a more positive attitude. Evola does not speak of the futility or meaninglessness of revolt. He recognizes that a metaphysical warrior who revolts against the modern world is likely to stand alone, condemned to suffering and unhappiness. In Hegel, the beginning of philosophy is rooted precisely in the unhappy consciousness — after all, happy, peaceful, comfortable consciousness is self-sufficient and does strive towards anything, but rather to preserve what already is. In the end, a happy consciousness is a general, complete absence of consciousness, it is in complete harmony with the surrounding world, a state in which we can observe animals, plants, and minerals. Plato's philosopher is also unhappy, as he is forcibly pulled away from the place where he could have happily observed the Ideas and the One, forced to descend back into the cave to bicker with aggressive, rude, ungrateful ignoramuses.

Julius Evola is much more solar and spirited. If you don't want to fall into a state of melancholy, then become acquainted with eschatological optimism through Julius Evola's works, such as his *Pagan Imperialism, Men Among the Ruins, Ride the Tiger,* etc. Unlike pessimistic heroism, the eschatological optimism we find in Evola always recognizes the higher meaning behind true war. True war cannot be meaningless. Moreover, it is real war that gives things their deep, living meaning.

Jünger: The Sea and the Forest

Let us move on to the figure of Ernst Jünger. Here I will dwell on only one of his works, *The Forest Passage (Der Waldgang)* from 1951.[44] From my point of view, this is a programmatic document of eschatological optimism. It represents a statement of the fact that: (1) the surrounding world is illusory; (2) the surrounding world is finite; (3) history is doomed; and (4) the world is hopeless, yet at the same time there is the need to resist it.

Jünger describes the material world as a sea, an expanse of water. Interestingly enough, he operates with geopolitical terms and draws on the opposition between "land power" and "sea power," or tellurocracy and thalassocracy. The sea element is matter, the "mundane sea," the element of heavy corporeal formation. The opposite principle is that of the forest. The forest is something solid, permanent, it is land and soil. It is also the paths that run through the forest (Heidegger's *Holzwege*[45]). It is not simply a symbol of rationality (as Deleuze interprets the figure of the tree in *The Logic of Sense*[46]), but also the territory of the axis. In Jünger, the forest represents the space where deep mystical experience takes place. The mystical experience of the forest is one of walking along paths that suddenly break off — "*plötzlich enden,*" as Heidegger said. These pathways have no continuation. This is the experience of facing the unknown,

---

[44] Ernst Jünger, *The Forest Passage,* trans. Thomas Friese (Candor: Telos Press Publishing, 2013).

[45] See Martin Heidegger, *Off the Beaten Track,* trans./eds. Julian Young and Kenneth Haynes (Cambridge: Cambridge University Press, 2002).

[46] Gilles Deleuze, *The Logic of Sense,* trans. Mark Lester and Charles Stivale, ed. Constantin V. Boundas (New York: Columbia University Press, 1990).

an elusive mystical element, a philosophical experience and an experience of mystery associated with soil and forest. Jünger says that the catastrophe in which we live is finite and illusory. It is part of our thrownness into the world and it is inevitable. No one can escape this catastrophe, but freedom can still be found within it.

We take this to be a test. Jünger's approach is much closer to Julius Evola's than to Cioran's. The mode of the diurne is predominant in Jünger. It is frightening to imagine how many wars he went through and survived. He lived to be more than 100-years-old.

For Jünger, war is not a gesture of hopelessness, but a gesture of radical overcoming, of radical opposition to the world and restoring the true foundations of existence. Jünger is an optimist: he believes that this world is terminally ill, but, nevertheless, we have no other path than to try to restore its true proportions at any cost. This can be done by "passing into the forest," through self-transformation, through deep philosophical work.

Jünger's Three Gestalts

Jünger discusses several main figures, Gestalts, one of which we have already mentioned today: the "unknown soldier," to which he adds the figure of the "worker," and the "anarch."

The unknown soldier has no purpose in war and therefore cannot attain victory. He is merely an unfortunate subject who has been thrown into the periphery of this world, who is doomed to go into something empty and meaningless for him.

The "worker" is a more conscious type who is aware of the need for war against the exploiters. The worker fights for world revolution, but remains within the framework of the system. The worker accepts the modern world, but completely apart from its petty-bourgeois wrapping, which he understands to be a cold, tragic challenge, like fate.

The figure of the "anarch" is the peak of human capacity. The anarch is like a transcendental axis crossing the plane, the horizon of illusion, the field of turbidity. The anarch is the flight of an arrow aimed and shot somewhere into the sky.

In *The Forest Passage*, Jünger says that man is thrown into the world and needs to break out of illusion. Man must wage battle inside this illusion.

The Transcendent Vertical

What is the "forest passage"? Obviously, it is not actually a physical retreat into a forest, it is not reclusion or escapism. Unlike another Jüngerian Gestalt, the "partisan," the forest dweller does not represent the organization of a grassroots network of resistance. This figure represents the decision, here and now, to reject identification with one's surroundings. Passing into the forest means renouncing and proclaiming a decisive "No!" to everything we see around us.

Here, Jünger sometimes lets some disturbing things slip. Yes, it is possible that passage into the forest will be tragic and end in misfortune, but, nevertheless, it is necessary to make this gesture. We need to make the irreversible decision, we must resist and enter into a battle, even if it is most likely hopeless.

Nevertheless, this act is in itself one of active opposition: it is war. Passing into the forest is necessary for a person to become a human being. Jünger writes: "The locus of freedom is to be found elsewhere than in mere opposition, also nowhere that any flight can lead to. We have called it the forest. There, other instruments exist than a nay scribbled in its prescribed circle."[47]

Passing into the forest is an awakening. Jünger conveys to us that, in principle, man has the capacity to experience ontological mutation, but is not awakened. He is sleeping in the forest. Passing into the forest means deciding to recognize

---

47 Jünger, *Forest Passage*, 32.

one's "ontological mutation," to refer back to Lucian Blaga's term. Here arises an interesting point of consideration: Jünger says that the forest passage does not technically imply abandoning one's habitual living and dwelling space, but rather constructing a transcendental vertical in the very same space where we already find ourselves. How is such an axis to be built?

Here it might be appropriate to refer to the myth of how Dionysus attempted to escape a group of pirates who had abducted him. Dionysus, captured by these globalist sailors, commanded vines and ivy to tie the oars and sides of the ship, to grow higher than the masts. A tiger then leaped out of the thick overgrowth and tore apart the marauders. We find ourselves here in the raging sea of the mundane. We are on a ship that is constantly on the move and has long since lost any orientation — much like Rimbaud's "The Drunken Ship." The ship is made of wood (ὕλη means both wood and matter in Greek). This is the corporeal world, the bodily shell. But our soul, our inner spark, our internal fire, can ignite, and then this wood will catch fire. Thus we embark on an uprising, we launch our resistance, and we repulse the civilization of the mundane sea. We have the chance to not fade away and be extinguished, but the decision must be made consciously. We must move towards it consistently. The eschatological optimist will declare a decisive "Yes!" to transforming the ship into a forest, into riotous vegetation, and even to the tiger jumping out of the thickets — "Yes, I am awake! Yes, I am getting out of this illusion! Yes, I choose freedom!"

The Salvation of the World in the Eschatological Optimist's Hands

What we have talked about today is not a finished doctrine. It is no more than a philosophical hypothesis based on the texts of a number of authors who have in one way or another responded to the problem of nihilism that is rapidly growing in our world. But this hypothesis might help us in some way, it might motivate us to live on, to fight and win in the context of the modern Kali-Yuga, in the conditions of the end times.

If even one of us, including myself and everyone gathered here today, commits to seeking this "forest passage," to becoming the anarch, or to making the strong-willed decision that we must break with the modern world and cultivate the warrior and hero within ourselves, then it seems to me that the world is already saved. Because even a single person can save all of mankind, as we know.

III. Out of the Hell of the Modern World

Question: Do I understand correctly that we can interpret eschatological optimism to be an attempt to bring Modernity back into the fold of tradition, like some kind of simulation of tradition…?

Daria Dugina: No, not at all. Eschatological optimism today must be placed within the structure of Postmodernity, Modernity has already been overcome. Nietzsche called the *Übermensch* the "victor over God and nothingness." Modernity overcomes God, whereas the eschatological optimist must then overcome nothingness. Regarding Traditionalism, it too is partially a phenomenon of Postmodernity. While it does not coincide with Tradition, it is in no way a simulation. It is incorrect to discuss eschatological optimism within the terms of Modernity/Tradition. We are not talking about a "plane," but about a kind of "volume." In Evola — both the early and later Evola — there are paradoxes that resonate with eschatological optimism, although he remains a Traditionalist. If we want to talk about the simulation of Tradition, this might refer to neo-spiritualists like Blavatsky, Mintslova, Bely (my favorite figures of the Silver Age) or later figures, for instance Castaneda. By the way, there is something quite interesting to be found in Castaneda. For example, he talks about what it means to be a warrior. His practice of contemplating his palms in his dreams is also interesting. Julius Evola represents an authentic revolt within Postmodernity. Guénon is even more fundamental. They show us the paths we can take. For myself, this path is, without a doubt, Orthodoxy and Edinoverie. For others, it is Sufism or Shiism. Eschatological optimism is not a religion, it is a metaphysical standpoint. There is nothing simulacral in it. Rather, it is strictly the opposite. However, the question as to whether Traditionalism is to some extent a "threat" to fully-fledged tradition, whether it could turn into a simulacrum, should be asked. Talentless or simply mediocre disciples are often capable of distorting the thought of genius teachers beyond recognition. Evola was more fortunate than many in this sense. In contemporary Italy, there are many convinced and fully-fledged Traditionalists who are oriented towards Evola and continue his ideas. I am friends with many of them — in particular with Rainaldo Graziani, whose father was very close to Evola, although he was much younger. They are wonderful people. But in Russia, everything is a bit different, and not for the better, alas… Perhaps this is because European Traditionalism is not very organic for us.

Question: As far as I've understood, your interpretation of eschatological optimism has fundamental differences from eschatological pessimism and, strictly speaking, these differences lie in the hope for the presence of some kind of echelon that is beyond reality, of which nothing is known, yet for which one can hope?

Daria Dugina: Yes, that is entirely correct. This purely transcendent echelon is described in different ways across various traditions. For example, in Christianity, in apophatic theology, it is held that we cannot know anything about God, because we are created human beings, we are in this world, we are born here and are limited by the nature of creation. In Orthodox mysticism, there is a particularly elaborate version of apophatic theology, according to which we can know God only through the experience of mystery. In fact, the term "enthusiasm" (ἐνθουσιασμός) that is often encountered in Cioran's texts etymologically means "inspired or possessed by a god," referring to a mysterious, mystical experience. Eschatological optimism is the experience of mystery.

Question: Daria, can I ask a question regarding culture? There is modern culture and there is traditional culture — what is the best way to approach and interact with them?

Daria Dugina: Let's recall how Lucian Blaga interprets culture. He says that culture is a pact between the "Great Anonymous," that is the "evil demiurge" who has created the imperfect world, and the human being, who must break out of it to reach the truth. Accordingly, the further a person strives to know the truth, the more perfect culture will be. But is there even one such heroic gesture in contemporary Russian culture, if we look at our most famous books, collectives, venues, and TV channels? Everything is, in the very least, marked by vulgarity or reduced to a simplified political agenda. How can one speak of Evola or Eliade in this context? I once went to Strasbourg to speak in the European Parliament, and I began my speech with a quote from Guénon. Everyone looked at me rather strangely. Here's what I'm getting at: even though there are no points of intersection between Tradition and "culture" in the modern world, you should not just shrug your shoulders and give up. Everything can always be changed. Even the most insignificant shift of the Overton window can have enormous consequences. Everything can be decided by a single heroic gesture if we are determined to break through the blockade of the "evil demiurge." One gesture can change culture. Modern culture, a culture of decay and vulgarity, needs to be resisted, to be met with a resolute "No!", but this does not mean that one should run away and retreat from it, but rather earnestly work from within it. In this lies the essence of eschatological optimism.

Question: I'll clarify my question: What I have in mind is whether it is possible through modern culture or, say, more broadly through European culture, such as through Renaissance culture, to establish a connection with the beyond?

Daria Dugina: Through modern culture? Which one? Through the culture of object-oriented ontology, cyborgs, and mutants?

Question: Well, let's say 20th century culture in general, or through the culture of the Impressionists in particular?

Daria Dugina: A connection with the beyond can be established through anything. Everything has meaning and a higher meaning. Higher meanings are manifest everywhere, and tradition can be found in everything. You only need to have an elevated and active concentration of knowledge of tradition, a verified Traditionalist view, a Traditionalist perspective within yourself to find it. Sometimes, behind the absolute chaos of modern culture and its products, one can see the traditional background that was the mainstay of human culture until its collapse in Modernity (New Time) and Postmodernity. Modernity is always bound to Tradition, whether by challenging it, parodying it, distorting it, or completely denying it. The philosopher Whitehead once said that "all of philosophy is nothing more than a series of footnotes to Plato." We could say that modern culture is a disputation of principles, a distortion, a twisting, and a reversal — but of what? Of Tradition, that most powerful foundation of all mankind that ensured its survival and flourishing for millennia. Returning to Tradition is not as impossible as it might seem. It is necessary to commit to the "Turn" of which Heidegger wrote.

Question: I'm also interested in how the archaic culture of primitive tribes (like the Aboriginals of Australia, for instance) relates to great classical culture — let's take Bach, for instance. In archaic societies, culture is improvisational, whereas in high cultures it is harmonious and orderly. Could we say that there is some kind of revelation in both?

Daria Dugina: Revelation is everywhere. But the best thing of all — and this is my totalitarian recommendation — is to seek revelation in the culture into which we are born. It is no coincidence that we are born as those who, in an altogether specific era and in an altogether specific territory, have concluded an altogether specific pact with the "Great Anonymous." So we must live in our culture, and meaning will be revealed to us in it and through it. But, purely theoretically, yes — you could productively interpret Impressionism, Bach, and even cyberfeminism. Something important can be found everywhere.

Question: Is there anything human left in cyberfeminism?

Daria Dugina: Of course, the living cyborg. In general, the term "cybernetics" is very interesting. It is derived from κυβερνήτης, which literally means "helmsman," i.e., the one who pilots a ship. In Plato, the helmsman is the intellect, the observer in the soul and the subjugator of bodily elements. Perhaps such a "helmsman" could be identifiable within cyberfeminism, but here we might easily become the victim of certain tendencies, i.e., we won't be helmsmen, but victims, tools, and ultimately simply spare parts. Therefore, it is better to look for reference points in your own culture. The foreign authors whom we discussed today leave us with their blessings to search for meaning within our own culture. They acknowledge that Russia is blessed in the search for the mystical horizon, for ontological mutation, and for the forest passage. Russia is blessed by the eschatological optimists for a great uprising.

Question: Didn't Nietzsche overcome ressentiment, eschatological *pessimism*, and historicity when he went mad towards the end of his life? Isn't this a real "non-fitting" into the system, a real negation of modern values?

Daria Dugina: Possibly. It cannot be ruled out that this is one of the options for overcoming the laws of illusion and inertia in a completely nihilistic world. For me, Nietzsche is a figure on the border between eschatological optimism and eschatological pessimism. His gestalt of the "child" in the three transformations of the spirit at the beginning of *Thus Spoke Zarathustra* and the overcoming of the previous stages of the camel and the lion embody precisely eschatological optimism. The Nietzschean child Dionysus is the *Übermensch*, the "victor over god and nothing." The victor over god and nothing is the victory over illusions. His death, his end, might look like madness from the outside, but we do not know what the inner content of this madness was. Perhaps it was a completely unique and mysterious experience that is closed to us. We are used to analyzing everything. We see a person who says strange, confusing words and we think that they are crazy. We see something deviating from the norm and we immediately take it to be a pathology or hallucination. We can't figure these things out, but, in the end, they might carry a higher meaning, like the prophetic mumbling of a holy fool. There was a special attitude toward holy fools in Rus'. They were special people, witnesses of some other world. So this is a difficult question.

Question: Object-oriented ontology and similar trends in principle convey a similar view of reality while at the same time happily, absolutely accepting this reality, the Kali-Yuga, and wanting to bring it to its logical end. Is this the reverse side of the same thing or is it a different view of reality?

Daria Dugina: Incidentally, I've been wondering who to call an eschatological pessimist. Baudrillard came to mind. But then I found a more vivid example: Nick Land, with his idea of completely accepting decay, submersion into matter, turning into monsters, accelerating the destruction of man and life on earth. Even more exhibitory here would be Reza Negarestani, who fascinates me. Deleuzeianism (or, as it is called in certain circles, "Dark Deleuze") is also eschatological pessimism. It is an agreement with dissolution and entropy, a rejection of the Logos and its struggle, and a consistent, uncompromising, and in some sense "internalized" decay. You are absolutely right. OOO is eschatological pessimism, so it resembles eschatological optimism with directly opposite signs. The common denominator is eschatology, i.e., the acknowledgement that perversion has already permeated the world and can now only be whipped up to this world's imminent end. But when it comes to understanding the end, our views differ.

Question: Thank you for the magnificent lecture. My question is the following: in the beginning, you mentioned Julius Evola's interesting concept of the "rupture of level." In connection with this, I'm interested in how eschatological optimism corresponds to initiation. Is initiation the aim? For example, in Evola the topic of initiation is one of the central themes, whereas this cannot be said directly with respect to Cioran and Jünger.

Daria Dugina: I think that initiation is the key point in eschatological optimism. There is some hint at this in Jünger's *Forest Passage*. He says that there are three foundations, or three great powers, that might save the person who passes into the forest: art, theology, and philosophy. Take note of theology. In Jünger, we repeatedly encounter an appeal to mystical experience. Sure, this is not directly about initiation, but it comes close. As for Cioran, the question is much more complicated. In my classification, he balances on the border between eschatological pessimism and eschatological optimism. In his Parisian period, he gravitated towards the former. But he makes no reference to initiation. Julius Evola is a pure example of eschatological optimism, and, as you correctly noted, initiation plays a central role in all of his philosophy. Appealing to hierarchy and initiation, verticality, and activating the transcendent dimension in relation to the surrounding world — this is the main, orthodox strategy of the eschatological optimist.

Question: I've always wondered: How does Evola's notion of initiation correspond to the rupture of level? In your view, are these synonyms or phenomena of the same order? For example, can we take the rupture of level to be the self-initiation of which Evola speaks in contrast to the regular initiation of René Guénon?

Daria Dugina: Yes, I think so. Initiation is something instantaneous, like a flash of light in the night, when both levels of reality — this one here and the one beyond — are exposed and there is a gap, an explosion, a kind of short circuit.

Question: While speaking of Julius Evola today, you noted that, compared to Cioran, Evola's optimism is pronounced and he calls for waging war against the modern world, launching a great resistance, and heading in this direction to the very end, the victorious end. But in his later works, specifically in *Ride the Tiger*, doesn't Evola in some sense come to recognize the uselessness of such struggle and accept modern reality?

Daria Dugina: No, he does not. Evola changes the forms and degrees of his optimism which he attached to one or another phenomenon at different stages, but he always remains an eschatological optimist — in his early Dadaism as well as in *Ride the Tiger*. Sure, there is some despondence. He feels pain at the impossibility of fully-fledged spiritual and initiatic realization. But, nevertheless, the most important thing for Evola is his stamina, the fact that he never shrugs his shoulders and gives up. This is precisely why I see in him the key to eschatological optimism. Naturally, this depends on my *grille de lecture*. I want to see and I do see in him the solar struggle, the uprising of solar man. Every author we've spoken about today has, on the one hand, a deep despair in the face of the surrounding modern world, while on the other, they have the determination to wage struggle — albeit hopeless! — against it. Something is happening with these thinkers which is like a ship in the mundane sea being tossed around by the waves. When the ship goes up on a wave, they talk about what needs to be fought; on the other hand, when this wave breaks and the ship slips down and a crash seems inevitable, we see an overwhelming feeling of black, deep melancholy. Therefore, in all these thinkers, we can find some tossing back-and-forth. Jünger also harbors some despair, but at the same time, he has the courage of a warrior and calls for revolt.

Question: You said that it is necessary to treat a person who passes into another tradition as a kind of freak. But how about the Japanese samurai who have lost the Japanese state, lost what they served? What if they decide to serve eternity and the God of Christianity? What is their status? Are they freaks?

Daria Dugina: No, they are not. I believe that tradition exists in different versions, and Western man, for example, might turn to Sufism and find realization there. I have an example of this: my good friend, the Sicilian princess Vittoria Alliata, a foremost specialist on Sufism and a faithful follower of René Guénon. She herself is a Sufi, an excellent expert on the Middle East — on Syria, Lebanon, and Libya. She was friends with Muammar Gaddafi and helped him write his *Green Book*, particularly the part on women's rights. Being from an old royal family dating back to the Langobards, she fully realized herself in Sufism. However, if a person sets out on the path of Traditionalism, then it might be easier and more natural for them to go through their own tradition. I am not opposed to someone passing into another tradition. I believe that every tradition can give meaning. If a person is drawn to some other tradition and they fail to find the required answers and ways within their own tradition, there is nothing wrong with this. But it is still necessary to find out whether this person searched thoroughly. Did they do everything to understand their roots, their origins, their people, their culture? If it depended on me, I would approve a strategy for education where a person would first be obliged to properly study, research, and understand their own tradition and only then turn to others. Already in school, it is necessary to fully acquaint oneself with Russian culture. And this should be continued at university. And only then, once a person has traversed this difficult path far enough, do they have the right to study others. Otherwise, they will remain half-hearted, they won't understand their own traditions, and they will only pick up the surface of another. But there are, of course, e always exceptions.

Question: Can we even talk about culture as "ours" or not "ours"? Isn't it all the same?

Daria Dugina: No, it is not all the same. Everyone has their own place in the world, their spiritual Homeland. This is not a purely physical value. Our roots, the origins of our language and our soul are here. There is a spiritual Homeland, and it is "ours," native and dear to us. For me, this is Holy Rus', Orthodoxy, Edinoverie, the Old Believers' Rite. But, in some sense, maybe we are all wanderers in truth. This is a very difficult question. What is certain is that wherever we find ourselves in the modern world, we are in the center of hell. It is difficult to see authenticity anywhere. We are cursed. But this is no reason not to rush toward salvation.

***

Athos, the Feminine Principle, Apophaticism, and Eschatological Optimism

"Feminine Athos": The Peculiarities of Feminine Consciousness[48]

It is well known that women are not allowed on the Holy Mount. There is something right about this. Here we might recall the Elder Paisios of Mount Athos. I recently read one of his texts and found a quote which accurately describes the ordinary state of feminine consciousness. If this consciousness is not in a state of prayer, then it operates in the following way:

> See what temptation can do? It can turn the switch back and forth from one frequency to another. Just as a fighter is about to receive a message and benefit from it, the dial is switched to another frequency, and the person is distracted by something else. Does he think of something spiritual again? Right away, the dial is switched to other thoughts, and man is never left at peace to focus. If man could only learn the devil's ways, he would be spared a great deal of trouble.[49]

This passage concerns the devil and the devil's tools. The devil tries to distract a person by constantly switching the focus of their consciousness. Analyzing our own and, more broadly, feminine consciousness, it could be said that this switching of the dial is what constantly happens within us. The very fact that women are not allowed on Holy Mount Athos makes it possible to anticipate the unique world of the male mind, the male miracle, and this is valuable. This grants them the ability to concentrate on what is most important, Christ.

---

48 The present text is based on the manuscript and transcription of a presentation given at an unidentified conference "on the topic of Mount Athos with Athonite monks and Russian theologians."

49 Elder Paisios of Mount Athos, *Spiritual Counsels, Volume II: Spiritual Awakening* (Souroti, Thessaloniki: Holy Monastery Evangelist John the Theologian, 2008), 130.

If we consider woman from another angle, she harbors another very important dimension of which Tatiana Mikhailovna Goricheva wrote.[50] This is woman's natural receptivity to apophatic theology and mystical experience. Despite woman's distance from the analytical male mind, from dry reason which can divide the world in accordance with the diurnal method into "yes and no," "enemy and one's own," she has an openness to apophatic theology. She bears and nurtures this within herself as if it were her own "feminine Athos." This is her ideal space. If she manages to overcome the mode of constant temptation and switching of attention from one thing to another, if she moves from this to the magnificent, mystical inner world, and if she tries to go to another deeper, but still essentially feminine, level, then she can participate in apophatic theology.

Tatiana Mikhailovna Goricheva says that the depth of woman's penetration into the inner dimension can at times even exceed the scale of falling and taking off among males. She cites the example of Mary of Egypt. This stunning figure of a great, righteous Christian woman proves that a woman's rise up from the abyss of falling, from the very bottom, is incredibly difficult, but still possible.

Alongside her mutability, woman can also be unusually sensitive to apophatic theology and the mystical experience of leaving this given world for another. This happens in her through prayer, through the capacity for spontaneous vision. If we read the lives of the saints, we can find examples of the appearance of the Divine, divine energies, and instances of higher contemplation to holy women.

The Paradoxes of Thrownness

I would like to mention one interesting hypothesis which I have been thinking about lately and to which I've dedicated several lectures and presentations: eschatological optimism.

---

50 T.M. Goricheva, *Docheri Iova. Khristianstvo i feminizm* (Saint Petersburg: SP Alga-Fond; TPO Stupeni, 1992).

How did this hypothesis arise? It was first born upon my acquaintance with the seventh book of Plato's *Republic*, which deals with the necessity of the philosopher descending back into the cave after his ascent and exit. There was one point here I couldn't understand: If the philosopher is to be so deeply unhappy inside the cave, why should he return to it, why should he descend back after he has discovered the true world of ideas beyond the dark, damp, gloomy cave filled with phantoms and shadows? Few scholars of Platonism have paid enough attention to this question. Why does the philosopher descend? I came to the conclusion that this descent is what is most fundamental in Plato's myth of the cave.

Later on, while reading the Neoplatonists, I noted their ontological frustration with the fact that they have been thrown into this corporeal, material world, one which, compared to the intellectual worlds of ideas and true being, is miserable and insignificant, carrying only decay and distortion. But one can also find in them an apologetics for such thrownness in the world, a recognition of the need to be in the body as part of the harmonious plan of the universal Intellect. This can be considered eschatological optimism.

Later on, already immersed in Christian theology, I got acquainted with the works of the holy fathers and the great theologians, and once again discovered the theme of man's thrownness into this sinful world alongside the need to abide and live within it while resisting it. Despite all the constraining conditions of this world, it is necessary to resist evil and accept the world while cultivating goodness within oneself.

And then, when I read modern post-Christian philosophers such as Emil Cioran and Friedrich Nietzsche, I saw the same problem: despair over being thrown into the world of matter, but equipped with a will to overcome it. The term "eschatological optimism" thus gradually came to mind.

Three Postulates of Eschatological Optimism

I've traced eschatological optimism from Plato through the Neoplatonists, Christian Neoplatonism, Hegel, and onwards to Nietzsche, Evola, and Cioran. This phenomenon, in my opinion, can also be found at Athos. Its pinnacle is Silouan the Athonite's maxim "Keep your mind in hell and do not despair," a beautiful interpretation of which has been offered by Elder Sophrony (Sakharov).

What are the grounds of this eschatological optimism? The first postulate lies in the following: the given reality around us, everything that we perceive as direct reality, is an illusion. In the words of Silouan the Athonite, it is hell.

The second aspect of this vision of the world is that the end of the world is the end of an illusion. Here we might recall René Guénon, who wrote that "The end of a world never is and can never be anything but the end of an illusion."

And the third postulate: knowing that everything is finite, that we are thrown into this illusion, that we are separated from our primordial source and that we are in hell, and that it is still necessary in spite of everything to act in the name of eternity. Being here, we must create a transcendental vertical axis of opposition to this world — a world of sin, illusoriness, and evil. It is necessary to resist hell, the switching of the dial in Paisios' words, which the devil provokes in us — especially in women — every day, every minute, and every second in order to distract us from our contemplation of what is most high. What is higher than us and above us is the soul, the Intellect, and the One — Plotinus' Neoplatonic hypostases. What is important is not the apophatic One alone. In order to get to the One, we still need to make the long and difficult ascent which demands of us a rupture of level, an overcoming of the human horizon, a passage from the body to the soul, then to the Intellect, and further beyond the inner limits of the Intellect to direct contemplation of the divine energies. This highest rupture of level pertains to the realm of apophatic theology.

Eschatological Optimism and Christian Apophaticism

When I began to reflect on the correlation between eschatological optimism and Christian tradition, I realized that it is precisely in apophatic theology that eschatological optimism manifests itself to the fullest. Here we have a consciousness of futility, of ontological poverty, of the finitude of the world, the perishability of everything "given" that surrounds us, and seems to us to be natural. At the same time, the apophatic act flares up in the world "here," but it is directed towards the world "there." This throw of consciousness is desperate and sharp. It corresponds to the third postulate of eschatological optimism: knowing that everything is finite, that everything is illusory, and yet we must act in the name of eternity. It turns out that the most basic standpoint of eschatological optimism is tightly bound up with apophatic theology. Mystical experience begins in the world of illusions, not beyond it.

This is an important point: apophatic theology cannot be taken as a certain stage. It is a commonly held opinion in the history of philosophy and theology that we must first master the method of cataphatic theology — speaking of God through the categories of the world and raising them up to the perfect degree — and only then can we pass to apophatic theology as the next, higher stage. In the sphere of mystical experience, however, there is no linear time such as we are accustomed to in our world, for it, let us recall, is nothing more than an illusion. The sequence "first cataphatic, then apophatic" is not temporal. Both approaches are synchronous, simultaneous. They are not different phases of one and the same process, but two primordially different orientations.

A person begins their return to the source when they ponder how they have already reached the extreme point of matter and how they now need to turn around and begin the process of ἐπιστροφή, that is, ascent to the One. This turn begins the very instant they understand that they have plunged into the illusion to the greatest possible depth. Now they must push off from the bottom, set off, and rise back up. This is where a person commits the rupture of levels by bluntly electing that which is absent instead of that which is present and given. Already with this first gesture, a person is no longer oriented towards the cataphatic, but to the apophatic. This is where apophatic theology begins. Everything becomes hell and nothing else. But the eschatological optimist does not despair. They entrust their hope to our Lord Jesus Christ.

In the proper Christian context, the model of ascent is very similar to the Neoplatonic model. The path of contemplation and leaping towards eternity is described in detail in John Climacus, Symeon the New Theologian, Gregory Palamas, and the authors of the Philokalia. Especially close to apophatic theology, indeed directly connected to it, is the Palamite doctrine of the uncreated energies of the unknowable God. Palamas' philosophy can undoubtedly be considered a version of eschatological optimism. First and foremost, this concerns his idea of subordinating the mind to the heart and the heart to God and the divine energies.

These are merely initial outlines and sketches of what I'm currently working on. Perhaps I'll develop a course of lectures devoted to this question, but I hope that my idea is clear in general terms. This is what I wanted to share with you.

And one more thing: I would like to thank all of the participants here, because today's conference led me to fill up an entire notebook with notes, and in every presentation I found theses which are very important to me and which need to be developed further.

And finally: this conference is distinct in that it has been at once very close to and very far away from life — close to the extent to which we participate in eternity, and distant to the extent to which our surrounding world is an illusion.

***

PART II:
THE FEMININE PRINCIPLE
AND THE PROBLEM OF THE SUBJECT

Woman and Tradition

Tim Kirby[51]: The ball is really in Russians' hands to show us what the family is going to look like, what relations between men and women are going to look like in the 21st century — will Russia take that opportunity or just squander it? Well, we'll see, but what we can do is take a listen to Daria Platonova, who is a researcher of Orthodox Feminism. She's going to tell us all about the true nature of Feminism in Russia. Ms. Platonova, so, roughly speaking, what are some of the key differences between Feminism in Russia and the West?

Daria Platonova: I've seen huge differences, because it depends on the context of where I have been: in the West, there is a kind of process of secularization, and religion is very, very far away from the state, so the problems of Feminism are not at all connected with any religious topics.

Tim Kirby: It's important to know that Russia does not practice separation of church and state but a symbiosis of church and state where the entities remain separate but work together very often — that's an important nuance and one big difference between Russia and, say, America.

Daria Platonova: Well, in Russia we have a very interesting phenomenon where the context, the Orthodox context, somehow influences even Feminism. That means that all the topics which are broadly described in Western Feminism, like the war for equality and the war for rights, in Russia have another degree, because Russia is more traditional, it stays more traditional and the influence of the Orthodox religion is much more complicated and interesting. So here we have a very interesting phenomenon in Russian Feminism which appeared with the name of Tatiana Goricheva, and it is called Christian Feminism.

---

51 The present text is an abridged and edited transcript of an interview in English conducted by Tim Kirby for the YouTube channel "Tim Kirby Russia" in May 2021.

Tim Kirby: Tatiana Goricheva, at the age of 26 during the height of the Cold War and Communism in Russia, converted to Eastern Orthodoxy. She later founded the idea of Orthodox Feminism and had to survive as a dissident in the 80s in the West. When the opportunity to come home arose in the 1990s, she came right back and is here to this very day, but unfortunately there is very little if anything written about her in English, as about all good things that come from Russia.

Daria Platonova: I think this sounds believable. It's very, very interesting to speak about this in the West, because nobody can understand how religion, which according to Western Feminism is a way of installing domination on women, can be connected with Feminism, like it's two opposite sides, controversial concepts. Here in Russia, we have this version.

Tim Kirby: That's interesting! Because in the West it seems almost natural that femininity and Christianity are always at odds. But does this really have to be the case? Maybe they can actually work together and find some sort of middle ground?

Daria Platonova: Actually, Tatiana Goricheva herself notes that in Christianity there is no hierarchical type, no hierarchy of woman and man; there is more dialogue between them. As she quotes the Bible, she says that there was Virgin Mary, really the prototype of woman, and there was Christ, and there was no hierarchy between them. She gave birth to Him, He is Her son and there was no inequality in this, there was a balance. There were two worlds: the world of woman and the world of man. Then, Tatiana Goricheva does an analysis of the biographies of women saints, and she finds there were a lot of women saints who had overcome the huge root of a great existential war and that they are really similar to the way which was taken and overcome by men saints. She says there is a special role in Christian Orthodoxy for women's suffering, and she thinks that there can be not only one world, like man's world with woman as a reduction of this world, but two worlds.

Tim Kirby: And here is the key point. When Western society moved from Monarchy to Liberalism, who got their rights first? White landowning men! They were the political actors and everyone else was a non-actor, you know kind of like how minors don't really have any responsibility today, or worse in the case of slavery. But as time went on, other types of men, other ethnicities and non-landowning men were sort of grouped into this male category as big political actors in society. Now the interesting thing that happened was when women also wanted to be reflected by the law, by constitution, rather than having a separate entity and a separate nature for women, women shoved into the male category. So, the interesting thing is when women did get their rights, they didn't get their rights by raising women from the status of non-entity to a separate woman entity of equal value to men. But they essentially became men. That is probably where Feminism took a very wrong turn and why there's so much desire among awful feminists today to essentially replace men, take the place of men or just become men. So, is this key oversight in the logic of, but that was a long time ago, about a hundred years ago, maybe this key oversight in the concept of Feminism really isn't relevant today, or is it?

Daria Platonova: Simone de Beauvoir says that women is another, an Other, she's the figure of another and this another is created by the man's world, and now women have to do a revolution against this man's world. This is Simone de Beauvoir, the so-called second wave of Feminism in history. But Tatiana Goricheva notes that it is fantastic that woman is an 'other', but she is not the other created by men; she is an 'other' created by God. And here she points out that this other has a separate, other world and there is no possibility to do a hierarchical type of hierarchization between men's and women's worlds, because these worlds are different. Here, Tatiana Goricheva says that it can be based on the religion of Christianity: when it comes to God, man and woman are equal. But they are not equal in that woman has all the rights that man has. Or a man is not equal to a woman, and he doesn't have the similar rights to those a woman has. These are two worlds and they don't cross, they are two separate worlds.

Tim Kirby: Men and women being of equal value, but completely different natures, is ironically a pretty radical version of Feminism for today's Western society.

Daria Platonova: This idea has existed not only in Christian Feminism, but it has also been presented in standpoint Feminism — it's not connected with religion, it is widely presented in the West. But here we have the main topic: that women's world has nothing in common with men's world. They are different. This is a very paradoxical thing, because the idea is quite obvious: really, they are different, even from consciousness, psychology, or even physical appearance, we are different. But the problem is that liberal Feminism, the Feminism which dominates the West, is focused on creating the equality of women and men, even up to the era of having the same psychological and physical appearance, like the androgyne figure is making the real equality of woman and man becoming true.

Tim Kirby: The current trend of androgyny, while forcing men to be sort of wishy-washy and passive while praising women who are strong bosses, has really confused Western society. It's kind of like we are all square pegs being forced into round holes. Why should we do this and why is this not happening in Russia which is open to all the big cool trends in Hollywood movies? Why does Russia have some sort of weird immunity to this?

Daria Platonova: Well, for Russia that's a very interesting case, because when we watch how Feminism has been developing in the world, we see that in Russia women's suffrage was accepted in 1906[52], so in the beginning of the 20th century, while in France, we have it from 1944. This is an incredible situation that means that we have already lived in the feminist world

---

52 [Platonova is here referencing the 1906 Parliament Act of Finland which granted voting rights to men and women in what was then a territory of the Russian Empire. Universal suffrage was instituted in Russia as a whole shortly after the revolution in 1917, two years before the United States. -Ed.]

and now we go to the new strategy of this Christian Feminism, Orthodox Feminism. As for Russia today, contemporary Russia, I think we are still trying to copy the West. We still try to be as liberal as the West is, even if in geopolitics we have a little bit of the course to multipolarity, but still, we are in this world where there is men's domination and woman is some kind of other created by a man. So, I don't think we have already overcome this liberal Feminism in Russia. I just think we are still in the trap, we still exist in the liberal paradigm. But we need to always understand that Russia was in the avant-guard of the feminist battle and today we have a regression to this Liberalism. So, we had a Soviet avant-garde, cyborg-like Feminism, with the idea of the real resistance of woman against the bourgeois liberal landlords and totalitarian hegemony, and now we are somehow softening our discourse to the liberal model, which is regress, and at the same time we have this Christian Feminism which is appearing.

Tim Kirby: But why did Russian women themselves, not under coercion, willfully choose to reject Feminism?

Daria Platonova: Well, actually I think it's because of the context. We're more classical and maybe here women decided to be some kind of saviors of the patriarchy, maybe they started to feel that men are losing a bit of the wheel and they decided to be the patriarchal saviors, maybe this is the explanation. At the same time, the thing is that Russia was communist more in the geopolitical way and I'm not sure that we can say that we had this cultural Marxism. The West is not suffering from communism now. As far as I've analyzed the conservative media in the United States, I see a lot of anti-communist speeches, but these are not anti-communist but more anti-cultural-Marxist. We had a communism which was mainly the economic direction of communism or socialism. But this communist politics, we didn't have it a lot, we didn't have this focus on Feminism, on the rights of LGBTQ and all that is happening now in the West, so our communism was really different.

Tim Kirby: Interesting, but then why does Russia, a formerly Marxist nation, seem to be immune to the effects of cultural Marxism?

Daria Platonova: There was even the possibility that communism could never exist in Russia, but that it could only exist in the form of Christian socialism. The thing is that our mentality didn't accept Communism as it was in the West, so we did a small re-editing of that. The thing is that for now, for Russians, it's quite interesting to see the cyborg feminists which can exist in the Communist Parties and are for the destruction of the woman, while we don't see Communism as the destruction of women.

Tim Kirby: In closing, are there any key differences between the mentalities of today's Western and Russian women and their desires, hopes, dreams and political views?

Daria Platonova: I just think we don't have this obsession of fighting men, and I think we like dialogue and harmony between men and women. We think that when a guy is helping you in the street, with handling something, maybe a big suitcase, that is not a kind of domination on us, that's a kind of help and this is normal. That means a person helps us in this way and we help men in another way. If it's a family, then we create a psychological balance, we help with our "kitchen magic" — you know there exists such a kind of magic; you can even find books now in the West which write about the garden witch or kitchen witch, even calling it a witch! So, we are helping in all these different ways, and I think in Russia this idea of a dialogue between the two, women and men, is very widely accepted, while in the West the dialogue of man and woman causes a problem, because women in the West already have the problem that they can be dominated by men, they will be dominated by men, and they have this theme in their heads and they don't create a dialogue, but a war. Feminism in the West is concentrated on the war against men, while Russian Feminism, as I see it and my friends see it, is concentrated on the happiness of the woman.

Women in the West who are fighting for their rights and receiving them are not happy, because they live in a paradigm in which there is no dialogue, only non-stop war. They become instrumentalized women. The problem is that the West has politicized the phenomenon of woman. Liberal feminism is trying to instrumentalize and make one unique woman, but there are multiple women. If we are to create Feminism, then we need to make a multipolar Feminism, where all the women of all countries have the right to speak. I think there is a permanent dialogue and war between women and men, and I don't think that it must be eliminated. In this war, there is the construction of both, so if we win this war, that will mean that both will end, because there will be no dynamic. Victory is in dialogue, in a soft way like tango. The dance of tango is a very good example, because on the one hand it's aggressive, on the other it's a love story. It's a compromise. These worlds will never be the same, so the war of one against the other will not create one world, but will create two destroyed worlds, as it is in the West. When woman fights against man, she destroys man, and then there is no more woman and no more man.

***

The War of the Sexes

Gender in Tradition: The Creation of the Universe

Today, I would like to talk about a complex array of problems pertaining to feminism and the feminine principle. Specifically, I would like to talk about what Bachofen called the "bloody war of the sexes." I will also try to examine a kind of logical sequence leading from the Traditionalist view of the confrontation between the masculine and the feminine (from the very same "bloody war of the sexes") through an unstable balance (a kind of tango where the partners change places in a harsh but beautiful dance) to the inverted androgyne of the *Cyborg Manifesto*.

When it comes to Tradition and Traditionalism, what is important for understanding the feminine principle here is context. What Bachofen calls the "bloody war of the sexes" is an ontological confrontation. It is not a confrontation over the course of which one must claim victory, but confrontation as a process. It is war for the sake of war. It is not a war that is to be won by one side, but the war that essentially constitutes the world. Whenever Tradition speaks of the characteristics of the feminine and masculine, cosmological or ontological terms, notions, theories, and plots are at play. In Hinduism, for example, there is the confrontation between Purusha and Prakriti, or the active and passive principles. This inevitably gives shape to and creates the world precisely by virtue of the interplay of mutual attraction and repulsion.

Interpreting such a cosmogonic and ontological confrontation as a will for the linear dominance of one principle over the other seems to be deeply erroneous. There is no end goal here of establishing the diktat of one principle, for instance the "masculine" over the "feminine." The whole dynamic of this confrontation is the leitmotif that constitutes the world. If one of these principles decisively wins this war, then the world will lose its balance, collapse in one direction, and its complex, organic structure will turn into a flat, alienated system that can only lead to the world's end and destruction.

Modernity: The Advent of Feminism

As for the subsequent models of interpreting sex and gender that arose in Modern societies, i.e., after Tradition was marginalized and discarded, the most striking formulations were put forth by feminism in its first, second, and third waves. Here, the point was for women to win the war of the sexes. At some point, women recognized that patriarchy as the fixed victory of men over women, and they resolved to rebel. Women now wanted to win this war — but in completely different ways. Most often, feminists choose the strategy of fighting for full equality with men, which means that they strive to take on the male function by entering the male sphere, the masculine paradigm. Women achieved the right to equality, to participate in social life, in politics, in state affairs, and demanded access to vote (the Suffragist movement) — all because they wanted to be like men, to become men.

It is curious that women gained the right to vote in elections in Turkey in 1930, while in France this only occurred in 1944. Which of these countries would seem to be more "progressive" in the Western sense of the word?

The war waged by feminists, suffragettes, and later the war waged by the feminism of the 1960s for the right to choose, i.e., the freedom and legalization of abortions — all of this was a reinterpretation, a turn of the war of the sexes not as a cosmogonic, eternally lasting process (as is the case in Tradition), but as a kind of historical task in which there must always be a clear winner.

Feminism as a Betrayal of the Feminine Principle

The women who have embarked on the path of feminist activism, provoking the oceanic tidal waves of a worldwide women's struggle (against men), have (more often than not) themselves consciously become "men" (or more accurately, their surrogates), pushing themselves into the masculine paradigm. In so doing, they have displaced the traditional, balanced model of interaction between these two principles, these two paradigms, which are, on the one hand, different from and contrast one another, while on the other hand being closely intertwined, constituting the world in their symbiotic dance.

By going over to the masculine side, feminist women create a gap without realizing it. In so doing, they betray the feminine, abandon the classical Traditionalist vocation of the mother or devoted daughter, and lose touch with the most important classical archetype of Tradition: the role of the wife, the bride, the lover. Women thereby move into a new, completely unbalanced world which arises due to a shift in the structure of the metaphysics of sex.

It would seem that things are generally clear at this point, that this is what we are now seeing everywhere. Up to this point, we have predominantly been witnesses of this brand of feminism. Of course, there are other variations, like socialist feminism, which insists on equality in labor and fighting against bourgeois exploitation, or anti-racist feminism, which identifies the fate of minority groups and underdeveloped societies in global politics with the position of women under patriarchy. But the principle remains the same everywhere: the demand for complete equality with men, for abolishing the ontological and corresponding social differences between the sexes. Without a doubt, all of this leads to women themselves adopting masculine archetypes and functions. Feminists start by calling for protection of women from men, but they go on to destroy women themselves by turning them into men.

Donna Haraway Changes the Agenda

Something astounding happened in feminism in 1985. In the journal *Social Review*, the famous feminist Donna Haraway published an essay entitled "The Cyborg Manifesto."[53] It should be said that in 1985 this model was absolutely avant-garde, and even today this work is an absolute breakthrough, comparable only to the writings of Reza Negarestani or Deleuze's works in the 1960s. The point is that if first- and second-wave feminism tried to shift the Overton window in society's understanding of women by bringing women closer to the masculine archetype, then Donna Haraway in essence shattered this window. She took the sheet of paper on which the whole paradigm of feminist thought had been sketched out — the whole history of the confrontation between the masculine and feminine principles from Tradition through the stages of the "bloody war of the sexes" all the way down to the appearance of the first feminists who proclaimed that women should win this war once and for all and wrest equality from men — and suddenly turned it over, drawing her own paradigm on the other side. In this new paradigm, Haraway argues, the very notion of "woman" as such is an artificial construct. The feminine experience, feminine identity, female sex, Haraway says, is simply a fantasy, a projection. There is no woman. "Woman" is simply a sociocultural role assigned to those who are weaker. Even if feminists defeat men, this role will not disappear, as women will simply become men, and men will become women. The asymmetry will remain, because sex and gender are an asymmetry where the one who is weaker, smaller, and lower down in the hierarchy is the "woman."

Proceeding from this, Haraway concludes that we must now move on from the first and second phases of women's war for equality, the war for the feminine, to the stage of the

---

53 See Donna Haraway, *A Cyborg Manifesto: Science, Technology, and Socialist-Feminism in the Late Twentieth Century* (Minneapolis: University of Minnesota Press, 2016).

cyborg. True equality cannot be achieved as long as sex (which always implies asymmetry) exists. This means that sex must be abolished and completely abandoned. Only then, when men and women are no more, will women be free. But this is not possible in humankind. This means that humankind must be abolished and replaced by sexless cyborgs.

The Cyborg, the Inverted Androgyne

The cyborg is a hybrid that is beyond sex. Through this figure, Haraway's work contains the most important and most existential essence that constitutes Postmodern or third-wave feminism. We have arrived at the radical figure of the inverted androgyne. Such a move, so innovative for feminism, perfectly fits into the context of "Dark Enlightenment."[54] Here, the principle of post-gender comes to the fore, wherein sex (gender) as such is recognized to be a deliberately denigrating system that inevitably creates inequality, hierarchy, and, in the feminist optic, domination, repression, suppression, exploitation, and harassment. In Haraway's work, sex and gender are recognized to be synonyms for totalitarianism. The conclusion: sex, gender, and the hierarchy, rigidity, and oppression inherent in them must be disposed of. For Donna Haraway, the figure of the cyborg is the opportunity to transition to a new world, to a society of victorious posthumanism.

Haraway describes the cyborg as follows. The cyborg is a creature that does not want to unite with another, does not want to love, does not want to give birth. It doesn't need anyone else at all. The cyborg is the absolute individual that needs no one but itself. The cyborg lives by regeneration. If it loses an arm, it grows another one. The cyborg lives neither in the sphere of nature, nor in the realm of technology, but belongs to an intermediate zone. It is ironic, not logical; it is fluid, not fixed; it is perverted, not straight.

---

54 Nick Land, "The Dark Enlightenment" [http://www.thedarkenlightenment.com/the-dark-enlightenment-by-nick-land/].

Further, alongside the philosophers of Modernity, Donna Haraway recognizes that "God is dead," but adds that "the Goddess is dead, too." It is not enough to overthrow the patriarchal figure of the Father, Son, and Brother — the triad of the Christian religion and the Greek classics. It is necessary to destroy the Mother, the Spouse, the Sister. Both come at the cost of each other. Emancipation must be full and complete. This means that the human itself must die. Therefore, the transition to the cyborg is the only solution. This is the most logical and consistent conclusion of feminism.

In this version of cyberfeminism, the feminine becomes something completely new that exists beyond sex and ceases to be feminine, instead coming to represent the inverted androgyne. Man is not suitable for this, because he is too human. Only the female feminist is capable of overcoming the human as such. Haraway later developed this idea into the theory of the "Chthulucene,"[55] a new phase in the evolution of the earth in which humankind will die out after a nuclear bombardment, leaving only surviving women who undergo mutation and turn into creatures consisting of cobwebs, algae, torn plastic bags, and other garbage thrown into the World Ocean.

Gender and Katechon

Let us reiterate the main phases in the development of the metaphysics of sex. At first we see how a war of the sexes is postulated in Tradition and in Traditionalism: the feminine and the masculine are in ceaseless, processual confrontation which constitutes and creates the living, orderly world that is always balancing on the edge of chaos. Then this struggle, this war, is cut short, because it is no longer conceived as a process, but is instead recognized to mean the necessary victory of one over the other. The delicate balance of the dialectic of sex

---

55 Donna Haraway, "Anthropocene, Capitalocene, Plantationocene, Chthulucene: Making Kin", *Environmental Humanities* 6:1 (2015): 159-165.

that prevailed in traditional society is frozen. Henceforth, the war must be won by one side. Man becomes a rapist and exploiter — this is how female feminists portray patriarchy. Then, within this paradigm, there are calls for violence by women against men.

The last stage of feminism comes when the war of the sexes is completely eliminated. Henceforth, it is simply crossed out — there is no more war, no more play, no more dialectic, no more relationships, no more love, no more marriage, no more birth, only self-regeneration. There is no subordination of one to the other; instead, there is hybridization. Donna Haraway's ideal is a world without sex and gender. In many senses, we are already heading in this direction.

It seems to me that Donna Haraway's model remains amenable, even if too avant-garde. Sure, we can notice the appearance of the first mutants on screens — performers like Sevdaliza in the ironic clip *Human* or Anohni from the band Antony and the Johnsons. We see examples of strange androgyny, transgender people, and half-human, half-animal entities. These are the prototypes of the Chthulucene. Nevertheless, it is noteworthy that the masculine and feminine, the human and the animal, the humane and the metallic, are still fighting within them. The two principles still coexist within them, and there is always some kind of painful, tragic imbalance. They are still in this great world war of the sexes. Although they strive to get out of this war, they come out of it merely deformed and incomplete. But a completely balanced, self-sufficient cyborg has yet to arrive. Its time hasn't come, but it could, and I think it will arrive rather soon. When the feminine and the masculine are finally abolished and replaced by cyborgs, it will signal the End of the World.

What conclusion can we reach from such a brief overview? In the sphere of sex, we are called to fulfill the mission of the Katechon, to save humankind from approaching death, which means saving sex in its ontological, metaphysical depth. If the war of the sexes ends, it will mean the end of the forces that create and maintain the world. Together with the loss of man and women, we will lose being itself.

***

Homo Hierarchicus: Tripartite Anthropology and the Experience of Hierarchical Society

Hierarchy and Integrality: Methodological Clarifications

I propose that we reflect on a model of sacred order and the reproduction of this divine model in the world, in the Church and the angelic ranks. Today, we will be talking about hierarchy, and in the course of our discussion we will touch on domains that are ultimately inseparable from one another — politics, economics, and religion. As a follower and scholar of Neoplatonism, I naturally adhere to the position that it is impossible to consider the religious separately from the political, the political separately from the psychological, etc., because everything is tightly bound together.

We will try to approach the question of tripartite anthropology and hierarchical experience holistically, from the standpoint of integrality. We will briefly dwell on the very notion of hierarchy, how it appears, develops, and is understood in Indo-European society — that is, in India and ancient Greece. Then we will move on to hierarchy in Neoplatonism, to how hierarchy is transformed in Christianity, we will touch on Dionysius the Areopagite, then we'll move on to the Middle Ages, and finally to the era of Modernity. Everything will be outlined in broad strokes, because, in order to build an overall picture, it is necessary to go through several paradigms and historical eras. We will end with Postmodernity, where hierarchy is completely abolished and disappears in favor of universal equality, anti-patriarchy, and the revolution of the fourth estate.

In this historical-philosophical survey, my own preferences are obviously on the side of Tradition, but one should not be surprised at the mention of "hypo-objects," "object-oriented ontology," or "cyberfeminism." This is necessary, because even if we have chosen the side of Tradition and we intend to defend it in the modern world, we are obliged to be up to date with the current agenda and feel the pulse of modern civilization. Here we will be forced to work with the depths of philosophical seeking as well as the superficial anti-hierarchical experience that has prevailed in modern society for at least several centuries. The faint light at the end of the tunnel of this lecture will be a small futurological projection of how hierarchy might possibly be restored in the modern world.

My reflections are not concerned with specific political forms, but rather with philosophical concepts and paradigms that are as far removed as possible from ordinary practices and facts; in order to comprehend history, it is necessary to begin with paradigms and only then move on to particulars. This principle of moving from the general to the particular will equip us with our main method of examination.

Defining Hierarchy:
Sacred Order and the Principle of Integrality

Hierarchy is a notion that arose in Hellenistic Greece, or more precisely in the Roman Empire, and was developed in the heyday of Eastern Christian theology, during the time of Dionysius the Areopagite (approximately the 5th-6th centuries AD). The term comes from two words. The first is the Greek ἱερός, "sacred," from which is derived the word "hierarch." The second word is ἀρχή, that is "principle" or "authority." Among the ancient philosophers, the word ἀρχή referred to the first principle of everything and designated a certain ontological point in the creation of the world. The very word "hierarchy" was introduced in the 5th century AD by the Greek author known as Dionysius the Areopagite, who was significantly influenced by Neoplatonism in his works *On the Celestial Hierarchy* and *On the Ecclesiastical Hierarchy*.

It is important that the notion of hierarchy has always carried a holy and sacred character.[56] It is a religious term. Even in the mid-20th-century *Oxford Dictionary*, the "sacred," i.e., that which is connected with the religious side of life, with the systematization and establishment of order in the religious sphere, is acknowledged as central to understanding the notion of hierarchy. Today, the very same dictionary no longer treats hierarchy through the notion of the sacred, but instead explains it as the systematic organization of society, government, economy, class and estate relations, and military subordination from the commander-in-chief to the ordinary soldier. In other words, the term hierarchy has had its nature changed in modern dictionaries: the sacred has been removed from the notion, it has been desacralized, reduced to superficial, secular, exterior characteristics such as economic, class, sociological, etc.

We intend to emphasize the traditional, inner understanding of hierarchy and its sacred significance connected to religious cult and spiritual gradation in contrast to the exterior, purely external, superficial side of life. If we use the methodology of René Guénon, we must mention two hierarchies: esoteric hierarchy, that is inner and sacred hierarchy, and exoteric hierarchy, which is associated with the secular side of everyday social existence.

Under what conditions does hierarchy exist? Hierarchy exists when something is whole. Why is this so? If there is a whole, then the composition of this whole includes elements which can be arranged, ordered, and correlated in a certain way due to the fact that they belong to something singular and organic. If we do not adhere to holistic positions, and instead proceed from the thesis of atomism, from the idea that the

---

56 Some authors distinguish between "holy" (*sanctum*) and "sacred" (*sacrum*). The distinction lies in that the holy encompasses the direct experience of encountering the spiritual world, which includes contact with its dark sides. The sacred, on the other hand, and to a lesser extent in Christianity, encompasses only the luminous, pure sides of such an experience. See Rudolf Otto, *The Idea of the Holy: An Inquiry into the Non-Rational Factor in the Idea of the Divine and its Relation to the Rational*, trans. John W. Harvey (Pantianos Classics, 2017).

cosmos is originally fragmented, prioritizing the individual in society, then there can be no hierarchy, since, according to this outlook, there is no whole within which the particular, the part, the atomic and the individual could be in a structured, harmonious, and orderly relation with other particular elements or the whole itself. In the absence of the whole, each individual represents only itself and has nothing to do with any whole. It is nothing more than an insignificant unit, an alienated atom, a separate fragment. Hierarchy, therefore, exists wherever there is a whole. Hierarchy may be defined in Louis Dumont's words "as the principle by which the elements of a whole are ranked in relation to the whole."[57]

Louis Dumont as a Source of Sociological Inspiration

One of the important thinkers who prompted and inspired me to deliver this lecture is the French social anthropologist Louis Dumont, the author of the remarkable book *Homo Hierarchicus*. Dumont is an outstanding European Indologist, a scholar of hierarchies, castes, and other societal structures who worked in his time with Roger Caillois, Marcel Mauss, and Georges Bataille. He had vast experience in studying the caste-based hierarchical society of India. Dumont is interesting because he was a social anthropologist with an accentuated Traditionalist position, which is rare among thinkers in the 20th century and is, alas, almost completely absent in the 21st century. Dumont professed a well-defined "macro-narrative" that stood for hierarchical society and critiqued modern society from the standpoints of the Traditionalist worldview. In the West today, such "grand narratives" are no longer possible and are even unacceptable. An energetic fragmentation of consciousness is taking place in Western society, one that is deliberately, purposefully, and aggressively practiced and supported both in the scientific community and on the level of ordinary laypeople. In our times, university lecturers refrain from any serious

---

[57] Louis Dumont, *Homo Hierarchicus: The Caste System and its Implications*, trans. Mark Sainsbury (Chicago: University of Chicago Press, 1974).

generalizations and value judgments, and even more so from projects and setting goals.

Louis Dumont engaged in impartially analyzing individualism in the era of Modernity and the egalitarian theories built on such principles.[58] According to Dumont, individualism is the antithesis of hierarchy, and it is on individualism that all modern theories of democracy, which Dumont saw as flawed, are based. Louis Dumont is the authority towards which we will orient ourselves today. He is the central character of our lecture, the inspiration and mentor of today's survey. His works *Homo Hierarchicus* and *Homo Aequalis* can be found in English, French, and even Russian.

And so, hierarchy exists whenever something is perceived as a whole, within any holistic model, whether we are talking about the entire cosmos as a whole, a community, collective, or society as fully-fledged structures that operate as the measure of things. If the individual becomes the measure of all things, then, of course, no hierarchy arises. On the contrary, hierarchy is abolished both in theory and in practice.

Dumont takes Indian society, which he meticulously and thoroughly studied, as a model and examines its intrinsic system of varna and jati (which are inaccurately generalized and defined in Western terminology as "castes") as a classic example of a society structured on a hierarchical principle. From Dumont's point of view: "the castes teach us a fundamental social principle, hierarchy. We, in our modern society, have adopted the principle contrary to it, but it is not without value for understanding the nature, limits, and conditions of realization of the moral and political egalitarianism to which we are attached."[59] "Why," Dumont asks, "should we travel to India if not to try to discover how and in what respects Indian society or civilization, by its very particularity, represents a form of the universal?"[60] He

---

58 Louis Dumont, *Essays on Individualism: Modern Ideology in Anthropological Perspective* (Chicago: University of Chicago Press, 1986).

59 Dumont, *Homo Hierarchicus*, 2.

60 Ibid., 3.

points out that modern anthropology does not do justice to the Indian theory of varna, which it views as a mere relic.

The Theory of Varna

Let us move on to examine the Indian caste system. Here I will also draw on Louis Dumont, whose works *Homo Hierarchicus* and *Homo Aequalis* set the task of "retrospectively tracing the path traversed by our civilization from hierarchical society to the modern egalitarian one,"[61] as well as on the works of other scholars of Indian society (first and foremost René Guénon[62], Julius Evola[63], and Mircea Eliade[64]).

India's caste system or system of hierarchy is represented by the theory of *varna*. Translated from Sanskrit, varna means "color," i.e., a certain quality. There are four varnas. They are first mentioned in the *Rigveda*. A myth is expounded therein about how the world and the human types, the estates or varnas, were first created. In Indian mythology, the main element was the Primordial Being, Purusha, out of whose body the universe was created. The varnas (the castes or estates) were created out of him. Purusha is the One Being, the Integrality, the Whole that gives rise to hierarchy. We can see here that holism is inseparable from hierarchy. Wherever there is holism, there is also hierarchy, and vice versa: where hierarchy is present, there is necessarily holism, and this means that individualism is absent.

One of the Rigveda's hymns, the *Purushasukta*, tells in detail of the dismemberment of the All-Man. The text says that the

---

61 Louis Dumont, *Homo aequalis I: Genèse et épanouissement de l'idéologie économique* (Paris: Gallimard, 1977).

62 René Guénon, *Introduction to the Study of the Hindu Doctrines*, trans. Marco Pallis (Hillsdale: Sophia Perennis, 2004); idem., *Man and His Becoming according to the Vedanta*, trans. Richard C. Nicholson ((Hillsdale: Sophia Perennis, 2004).

63 Julius Evola, *The Yoga of Power: Tantra, Shakti, and the Secret Way*, trans. Guido Stucco (Rochester: Inner Traditions, 1992); idem., *The Doctrine of Awakening: The Attainment of Self-Mastery according to the Earliest Buddhist Texts*, trans. H.E. Musson (Rochester: Inner Traditions, 1996).

64 Mircea Eliade, *Yoga: Immortality and Freedom*, trans. Willard R. Trask (Princeton: Princeton University Press, 2009).

highest varna of Brahmins (priests) was created out of Purusha's mouth. The varna of warriors, the Kshatriyas, from whom the rulers and kings come, was created out of his chest, shoulders, and arms. The laborers, peasants, artisans, and merchants, the Vaishyas, were born out of his thighs. From his feet appear the Shudras, the lower caste called only to serve the higher ones. This is how the four varnas, the four castes, the four estates, arose. There is also a fifth category, the "untouchables," the Chandalas or Dalits, who are outside of society as such and have no sacred archetype.

One of the first versions of the origin of the varnas is contained in one of the oldest records of Hinduism, the *Laws of Manu*, which describe the functions of each caste down to the details. The system of varnas in Indian society was designed to ensure integrity and order — for example, the "order of increasing statuses" from the service of the Shudras to the economic activity of the Vaishyas and further to the political rule of the Kshatriyas and the sacred doings of the Brahmins. As one moves from the lower to the higher varnas, the degree of religious purity of the varna increases, the highest expression being the Brahmins.

According to the logic of Hinduism, society in general, encompassing all of its varnas, is a single living being, not merely a mechanical agglomeration of separate individuals. Just as different organs in the human body fulfill different functions without infringing upon one another, so do the varnas form a holistic organism, a body, in which one part harmoniously complements another.

We also encounter holism in Plato's examination of the idea of justice. He insists that society itself and its division into estates is possible only when there is a common whole. Plato names the three virtues of the three estates and says that there is a fourth that holds these virtues together: justice.

Brahmins: People of a Pure Light

The highest and oldest varna that is as close as possible to the Absolute and which originated from Purusha's mouth is the caste of Brahmin priests. They are the ones with the right to perform rituals and enjoy immunity — murder, execution, beating, punishment, exile, and prosecution do not apply to them. Killing a Brahmin is equivalent to destroying the sacred itself. The duty (*dharma*) of the Brahmin is to "teach and learn, to sacrifice and make offerings, to give and receive."

Brahmins are not on equal footing with other varnas. They are a completely separate priestly caste that can interact with everyone except the "untouchables," who no one can interact with. Brahmins have a developed system of taboos, such as in regards to marriages, and they have a special dietary system with a prohibition on consuming meat — as a general rule, they are vegetarians. Brahmins are obliged to strictly observe the principle of not causing harm to any living beings.

Brahmins correspond to "spiritual authority" (*autorité spirituelle*) and are the highest instance of such authority.[65] This authority is symbolized by the color white. The Brahmins are associated with pure light, and among the three cosmic principles (the *gunas*), their souls consist of the element of *sattva*, meaning pure light. This is the contemplative principle of the soul. The aim of a Brahmin's life is knowledge, *jnana*, and upholding the sacred law (*dharma*).

Kshatriyas: Warriors of Fire

The Kshatriyas are the second varna. This caste consists of warriors and influential princely and royal families. This varna is associated with action, the *rajas guna* and the color red. The Kshatriyan spirit corresponds to the chest, shoulders, and arms of Purusha, as well as to the heart, since this area is associated with fire in Indo-European myths. The heart is a source of heat,

---

[65] See Rene Guénon, *Spiritual Authority and Temporal Power*, trans. Henry D. Fohr (Hillsdale, NY: Sophia Perennis, 2004).

and among the Greeks it was the seat of the inspirited element, θυμός. According to the Vedas as well as ancient Greek Pre-Socratic medicinal notions, fire is to be found in this area. Purusha spews fire and thus unleashes *rajas*, the color red and the caste of Kshatriyas into the world.

Between the Brahmins and Kshatriyas, as Dumont writes, there is a complex relationship of "two forces" — "status" and "power" or "authority." Here we are dealing with an absolute difference between the rank of the priest and royal authority. Status, authority, and sacrality are the inalienable qualities of the priest. Although the priest does not have power like the warrior and king, the latter are obliged to honor his authority and recognize his spiritual dominion. The warrior in and of himself is not sacred; he needs sacralization, initiation, dedication. Genuine, legitimate power and authority in the hierarchical system is always sacralized by the priesthood. At the same time, however, the ritual supremacy and purity of the priest should not detract from or diminish the dignity of the king or warrior; it should not cancel out the significance of the functions they perform. Royal power is seen here as an instrument of mediation between the divine world of *dharma* (spiritual law) and the realities of this earthly world. Warriors are subordinate to priests in spirit, but in worldly affairs the priesthood is subordinate to secular authority.

Kshatriyas, like Brahmins, belong to the category of the "twice-born," i.e., those within whom the heavenly and earthly natures are combined. Therefore, they are not only immersed in earthly life, but also obliged to master the sacred texts (to go through training), to receive initiation, to participate in sacrifices, and to bring gift offerings to Brahmins. The ritual aim of the Kshatriya's life is love, *kama*.

Vaishyas and Shudras: Submersion in Materiality

The third varna of Vaishyas comes from Purusha's thighs and consists of pastoralists, farmers, merchants, and artisans.

They are also considered to be sacred, but this time the earthly element is predominant. Their souls, according to Hinduism, are a mixture of fire (*rajas*) and material darkness (*tamas*), which pulls them down. The lot of the Vaishya is the organization and order of earthly life. At the same time, they are also fully-fledged participants in the hierarchy of varnas, and they have their own rites and symbols, their own traditions and rules. Vaishyas are subordinate to the authority of the Kshatriyas and accept the authority of the Brahmins. The Vaishya's life purpose is *artha*, that "well-being," "prosperity," success, wealth.

Indian society, its hierarchical axis, is built out of the harmonious combination of these three varnas. We mentioned that the souls of a fourth estate — the Shudras, servants, hired workers, whose purpose is "to obey and serve without envy" — came from Purusha's feet. They too have their place in the hierarchy, but without any specific archetypal function, form, or vocation. It is important to note, however, that in the earliest stages of Indian society there were only the three higher varnas. The Shudras, and below them the pariahs (Chandalas) created out of the dust under Purusha's feet, are mentioned only in rather late hymns in the Rigveda. It is likely that the Shudras and non-caste Chandalas were the natives of Hindustan who were not integrated into early Vedic Indian society.

Chandalas

In India, there is yet another, fifth category of the population — the "untouchables," the "outsiders," the Chandalas. This is another story altogether. They have generally been struck out of the caste system of Indian society. We will only mention that the category of untouchables arose in deep antiquity and most likely refers to the local tribes who inhabited Hindustan before the arrival of the Vedic Aryans. In the early religious texts, however, they are practically not mentioned, while in the later *Laws of Manu* there are regulations on how they should behave. For instance, they are prescribed to handle affairs like collecting garbage and working with leather and clay. They lived in separate quarters, separate settlements, on roadsides, and generally did not have the possibility of interacting with the "pure" castes.

The theme of "pure" and "impure" in hierarchy and in tripartite anthropology is one of the main features of the predominance of the sacred in Hindu society. Everything below the third caste (the Shudras and untouchables) is "impure," which is to say not touched by divine presence. The first three castes are "twice-born," while the rest are not. The notions of "purity" and "impurity" in Hinduism are associated with passing through initiation. If a person went through a rite of *upanayana*, or second birth, the initiatic experience of discovering the universe, then they became "pure" or even "twice-pure." When they were on a lower level, they were "dirty" and could defile others. The untouchables lived in harsh conditions until altogether recent times, their lives consisting of numerous restrictions and prohibitions. They were denied access to temples, shrines, and some public places. This system lasted in India for quite a long time. Now, according to some sociologists' estimates, untouchables and Dalits make up around 18-19% of India's population. They are divided into various categories: tanners, washers, janitors, garbage collectors, sewage cleaners, masons, potters, slaughterhouse workers, basket and mat weavers, etc.

The caste and estate structure of Indian society is also reflected in the Indian philosophy of Samkhya. According to Samkhya, the world consists of three types of matter, three gunas. These three principles correspond to the castes. The subtlest and most luminous matter, *sattva guna*, is associated with the intellectual and contemplative function. This is the domain of the Brahmins. It is symbolized by the color white. *Rajas guna* is associated with fire, development, expansion, action, administrative functions, the rational mind and the movement of the soul. Its bearers are the Kshatriyas, the second caste. Its symbol is the color red. The mixture of the *rajas guna* and the third guna, *tamas*, is characteristic of the Vaishya caste.

Here red is mixed with black. Finally, the third *guna* is *tamas*, whose name is translated as "indifference" and means darkness, death, ignorance, laziness, the realm of crude matter. This *guna* is predominant in the lower castes of the Shudras and the Chandalas.

If Purusha is the spiritual principle of the world, and this being is sacrificed at the beginning of creation, dismembered, and taken to constitute the basis of the forms of the universe, then Prakriti is the material aspect of manifestation. It is also made up of three *gunas*. The varnas are distinguished by their spiritual and material nature, i.e., by their relation to Purusha and Prakriti. The higher the varna, the more spiritual it is and the more subtle its representative's matter.

Thus, Hinduism exhibits a strict picture of caste societal structure associated with the soul, the principles and qualities of the soul, and the elements of the body of the Primordial Man or First Being, Purusha, who was dismembered. The theme of dismemberment of a god or sacred hero is encountered in many religions. This is the classic scenario of dismembering and sacrificing the Divine. In Hinduism, this is manifest in the form of the division into castes.

Cosmic Cycles

In Hinduism, the varnas are bound to cosmic cycles, Manvantaras. These are periods of time, epochs. There are several such Yugas or gigantic cosmological eras. There is the Satya-Yuga, the Treta-Yuga, the Dvapara-Yuga, and the Kali-Yuga. The Satya-Yuga is the golden age, the Treta-Yuga is the silver age, then comes the bronze age, the Dvapara-Yuga. Finally, there is the Kali-Yuga, the iron age, the period in which, according to the Hindus, we live today. This is the period of the world's decline, the era before the end of the world. In Hinduism, however, this end is followed by a new beginning. Therefore, Indians prefer to speak of the end of the cycle, not the end of the world.

This change of epochs or eras is characterized by the transition from one principle to another. When the intellectual, contemplative, priestly principle is dominant, we are in the golden age. When there is a transition to the phase of rajas guna, where the "fury" of warriors dominates, this is the era of the Treta-Yuga. When we move into the darker era corresponding to the Vaishya caste and a combination of rajas and tamas, that is, military fury and crude materiality, this signals the arrival of the Dvapara-Yuga. The most terrible time, the black era, is the Kali-Yuga, where the material civilization of the consumer society is dominant, that which we face today not only in the West, but, unfortunately, in Russia as well.

In each of these successive Yugas within the greater Manvantara cycle, morality and intellect fall and ignorance and vices rise. The end of the Kali-Yuga is supposed to be marked by the appearance of a savior and restorer of the golden age on a white horse, Kalki, the 10th avatar of the deity Vishnu. He will purify the world and initiate a new Manvantara. This is "the end and the beginning again." as Lev Gumilev titled one of his books.

The Regression of Castes

Scholars of India and Traditionalists who have written about the different orders of hierarchies associate the process of fully-fledged hierarchy's perversion with a revolution of warriors. The Kshatriyas rebel against the Brahmins, the warrior's revolution overthrowing the priesthood. The Brahmins then cease to be the highest spiritual authority. Henceforth, warriors rule by direct strength and might. Hierarchy has already been broken, as the secondary has been put in the place of the primary, and thus, the entire social order begins to undergo increasing entropy.

Then comes the next downward shift: the revolution of Vaishyas. The Vaishyas' usurpation of power is a total overturn of hierarchy: the economic, artisanal, lower element begins to rule over the higher and the spiritual. Priests and warriors begin to be subordinated to economic factors and become dependent on the material side of things. Power is seized by financiers, entrepreneurs, and managers.

Next comes complete disintegration, falling into the state of tamas, where there are no castes at all, and there is no place in society left for the fully-fledged human being. Man himself is now lost and fragmented. This is the end of the cycle. The human being is denied qualitative differentiation. Hierarchy collapses completely. Here appears the mythical idea of equality that is, in actual fact, a direct expression of dark, infernal matter.

Such an end of the cycle embodied in the collapse of hierarchy and wholeness is described in the classical Indian texts. This model of the historical process is also adopted by the Traditionalist philosophers. Thus comes the final age, the Kali-Yuga, the era of democracy and equality, the worst forms of socio-political organization. The term "democracy" is, of course, not used in Hinduism, but in René Guénon we encounter the thesis that the Kali-Yuga is marked by the transition from hierarchy to democracy, which promptly turns into plutocracy. Guénon says that the modern West has arrived at its decline precisely because it was the first to go through all the stages of the decline of caste. Forgetting the sacred nature of hierarchy, modern Westerners have forgotten their inner spiritual dimension while focusing entirely on the exterior. Hence, hierarchy collapsed and the West lost the sacred, divine principle manifest in this hierarchy.

Plato's Sacred Triune

Let's move on to ancient Greece. At times, various authors claim that caste society is characteristic primarily of India, and that wherever we encounter castes, we are dealing with Indian influence. I adhere to the point of view that philosophical knowledge has a similar structure in different traditions, and that this unity does not necessarily imply direct borrowing. This is what René Guénon believed when he spoke of the presence of one Primordial Tradition encompassing a number of primordial truths. According to Guénon, the sacred hierarchy of castes is one such universal idea. According to Dumézil, the tripartite model of societal structure (as well as the tripartite structure of the soul) is a typical trait of Indo-European peoples and the Indo-European worldview as such. It is not always correct and necessary to speak of direct influence by one Indo-European tradition on another.

In Plato's *Republic*, one of the most important dialogues of Platonism, we encounter the idea of a tripartite structure that completely coincides with the classical structure of Indo-European society. It is almost identical to the Indian version, or is at least very similar. The peculiarity of Platonism is that this hierarchy is conceived as more than a political phenomenon. It is important that the *Republic* is primarily devoted not to politics, but to the problem of justice and the structure of the soul. This is how the first book of the *Republic* begins. As the listeners and participants of the dialogue enter into discussion on the idea of justice in the soul, they understand that they cannot even comprehend it in full due to its fundamental nature and scale. In one particular case, they fail to decide on and understand the scale of the discourse, so in the second book the dialogue's participants move on to the topic of the ideal state. But, initially, the dialogue is about justice in the soul.

In Platonism (as well as in political Platonism), hierarchy and the tripartite division of society are connected to the soul. The soul, the cosmos, and the state are the three instances constantly echoing and interpenetrating one another. They have a common ontological structure. Whatever is true and just for the soul is true and just for the cosmos, society as a whole, and the Empire.

Philosopher-Guardians and Apollo's Laws

In the fourth book of Plato's *Republic*, there is a passage about the ideal state. It reveals the four qualities of the ideal state: σοφία, "wisdom," ἀνδρεία, "courage," σωφροσύνη, "prudence," and δικαιοσύνη, "justice," which holds everything together. These qualities are also found in the human soul. So, we have a single, grand, holistic, commensurate orb, a common ontological structure that applies both to the individual human being and the state as a whole.

What hierarchy and gradation of castes and estates is there in the Platonic State? Everything is ruled by the "higher guardians" — this is what Plato calls philosophers, thinkers, sages. He does not always use the term "philosopher" — the term "higher guardians" figures more often. Whenever "guardians" are mentioned, he has in mind the "higher guardians," that is, the ruling philosophers. They are the ones who care about the correct way of life for the citizens.

These philosophizing rulers, philosopher-kings, are first and foremost guided by and operate with the principle of contemplation. They develop their minds and contemplate the Ideas, especially the highest Idea of the Good. The philosopher guardians occupy the same place in the hierarchy as priests, Brahmins. They receive laws directly from Apollo. The legislation they create is incredibly complex, because Apollo's laws are prophecies that the Pythians receive and announce at Delphi, which are only then deciphered. In principle, this is a topic for a separate discussion on how Apollo's laws operate in Plato's ideal state. This does not mean that a strict system of actions is rigidly prescribed for any given situation. After all, the Delphic oracle was "something" whose mysterious utterances required skillful interpretation.

The philosopher is also a mediator between the higher world of the Intellect, the Good, the Ideas, and the world that abides here. The philosopher exits the cave of matter, the material cave, leaves this world, and discovers a new horizon upon encountering the Good. The philosopher's ascent out of the cave of confinement and ignorance to the sun of knowledge is beautifully described in the seventh book of Plato's *Republic*, where the ruler is educated and takes shape through the prisoner's liberation from his shackles and his advance to exit the cave and the world of shadows and reflections. The ruler is he who completes the entire initiatic path.

This path, unfortunately, is tragic for the ruler, because anyone who leaves the material cave, where there are only shadows and likenesses of things, and goes beyond the limits of matter and sees the wonderful and beautiful land of the true world, does not do so for long: after residing in the idyll of light and truth, he is obliged to descend back into the cave. He likely has no desire to descend into the vale of weeping, into the world of mirages and simulacra that reign in the cave, but he is compelled to do so. In any other state, Socrates says, he would not be forced to return, but rather would be allowed to withdraw into contemplation and withdraw from the world. But in the philosophers' state, he must be taken back into the cave. Socrates says in the dialogue:

> It is our task as founders, then, to compel the best natures to reach the study we said before is the most important, namely, to make the ascent and see the good. But when they've made it and looked sufficiently, we mustn't allow them to do what they're allowed to do today... To stay there and refuse to go down again to the prisoners in the cave and share their labors and honors, whether they are of less worth or of greater.[66]

Hence arises the problem of the unhappy philosopher and the unhappy consciousness. This is one of my favorite paradoxical themes in Plato: a person who has left the space "here" in the cave and has received initiation and found the truth, must then return to try to awaken and direct others towards the truth. But in doing so, he will be unhappy– it is even most likely that they will kill him, just as they killed Socrates himself.[67]

After the philosophers (the "higher guardians"), the next estate is simply that of the φύλαξ, the "guardians" or "auxiliaries"

---

66 Plato, *Republic* 519c-e.

67 "As for anyone who tried to free them and lead them upward, if they could somehow get their hands on them, wouldn't they kill him? They certainly would." — Ibid., 517a.

(ἐπικουρία τοῦ φύλἄκος). This estate is concerned with the internal and external security of the state and has a furious spirit, τὸ θυμοειδές. We saw the same thing in India in the *rajas guna*, the inspirited element of the flaming soul. This fierce spirit is the sense of honor that provides for such virtues as courage or the ability to resist, as well as meekness or the ability to be obedient. The latter capacity is also very important, for Kshatriyas ought to be obedient to the philosophical principle. If they are insubordinate, they fall into a destructive state, just like a horse that does not listen to its master and starts to gallop when its rider is trying to restrain it. A disobedient horse ruins everything — the chariot collapses and the rider is harmed. Therefore, Plato says, the warrior's obedience is very important: he must bend the knee before his superior. Here we are talking about two notions: spiritual, priestly power and worldly, exterior, external power. The guardians represent external power.

The artisans are the third estate corresponding to the Vaishyas in the Indian stratification. These are the peasants, traders, and craftsmen. In Greek, they are called the δημιουργιοκοῖος, with craftsman being δημίουργος. The notion of the "demiurge" is also used in Plato's *Timaeus* to describe the construction of the material world. The demiurge is the operator between the higher apophatic world and the material, earthly world. The demiurge engages in building and thereby performs the function of a craftsman. The main, dominant principle among artisans is the "lustful principle," ἐπιθυμητικός, which is also hierarchically distributed throughout parts of the body. This is the natural principle that can completely turn off the mind, and lead one to being dishonest and unreasonable. But if a person is kind, just, and happy, if this element is curbed and under the control of the spirit and the higher mind, then everything within a person will be in balance.

What is important here is that this tripartite hierarchy in the state (the elder philosopher-guardians, the auxiliary guardians, and the artisans) is analogous to the hierarchy in the human soul, which manifests itself in three principles:

- The rational, contemplative element — νοῦς
- The spirited element — θυμός
- The lower lustful element — ἐπιθυμία

If there is balance and order between them, then everything will be well. If there isn't, then everything will be truly regretful. The same goes for the state. If there is no order, or if the hierarchy of principles is turned upside down, then a catastrophic situation sets in, the Kali-Yuga, where hierarchies break down and the divine order is violated.

Why does a violation of the divine order take place? To answer this question, we smoothly transition to Neoplatonism and Christianity. The idea of hierarchy, like the term itself, appears in 5th-6th-century Christian theology under the strong influence of Neoplatonism. Neoplatonism is the continuation and development of the Platonic way of thought, a systematization of Platonism, an attempt at constructing a rigorous system on the basis of the works written by Plato. Firstly, this entailed the systematization of the process of learning to read the Platonic dialogues. Secondly, the point was to constructively arrange all of the dialogues and all of their concepts into a hierarchy. For example, in Neoplatonism, in Plotinus, there is the clear structure of the One, the Intellect, and the Soul. In Plato one can still find various models: in one place the Intellect is dominant, in another the Good, and in another the apophatic One. He had no final schema. The Neoplatonists came to seminars on the Platonic dialogues with pencils and drew beautiful, clear diagrams to show what follows from what. This systematization of the whole of Platonic philosophy had taken place by approximately the 5th-6th centuries AD.

Christianity: The Heavenly Hierarchy of Dionysius the Areopagite

The true identity of the author of the Areopagitic corpus associated with the name of the Athenian thinker Dionysius the Areopagite, a disciple of the Apostle Paul, is not known for certain. There are different legends about his persona. This is a fascinating area to explore — "Who was Dionysius the Areopagite?" Just as in modern culture we asked "Who killed Laura Palmer?", so in the history of philosophy and patristics we find the question, "Who is Dionysius the Areopagite?" The theories are completely different, ranging from the Monophysite Neoplatonist Severus of Antioch to a bishop of Maiuma of Georgian origin, to Peter the Iberian, to John of Scythopolis, who is known as an interpreter of the Areopagitic texts in the 530s, to Sergius of Reshaina. Although this question is not so important for us today, I want to note that Dionysius the Areopagite is a mysterious figure who is of great importance for Orthodoxy and for Christianity in general.

It was none other than Dionysius the Areopagite who put forth the notion of "apophatic theology," one of the single most interesting and mystical topics in Christianity. Apophatic theology holds that nothing can be affirmed about God, for He is above all being and beyond any comprehension. "God is not, because he is above all being," the Areopagite said. God is ἐπέκεινα τῆς οὐσίας. Conversely, cataphatic theology describes God on the basis of his creation, exalting this creation to the superlative degree. For example, there is a beautiful girl, a beautiful church, or something beautiful, while God is the most beautiful of all and everything. There is an intelligent person, an intelligent scholar, while God is the most intelligent Intellect. Cataphatic thinking starts from being and ascends from creation to the Creator. Apophatic thinking says otherwise: No, God is not the most beautiful, God is not the most intelligent, because He is beyond all attributes and we cannot say anything about Him in the terms of human language, for He is absolutely in nother realm.

In his examination of the question of cataphatic theology, Dionysius the Areopagite introduced the notion of hierarchy. According to the Areopagite, hierarchy is "a sacred order, a state of understanding and an activity approximating as closely as possible to the divine," whereby one imitates the divine beauty:

"Hierarchy causes its members to be images of God in all respects, to be clear and spotless mirrors reflecting the glow of primordial light and indeed of God himself."[68] Everything that exists, including angels, the heavenly orders, the Church, and the cosmos, dwell within the divine order. Someone in this hierarchy teaches, someone else learns. Some occupy a higher degree in terms of proximity to the divine light, as they stand closer to the sun of divine truth, while others stand farther away. Hierarchy is the establishment of a single chain between different layers and degrees of the cosmic cave or mountain slope. It is like the rope running between a group of climbers ascending a mountain.

Let us examine the meaning of hierarchy according to the Areopagite with reference to his work *On the Celestial Hierarchy* (Περὶ τῆς Οὐρανίας Ἱεραρχίας). I really recommend studying this work attentively. As a graduate with a degree specializing in the history of foreign philosophy, I'll allow myself to remark that the Prokhorov translation is not very good and leaves much to be desired. Learn Greek. Dionysius the Areopagite's texts are not very difficult, it will take you a year of working with a dictionary to read them. These texts are very important, but the Russian translation can be confusing.

The treatise *On the Celestial Hierarchy* describes the highest, middle, and lowest ranks of angels. There are nine in total and three triads:

+ Cherubim, Seraphim, Thrones
+ Dominions, Virtues, Powers
+ Principalities, Archangels, Angels

All of this is documented with great certainty and all the orders are described meticulously. There is a semantic and ontological connection between them. The highest ranks transmit light, intellect, and goodness to the middle ones, and

---

[68] Pseudo-Dionysius, *Pseudo-Dionysius: The Complete Works*, ed. John Farina, trans. Colm Luibheid and Paul Rorem (New York; Mahwah, NJ: Paulist Press, 1987), 164d.

these, in turn, transmit this to the lowest ranks. The radiance of divine glory is hierarchically distributed in heaven, enlightening and illuminating level after level.

This theory of the nine angelic orders was fully adopted by subsequent theologians and the Church as a whole. It was followed and developed by Catholics (Thomas Aquinas) as well as Orthodox (Gregory Palamas). It has fully entered the corpus of Christian theology.

Church Hierarchy

His work *On the Ecclesiastical Hierarchy* (Περὶ τῆς ἐκκλησιαστικῆς ἱεραρχίας) is no less important. This treatise speaks of the hierarchy of initiators, the bishops, presbyters, and deacons, and the hierarchy of initiates, the monks, laity, and catechumens. In Dionysius the Areopagite, this hierarchy carries a religious, sacred meaning. Whoever is a part of the hierarchy is fulfilling the divine mandate, the divine will. Therefore, hierarchy is salvational for man.

There are different ranks in the Church — bishops, priests, deacons, readers, *kliros* singers, and there are also the ordinary parishioners, the laity, and the catechumens who, for example, following the priest's exclamation "As many as are catechumens, depart", are supposed to leave the temple and no longer be present at the liturgy of the faithful. The practicing believer sees the whole structure of the hierarchical order every Sunday in Church. The fact that we are in the temple, in the place of a parishioner or clergyman, is also a fulfillment of the divine hierarchy. Our position in this hierarchy is our opportunity for salvation. Hierarchy is a divine institution. We are supposed to move along this hierarchy. Here is how Florovsky, a historian of theology, writes of the Areopagite's model:

> There are levels in the world, gradations which are defined by the degree of proximity to God. God is everything in everything, but not equally in everything. According to its nature, not everything is equally close to God. But among these entities, which seem to be constantly receding, there is a living, unbroken connection, and

everyone exists for others, so that only the fullness of everything realizes the goal of the world.[69]

Here, once again, we see fullness and holism. All parts and every point are needed in the Church. The catechumen is needed, the layman is needed, the cleric is needed, the reader, the deacon, the priest, the bishop, and so on, are all needed.

Everything external is connected to the internal — the hierarchy of the Church and the world are connected to the structure of the soul. Just as there is an external hierarchy, which we saw outlined in the example of the Church, there is an inner hierarchy in the soul. Just as in the soul there is both the *kliros* and the catechumen, so is there a higher principle, contemplative, within the soul. We need to aspire and strive for this contemplative principle, only then will we fulfill our mission as human beings who are God's creation.

In the third chapter of the treatise *On the Celestial Hierarchy*, it is said that the goal of hierarchy is "to enable beings to be as like as possible to God and to be at one with him."[70] In other words, by following hierarchy, but not rejecting the hierarchical structure of the world, we fulfill our mission: it is becoming of us to listen, and we listen; it is becoming of us to serve, and we serve; it is becoming of us to be priests, and we are priests. Through dwelling in the right place and showing true respect for it and to the whole bundle of such places, we live.

Hierarchy in the Middle Ages

Next come the Middle Ages. During this period, on the one hand, the principles of hierarchy formulated by the Areopagitic corpus, Plato, and the European classical tradition as a whole were preserved. On the other hand, a gradual fall away from them began. Hierarchy began to lose its contrast and its ontology.

---

69 Georges Florovsky, *The Byzantine Ascetic and Spiritual Fathers*, trans. Raymond Miller, Anne-Marie Döllinger-Labriolle, and Helmut Wilhelm Schmiedel (Büchervertriebsanstalt, 1987).

70 Pseudo-Dionysius, *Celestial Hierarchy*, 165a.

The Middle Ages accepted Areopagitic angelology and Platonism as well as the idea of the sacred character of ecclesiastical and political authority, i.e., of the Pope and the Emperor. This model worked perfectly for a certain period of time. In 12th-century Italy and for several centuries to follow, wars broke out in order to determine who is the highest link in the hierarchy — the Pope or the Emperor? Thus began the confrontation between two parties, the Guelphs and the Ghibellines. These major political factions fought amongst each other. The Ghibellines placed imperial power over papal authority, while the Guelphs advocated limiting the power of the Emperor of the Holy Roman Empire and strengthening the influence of the Roman Pope. This confrontation is even reflected in Dante's *Divine Comedy*. Dante was originally a "white Guelph" who later, in exile, joined the ranks of the Ghibellines. His most important political treatise, *On Monarchy*, described a Ghibelline hierarchical model.

There are a number of interesting facts related to the architecture of our Kremlin. The dovetails, the battlements on the Kremlin walls, are a symbol of the Ghibellines. Who was the architect of these walls? Pietro Antonio Solari of Milan, the most important Ghibelline city. The dovetail and the letter "M" are Ghibelline symbols. This is a very symbolic gesture, this is symbolic architecture. The Ghibelline line resonates with the Byzantine tradition of the Emperor as Katechon, which was later brought to Rus'. The modern stars on the Kremlin towers were created in Donbass, in Donetsk, in the 1930s and then brought to Moscow. Russia's role as Katechon and the battle for Donbass — how connected everything is!

The struggle between the Guelphs and the Ghibellines did not end with the victory of one side. This war was left unfinished. But the very foundation of the hierarchy of principles — sacred and earthly hierarchy, ecclesiastical and imperial power, Pope and Emperor — was shaken. During the Renaissance, political tendencies began to emerge which cast doubt on the sacredness of Papal power, i.e., hierarchy in the

Guelphian interpretation. With this we enter the 16th century, the period of the Reformation.

Protestants against Hierarchy: The Birth of Capitalism and Liberal Democracy

Louis Dumont, whom I've mentioned repeatedly and on whom I'm drawing in my studies, said in his *Essay on Individualism* that Protestantism destroys the hierarchical vertical. The Reformation was the time when the bourgeoisie, the "Third Estate," came to power and completely overturned the hierarchy.

Luther nailed his famous "95 Theses" to the church door. Here we see a sharp criticism of church hierarchy and the beginning of the transition to a new, de-hierarchized order. The vertical that represented the divine order and which, according to the Areopagitic works, was necessary for divine energy to pass into the world, like an ontological cord, broke and tore. It is no coincidence that the socialist Max Weber later noted that it was Protestantism that led civilization to modern capitalism. In his 1905 work *The Protestant Ethic and the Spirit of Capitalism*, Weber wrote that European Modernity was built out of an indissoluble alliance of Protestants and the rising bourgeoisie.[71] Protestants rejected at once church hierarchy and the ontological hierarchy of the world as a whole, putting in its place rationalism in matters of faith as well as everyday affairs. While Catholics, Weber wrote, were somewhat removed from this world and more indifferent to earthly goods, Protestants were oriented towards the material world. The other world, the kingdom of heaven, was much more important to Catholics than their temporary stay on earth. Protestantism, particularly through Luther's notion of "vocation," *Beruf*, created the possibilities for the emergence of the capitalist world. In place of monasticism and speculation turned towards the beyond, Protestants put an emphasis on earthly life and on the economic

---

71 Max Weber, *The Protestant Ethic and the "Spirit" of Capitalism*, trans. Peter Baehr and Gordon C. Wells (New York: Penguin Books, 2002).

practice that a person is called to perform. Personal enrichment and well-being were now turned into a measure of "holiness."

Thus, the destruction of hierarchy gave rise to the ethics of capitalism, which gradually came to reject any vertical whatsoever. Hence the market, democracy, the quality of opportunities, and other dogmas of liberalism. Next, with the development of capitalism, the fourth estate (the proletariat) gradually begins to come close to power.

Deism and de Tocqueville's Democracy

The next stage is New Time, Modernity, and its philosophy, including Rousseau, the idea of equality, and the complete destruction of castes. Henceforth, Modernity's thinkers proclaim: man is born free and equal, yet he is stuck in the snares of hierarchy, and this must be overcome. The whole philosophy of the Enlightenment declares that it is necessary to get rid of the hierarchies that dominate in society, religion (the Protestant motive), science, and culture. Humanity needs freedom of mind. The Enlightenment philosopher believed that he could deal directly with divine revelation and had no need for any mediating instances. This is how the idea of deism appeared, wherein God is relegated to the background and equated to a purely logical cause. We see this in part already in Descartes. Starting with Newton, Hobbes, Spinoza, etc., this tendency manifests itself with ever increasing intensity and leads to the total overthrow of the divine order within the world, replacing it with atomism and materialism. By the 20th century, this growing obsession with materiality will degenerate into outright nihilism.

Among the cases of the ideology of equality which Louis Dumont cites, there is one anti-hierarchical figure who was delighted by democracy in America and wrote a book on the subject in 1831: Alexis de Tocqueville. He argued that the "sacred idea of equality" is simply wonderful and is the future of mankind. Everything democratic, new, and best must be devoid of hierarchy. He fiercely criticized estate society and the very idea of hierarchy, and asserted that all people should be equal. At the same time, however, he allowed for the right of hierarchy for certain social functions.

De Tocqueville's caveat is of interest: despite the necessity of equality, there might arise the danger of the tyranny of the majority. This entails the cult of material prosperity, the growth of the individual's isolation and alienation, and the decline of the arts. De Tocqueville qualifies that under aristocratic regimes, certain aspects of society, such as art, for instance, can still be better than under democratic regimes. According to Louis Dumont, de Tocqueville represents the transitional phase that breaks the estate system but still doubts whether it should be broken completely and once and for all.

The Left against Hierarchies

Now let us skip a century: in the 20th century, nihilism fundamentally prevails. Man stands amidst the ruins of the collapsed edifice of hierarchy with an expression of despair on his face. There is no more authority for him, he is neither cold nor hot, he is abandoned by fate in a lifeless world, he has no God. "God is dead, you have killed him. You and I," Nietzsche's madman says, clearly citing Psalms: "The fool hath said in his heart: There is no God." Man no longer strives for anything, he no longer has any orientation. Everything is destroyed, and power is seized by the fifth estate, those carriers of pure *tamas* who stand at the very bottom of the hierarchy of being. The lowest castes begin their uprising. According to Louis Dumont, both liberalism and communism represent the power of precisely such lower elements — this is the uprising of the dark element, the material, decadent, and the impoverished that hold the economy and profit to be the highest good.

Louis Dumont says — and the New Right repeats this after him — that the main error of both communism and liberalism is betting on the economy, the conviction that the economy predetermines everything. This is a characteristic of the thinking of the lower estates of the bourgeoisie, the proletariat, and the Chandalas. In his work on revolution and modernity, Julius Evola speaks of a revolution of the fifth estate, i.e., the time of the Chandala. "The Advent of the 'Fifth Estate'" is the title of the text in which he points out the complete, final inversion of hierarchies in the era of nihilism.[72]

Modernity, liberalism, and communism proclaim universal equality. This is manifest to an even greater extent in Trotskyism. In the model that was implemented in Russia, everything grew into a phantasmagoric structure that reproduced a new hierarchy. We did not manage to build equality. In Russia, according to Berdyaev, socialism became a certain form of religious consciousness, a new religiosity. We also had an Emperor, albeit a substitute one, and there were certain cults. Some hierarchy was preserved in everything except money, but in sacred hierarchy material inequality does not play any role at all, since wealth says nothing about the essence of a person and is a criterion only for the lower castes, the Vaishyas and those below them.

At the same time, the Western model of revolution, such as the 1968 Revolution in France, openly denounced structure, hierarchy, and patriarchy. A new life was proclaimed, the hierarchization of the feminine and masculine was denounced, and there appeared anti-patriarchal movements and second-wave feminism. A fully-fledged and mass-scale uprising against hierarchy along with attempts to equalize everything then overwhelmed the West. The left declared the human being as such to be "too hierarchical," too cruel, too totalitarian, too grand. The human has a head, chest, and legs — this is unacceptable. The human moves vertically — this is arrogant. The human is hierarchical in his very consciousness and even in his organic body.

---

72 See Julius Evola, *Recognitions: Studies on Men and Problems from the Perspective of the Right*, trans. John Bruce Leonard (London: Arktos, 2017).

From Human to Mold

In recent times, we are encountering even more radical versions of anti-hierarchical philosophy, such as that of Timothy Morton. This ecologist and object-oriented ontologist came to Moscow and, during his presentation at the Garage museum, looked at his hand and was surprised, even downright upset, that it doesn't exist separately from him. In one instance in the lecture, he even spoke to his hand and treated it like a separate individual, trying to personalize it. The character Jerry Horn in the third season of David Lynch's *Twin Peaks* also talks to his leg.

Such a "marvelous," infernal, contemporary ontologist like Morton talks about the need to introduce the concept of the "hyposubject," that is a "sub-subject," a subject without subjectivity, a kind of personalized object. The human being has too much will, which he needs to give up. The human is too hierarchical. When he gets out of bed in the morning, he is already entering hierarchical territory, because his head is upright on top and his legs are below. Timothy Morton's hyposubject must necessarily be a feminist, a person of color, homosexual, ecological, transhuman, and intrahuman. As follows, man needs to get rid of the fully-fledged subject and turn into a rhizome. The rhizome is a concept pioneered by the French philosopher Gilles Deleuze, who argued that there are too many subordinations and hierarchies in the world, and that we all need to turn into a web-like mold, mycelium, or roots which spread out horizontally.

Practices aimed at transforming and de-hierarchizing the human being run like a red thread throughout the modern world. This is confirmed by the rampant proliferation of psychedelics — not only in the 1960s, when this was an element of "liberation" and flirting with shamanistic practices for hippies and other countercultures, but today, when they are available to everyone and especially, unfortunately, to young people who have not yet fully realized who they are and how they should live. The proliferation of narcotic substances and the general consumption of alcohol are meant to split consciousness, to shake up, decompose, and destroy human subjectivity. This is just a form, a means, a method for developing hyposubjectivity within oneself, for suppressing one's will, destroying oneself, and destroying the hierarchical principle within yourself.

Restoring Hierarchy: There Is No Other Way

What is to be done? There is really no clear-cut answer to this question. I would answer that hierarchy is inevitable. By recognizing this, you will always be subordinate to a higher principle. Even if you find yourself in oblivion, you will always be guided by this contemplative principle. It must be discovered and developed within yourself. If you develop it within yourself, it will be projected onto a larger scale, including politics. When you start working on your inner hierarchization, on subordinating the lust for rage and the fury of the mind, then the exterior world will begin to transform.

Hierarchy, in my view, is something natural. Rejecting hierarchy means rejecting life. Only where there is death is there no hierarchy. All the dead lie equal before God. The dead in a grave enjoy full equality. The dead have no hierarchy. It could be objected that, for instance, in Dante's *Divine Comedy* there is hierarchy. We will not delve into the details here. Only in the material sense are the dead and rotting corpses equal. Wherever there is soul and spirit, there is life and there will always be hierarchy and a vertical axis. It is necessary to restore and cultivate this verticality, to work with it. It does not need to be restored externally. I am not calling for the creation of a political caste structure. I am calling for restoring justice in the soul. I am calling for a clear structuring of these three principles, their hierarchization, for the qualities intrinsic to each of these principles of the soul to be seen clearly and correctly subordinated. Fury must be combined with obedience. Lust must be subordinate to fury. The mind will curb both rage and fury and sovereignly rule over our lives. Only in this way does the philosopher, the highest guardian, the true ruler, come to be.

Questions and Answers

Question: The line of the modern "left" on equality or of the "right" on inequality and hierarchy "runs like a red thread," as you said. If we are talking about hierarchy in modern society, about the talented, strong, and skilled being able to achieve something more than their less smart and less skilled colleagues, then why do "left-wing ideas" have such huge popularity, especially among young people? The very idea of hierarchy should be attractive to an adequate person, because it gives them the opportunity to use their potential to grow.

Daria Dugina: I think that what young people are attracted to in left-wing ideas is the possibility to remain who they already are, without the growth that hierarchy sets up and challenges. Hierarchy is always an effort, tension. Take Dionysius the Areopagite. He says that in order to receive the Divine, one needs to seriously work. It won't just happen. Perhaps the left just wants to enjoy the state of the given — they are how they are and that's good enough. Take the case of body positivity: girls do not take care of themselves at all, and they assume that this is unnecessary. Allegedly, we are all equal, and beauty is in every one of us. Maybe there is something to this thought. But you still must try, work on yourself: your body is also a product of God's creation. It needs to be maintained in order to pray, to work, to move, to perform penance in a monastery. It seems to me that the attraction to the left is due to the fact that it proclaims relaxation, effeminacy, languor, and ultimately apathy and weakness. There you'll be accepted as you are. Moreover, young people are not even drawn to the left, but to the liberal left. Today, there is no real anti-capitalist, heroic "left." There is a new hybrid formed after 1968 with the emergence of the "new left" which quickly transformed into "left liberals."

Question: What is the situation with hierarchy and left-liberal views in Russia? If everything is clear in Europe's case where left-liberal views are openly promoted and advancing, then what about in Russia?

Daria Dugina: Russia is a little behind, as always. Currently, we are still in the phase when the economic caste/varna of Vaishyas dominates over others. That is why we have such subordination of everything — culture, politics, war, even the Church, which is criticized sometimes justly, sometimes extremely unfairly — to the economy. This is also why we have the attitude towards the military that we do. They are not a central part of our society. They are marginalized, like the priesthood and philosophers, while economic elements, Vaishyas, are more involved in governmental authority. They are the ones with the largest share not only of the wealth of society, but also in administration and decision-making. This is an inverted model in relation to Tradition. At the same time, the figure of the sacred king has been preserved. Albeit in altered form, it is still the heritage of the place of the Emperor. Therefore, the highest subjectivity in the people's consciousness is attached to the President. It is as if he has his own mission. Maybe he doesn't know this, maybe he does. But everything besides the President himself is an inverted hierarchy. But still, we don't have liberal-democratic equality, there is no domination of the hypo-subject. We haven't "grown up" to this yet. Western communism was also transformed on Russian soil. The classical version of communism did not work out — neither the Trotskyist version nor any other. The result was a new sacrality, a new religious formation with Stalin's cult of personality and state paternalism. Many of the early communists were altogether strange mystics. Like Bogdanov and his Institute of Blood Transfusion — he died from transfusing himself with the wrong blood group resulting in blood poisoning. The idea was that equality would come only once all people share their blood and the blood of humanity becomes common to all. Perhaps our space itself is mystical. We are still not departing into hypo-subjectivity, although there are already some signs pointing towards this. If we analyze contemporary culture, then there are such figures as, for instance, Skriptonite, who doesn't even pronounce his words. In his album released a few years ago, there's only moaning and sounds. Through him, in fact, the absence of Logos manifested itself. Now, maybe he has begun to express his thoughts more artfully, but at that moment we could see hypo-subjectivity. There we also see the clip-consciousness or clip-thinking that is penetrating us and taking its place against the general backdrop of the poisoning of the young generation, unfortunately, with narcotics, alcohol, and "spices" — all of these are cells of the progressive anti-hierarchy designed to turn our society into a conglomerate of hypo-subjects. This is terrible. It needs to be fought, it needs to be confronted personally by one's own example. Everyone who thinks about hierarchy needs to set the example of how it is possible to live and think differently.

Question: Shouldn't the idea of equality be considered not only "from below," as an assertion of a kind of *"ressentiment,"* envy and one's own weakness, but also from above, as an assertion of magnanimity? Perhaps this magnanimity borders on some kind of Luceferian pride, but, nevertheless, it leads to apocatastasis and to the justification of everything.

Daria Dugina: Yes, therefore we can speak of two types of equality: equality which denies hierarchy and equality which transcends hierarchy, or apophatic equality. When I said that everyone is equal when they die, I had in mind a double model. On the one hand, indeed, all the dead are equal. On the other hand, they are hierarchical. When I was thinking about their equality, I imagined standing before the Last Judgment. Souls stand before God and are forgiven. Then everything just disappears. This might be the case, but it is also very strange. First, some kind of hierarchy would be established, and then everyone would move to some kind of equality. Why, for example, are Postmodernist concepts of the erosion of the Logos and the destruction of hierarchy inapplicable on Russian soil? We would first need to build a hierarchy and first obtain Logos, and only then would there be attempts to ruin it (why, though?). But what is there to ruin where there isn't anything in the first place? Here everything should come in phases. First, we treat hierarchy with awe and service, and then there will be the idea of magnanimity. Likewise, we consistently speak first of cataphatic theology and only then do we move on to apophatic. We cannot skip over it. Let all of us, all Russians, work on restorting hierarchy. First we need to restore this hierarchy, and we will always have time for it to fall apart. As for magnanimity — this is up to God to grant.

Question: If we look at the feminist agenda, then how justified is women's desire to become equal to men? Or should hierarchy be maintained in this context?

Daria Dugina: Thank you very much for the question. This is a topic that I really love and study. In my view, in order for us to maintain the correct balance, we do not need to insist on any rigid subordination of men and women to each other in contemporary society. It is necessary to adopt so-called standpoint feminism. This is a feminist theory that holds that man and woman are of fundamentally different worlds. Just like how in rhetoric there are opposite and equivalent concepts put side by side but not into contradiction. They cannot be placed into the same hierarchy, they must exist together, side by side, in parallel. The equality or hierarchization of woman and man that is happening in the modern world leads to killing femininity. When modern feminists put woman over man and assert that she will now avenge many centuries of humiliation, this is nothing more than the destruction of femininity, the destruction of the sacred role of woman. When woman is placed below man, who claims that it is necessary to save patriarchy and demand that woman serve man, almost as if she were his property, then this perverts the masculine principle itself through an incorrect formulation of the question of power and by humiliating female dignity. If we consider things from the standpoint of the metaphysics of sex, then a tense balance should be maintained between men and women, one that will not be destroyed by matriarchal or by excessive and straightforward patriarchal strategies. In classical hierarchy, the situation is somewhat different. In India, women were not "twice-born." Only those who went through the procedure of initiation were "twice-born," i.e., the first three varnas. Women were left out of this category. But even there, some types of female initiation existed. In ancient Greece, women played an active role in the higher principles and could even be philosophers. For example, Hypatia, who was a Neoplatonic philosopher, was very much loved by her students. In Plato's *Republic*, in the fourth book, Plato says that both women and men can fight together — they are "like dogs" (this is a metaphor) fighting in one and the same battle. Women might be a little weaker than men, but they are on equal footing. In many cultures, there is a female priesthood, such as the institution of the Pythia, the Vestals, seeresses, etc. In Christianity, there is female monasticism. I believe that it is impossible to linearly hierarchize woman and man. But we should not go into matriarchy. Sometimes, when asked whether we should accept patriarchy, I want to say "yes." But there should be some special caveats here. It should not be a materialistic patriarchy, a "cook for me now" patriarchy, but rather organic and harmonious form interaction and cooperation. That is why, out of all the feminist currents, I like standpoint feminism most of all, as women and men are put on different planes and are not subordinated to one another. They are two fully-fledged, autonomous worlds. There is another version of feminism that I really like, that of the philosopher Tatiana Mikhailovna Goricheva. She lives in France, having been forced to leave the country in Soviet times. She created an Orthodox journal here, *Maria*, which engaged in the articulation of Orthodox feminism. Tatiana Goricheva says that woman has a special mission. If man has, for example, the mission of Christ, the apostolic mission, and service is the highest realization of man, then woman has her own special figure for her female mission. Her archetype is the Mother of God, giving birth to a child, as well as serving, like the service of the myrrh-bearing women who followed Christ. There is also a third option: Mary of Egypt. She is a vivid figure of martyrdom, overcoming sin, and monastic ascesis. Goricheva says that these are different models and each has its own mission. It is not the case that in Orthodoxy women should blindly obey men. She has her own predestination.

Question: Could you go a little deeper into the question of the rhizome and how in some groups local initiatives are now preferable to giant, corporate ones? Although a corporation is a rather strict vertical, the rhizome, it seems to me, is associated with small local initiatives.

Daria Dugina: In Deleuze's work *Thousand Plateaus*, the rhizome is understood metaphysically as the overcoming of hierarchy. For Deleuze, it refers to the opposite of the idea of the tree, that is, the idea of the fundamentally vertical Logos which has roots and a crown. What you said is interesting and is more related to ideas about a network society, that is the organization of society in such a way that a centralized administration yields to various local and autonomous spaces. This is interesting, I like it. This seems to entail certain autonomy for regions, including on the political level. Large corporations, even state ones, cannot always handle regulating small issues. But Deleuze says that this is about metaphysics. He argues that the tree permeates our mind and entrenches totalitarianism, and that we need to get away from the vertical structure of "roots—trunk—crown" and move towards horizontal fragmentation. Local initiatives are interesting as a model for society, but they are risky, because hierarchy is what collects the human mind every day when it wakes up. The Russian philosopher Nikolai Fyodorov had the formula that every day, when man gets out of bed, he performs an act of consolidating his consciousness and gathering everything around the core of his inner hierarchy, as if sticking everything to him. When a person lies down to sleep (which is identical to death), they seem to fall apart into pieces. Therefore, Delueze's rhizome is about human existence, about the philosopher in a state of fragmentation and disassembly. While the network society is an interesting model, it can only be partially implemented.

Question: On the TV program *Russian Response*, Andrei Afanasyev talked with Krasovsky. Krasovsky pushed the thesis that any hierarchy, any Empire, is doomed to disintegrate, to fall apart. He prophesied that Russia will fall apart. What do you think — is this really the case?

Daria Dugina: When we talked about the Hindu model of society today, we mentioned that castes are associated with Manvantaras and Yugas, i.e., with cosmic cycles. In some sense, the Kali-Yuga, the dark age, is inevitable. This is also the case in Christianity: the End of the World is inevitable. We can see that the very course of history from paradise to hell deliberately presumes the end of hierarchy at some point in its finale. But, unlike the liberal version, the end of hierarchy does not end in the reign of equality or the victory of anti-hierarchy. It might be only an ephemeral moment, an illusion of the reign of the dark element. In fact, the cycle will simply end and a new, fresh hierarchy will be installed again. But I don't think that the living world is capable of existing without hierarchy.

Question: Are you a believer?

Daria Dugina: Yes, I'm a believer. I belong to Edinoverie. The Edinoverie Church is somewhere between the Old Believers' Rite and the ruling Church of the Moscow Patriarchate. We maintain the Old Rite, but at the same time we are part of the MP ROC, under the omophorion of the Patriarch of Moscow and All Rus'. I'm from a family of believers.

Question: How do you relate to the current ideas and trends about enlightenment? Many people are talking about this now, this knowledge is widespread. Is this some kind of spiritual phase of transition for society as a whole?

Daria Dugina: There are two sides to this. On the one hand, enlightenment and the practices people appeal to are very often traps. They are a simulacrum of the sacred. René Guénon warned of this when he analyzed neo-spiritualism and the trends of enchanted fascination with mystical teachings. Guénon said that people understand them too carnally, like a kind of algorithm or instructions on how to make life more fun and easier. To some extent, this is a simulacrum of genuine

Tradition. On the other hand, the desire for enlightenment and the craving for liberation are very good. "Enlightenment" is a term that comes from Buddhist philosophy. It is the achievement of inner clarity, getting out of the subject-object plane and trying to break the everyday functioning of life; it is a passage to the beyond, an appeal to something other. This is good, and very important in recent times. The main thing is for people to appeal to the right trends. If Orthodoxy and other traditional religions have clear-cut ritual, then they remain hierarchical, while other strategies offered today like "enlightenment" ones (shamanic practices and so on) can have a detrimental effect on the unadapted soul and undeveloped consciousness. So, one needs to remain within Tradition, to preserve it and preserve it within oneself. It has existed for centuries, it is fine-tuned with a full algorithm for adapting a person to certain difficulties, even physical ones. There are fastings where everything is fully planned out — there are four big fasts a year. There are morning and evening prayers, prayers for before and after meals. All of this contributes to consolidating a person both inwardly and exteriorly. The demand for enlightenment is a very good indicator. The main thing is for a person to not fall into the trap of artificial enlightenment. Sometimes it is scary where a person can end up in search of enlightenment.

***

The Man of Light in Iranian Sufism

The Body of Inner Man[73]

Today, I would like to dwell on the question of understanding corporeality in Iranian Sufism. First and foremost, to do so, I will be drawing on Henry Corbin's *The Man of Light in Iranian Sufism* and *History of Islamic Philosophy as sources*.[74]

When I set out to study Iranian sufism, I noted an interesting peculiarity: when Corbin talks about Suhrawardi's[75] doctrine and his notion of the man of light, he mentions the "body of the man of light." This immediately drew my curiosity, because it would seem that little space has been allotted to the problem of corporeality in Sufism. Nevertheless, I saw that Suhrawardi and Henry Corbin were both talking about a "body."

Let us recall that the "man of light" in Sufism is the spiritual counterpart of the manifest human. In some sense, it is the sovereign soul, the initial instance of ascendance to what in Neoplatonism is called the One. Suhrawardi says that man is initially thrown into the realm of black light, into the night of the unconscious. As he dwells in the world and comprehends this initial thrownness, he gradually begins to orient himself within the world, that is, he enters the clarity of the exoteric day, the exterior, rational, normative reality with ready-made solutions. A person who undertakes to escape the black light accustoms himself to dwelling in this exoteric day. Sometimes, he spends his whole life in this way and remains within it always.

---

73 The present text is based on a presentation at the eighth session of the online Plato Seminar organized by Alexander Dugin and Paideuma TV, "The Immateriality of the Body and the Incorporeality of Matter," on 11 June 2020.

74 Henry Corbin, *The Man of Light in Iranian Sufism*, trans. Nancy Pearson (New Lebanon: Omega Publications, 1994); idem, *History of Islamic Philosophy*, trans. Liadain Sherrard and Philip Sherrard (London: Routledge, 2004).

75 Shihab ad-Dīn Yahya ibn Habash Suhrawardi (1155-1191) was a Persian philosopher and mystic who founded the philosophy of Ishraq. He paid special attention to the metaphysics of darkness and light. He was executed for his beliefs.

The Night Above and its Body

The goal of every person, according to Sufi tradition in the interpretation of Suhrawardi and Najm ad-Din Kubra[76], is to exit the exoteric day and its rationality and to head into the night. This "night" refers to the night of super-consciousness, a night that transcends the exoteric day. Such a night is directly opposite to the darkness of the unconscious.

This higher night encompasses the sun — not the daytime, exoteric sun, but a special midnight sun. This is the initiatic sun. The path of ascent from the night of the unconscious through the day of consciousness to the night of super-consciousness, to the space of the apophatic, ineffable, supreme One, is the point of Neoplatonic henosis (ἕνωσις) or "union" and identity with the Absolute.[77]

This process of purely spiritual, metaphysical passage is, oddly enough, described in Sufism as a passage from one body into another. In Suhrawardi, we find a formulation describing the presence of different bodies — the "body of day" and "body of night." The body of night is the paradoxical "body" of the man of light. What is interesting and what struck me in Suhrawardi is that he describes this subtle body rather thoroughly and in detail. It is also called the "body of resurrection," that which remains hidden in the physical body, in the "body of day." The man of light's body also has subtle organs (*lataif-e-sitta*, اللطائف الستّة) which are the dwelling places of the seven prophets. Accordingly, the process of ascent, of spiritual transformation, of philosophical breakthrough from the (not yet illuminated) night of the consciousness to the super-night, the higher darkness (already past the entire zone of day) that transcends light, is associated with a paradoxical transformation of corporeality which is difficult to explain.

---

[76] Najm ad-Din Kubra was a Persian mystic, theologian, Sufi sheik, and poet who authored numerous philosophical and theological treatises.

[77] In Neoplatonism, *henosis* is union with the One (Τὸ Ἕν). This concept later became widespread in Christian theology, Islamic mysticism, the *Corpus Hermeticum*, etc.

If we turn to the Zoroastrian religion, we encounter the teaching that there exist two worlds: the corporeal world of *getik* and the luminous, spiritual, mental world of *menok*. Every embodied person has their luminous double, their angel. But even the brightest angel has a still higher ultra-luminous double. If an angel belongs to the light, then the angel's angel is above and beyond light. This corresponds to the figure of the *daena*, the clairvoyant, purely transcendental soul.[78] Somewhat paradoxically, in Zoroastrianism, this triple hierarchy of darkness (below), light (middle), and darkness (above) is described as the structure of the body or as three "bodies." Moreover, the body can be both corporeal and luminous, super-corporeal, spiritual, even apophatic.

Contrary to what materialists believe, the problem of corporeality in Sufism, as well as Neoplatonism, is not hereby eliminated. It could be said that in mystical teachings such as Sufism, which grew out of the soul of Neoplatonism, Zoroastrianism, and Mazdaism, as well as a number of other spiritual currents, the body is preserved at all levels of the manifest world. It is manifest not only in its coarse, primal element, but it also exists in the sphere of the spirit, light, and even beyond light and the world.

Initiatic Photism: The Mystery of the Green Light

It is also important to note that in Sufism the passage from the night of the unconscious to the day of consciousness and then even higher to the night of super-consciousness is accompanied by vivid, colorful, visual images. Throughout Sufism runs the thread of a green light which symbolizes the highest, apophatic, ineffable principle beyond being. The transcendent, supreme night, the "darkness above light" of which the Areopagitic texts speak, manifests itself through a visible green light.

Why is it green? I discussed the matter with my father — what kind of light is this, what kind of shade? I thank him

---

78 "*Daena*" is a Zoroastrian concept meaning "understanding" or "revelation."

for the hint: this green light is, in fact, barely distinguishable from darkness, barely tangible, it is a dark shade that only barely stands out against a dark background, it is light and not light. One could say that it is a result of compromise between night and light, thanks to which darkness becomes fixed and distinguishable.

Thus, in Iranian Sufism and the works of Suhrawardi and subsequent authors of the Ishraq school, the topic of the body is developed in connection with the concept of luminous consciousness, the man of light, and plays a most important role. The body is present not only in a person's initial state of thrownness in the world and creation, but also on their spiritual path and in their luminous, metaphysical becoming. This special — mysterious — body is of a barely distinguishable, dark-green hue. This is the appearance of the immortal soul or the figures of angels.

***

The Sublime and the Aesthetics of Great Pan

I would like to speak a bit about the great god Pan. With the word "great," I'm referring to Arthur Machen's work *The Great God Pan* (1890). Arthur Machen was an English writer, a forerunner of Lovecraft, who largely influenced the latter as well as decadent literature on the whole. Arthur Machen was highly acclaimed by Jorge Luis Borges, who is himself regarded as a classic of the "magical realist" movement. He also influenced modern cinema — for instance, Guillermo del Toro's films largely revolve around motifs and influences from Machen.

Machen's *Great God Pan* touches on the question of human contact with the sublime. Along with the beautiful, the sublime is one of the two foremost elements of aesthetics, although this is often forgotten. The sublime — *le sublime* in French and *das Erhabene* in German — is not simply something refined, exquisite, or aesthetically charged. Rather, it is a figure, an action, a history, a situation, or an experience that greatly exceeds the norms of ordinary human existence and experience. Therefore, this notion comes closest of all to the "sacred," in the sense that Rudolf Otto understood it, and after him Carl Jung, Mircea Eliade, and others.

An Operation to Expand Possibilities

The sublime and the sacred are manifest in the work *The Great God Pan* in a very interesting and unusual context. The story is based on Irish folklore. The plot is quite classic for the late 19th and early 20th centuries. The hero of the story is a scientist, a doctor, who by way of a surgical operation is capable of expanding the possibilities of the human perception of reality. The scientist conducts a test on a simple village girl named Mary. The experiment is not entirely successful. The girl plunges into madness. The patient is constantly confronted with something that radically surpasses and overwhelms her. While she does gain access to some kind of extra-reality, she is unable to control it. The scientist understands the girl to have met the god Pan, the personification of the forces of nature in all their diversity and power.

Further on, the reader is presented with an account of the life of Mary's daughter, whom she gave birth to after meeting Pan. The daughter, Helen Vaughan, harbors something at once inexpressibly beautiful and terrifying, capable of driving those around her insane to the point of suicide or murder. The faces of the people led to death by Helen Vaughan are frozen with panic, fear, and horror. This fear and horror are transmitted to anyone who sees their bodies.

Beyond the Human

This work is an excellent showcase of the problem of the sublime. Here, in full measure, we see the experience of facing the sublime, the numinous, which according to Rudolf Otto, is characterized at once by astonishment, admiration, and incredible joy, as well as wild fear and deep horror. This encounter is almost always fatal, or in the very least traumatic for a person who otherwise dwells within their comfort zone (although being in such a state should not be considered natural).

Beauty is interpreted in this book to be a kind of border that separates what we are capable of perceiving without special preparation, something in which we can delight in and admire on the one hand, and which exceeds our possibilities and capacities on the other, i.e., the sublime. If the experience of encountering the "beautiful" entails temporary charm and fascination, then the experience of encountering the sublime, as happens in Machen's tale, can be the opposite, i.e., one that brings with it horror, death, and madness. Thus, in this story, the god Pan himself acts as a generalized representation of the sublime, but by no means the beautiful.

It is interesting that Socrates was often compared to Pan. His exterior form, down to the wrinkles on his face, largely corresponds to Greek notions of how this god should have looked.

Thus, ever since archaic times, the encounter with the sublime has been associated with the experience of trauma. It can lead a human being to death and madness, but it also harbors the possibility of meeting that which lies beyond the human.

***

The Poor Subject

Russian as an Enigma[79]

Russian thought lives where night parts with the day, in the cold dusk of the Russian forest. There is no "Russian philosophy" as such, and such a thing could never come to be. Philosophy means touching upon secrets, upon what is concealed, and vertically ascending to the heavenly world beyond.

Where are we to go if the beyond is within us? Russians have no border between "there" and "here." We live in "here-being." And in here-being, we experience the sacred in every moment of our lives. Our thought is woven with dreaming and enmeshed in the structure of dreams.

Russians are spirit-seers. Our thought cannot grasp what it comprehends. It is what it comprehends. In our land, in the space of our soul, the comprehended and the comprehending merge. This is the mysterious, secret course of things, the frantic course of things. We have no subject — it is absolutely poor. We have no object — it is negligible and small. Perhaps, Russians today are in their thought and existence closest of all to authenticity. We do not comprehend this — we live it. It pierces the structure of the Russian soul, it cuts into our inner tissue, at times painfully.

Witnesses of the God-Forsaken

In the West, the subject stands at the center of everything, or rather, it once stood there before they destroyed it. First, the West was forsaken by God, and now it has been forsaken by the subject.

But us? We have something else. We are hurt by the God-forsakenness of Europe, we are the witnesses of Europe's having

---

[79] The present text was a speech delivered at the premiere of the late Andrei Iryshkov's multimedia project and documentary film *The Feminine Principle in Russian Philosophy* at the Gorky Art Theater in Moscow on 27 January 2020.

been forsaken by God. We are God-bearers. We are the witnesses of subject-forsakenness, but… the Russian subject — what is it? A poor subject. So big that it starts to seem too small and poor. This poverty is not poverty in the sense of lack or need, but rather a poverty that surpasses riches and emeralds. It is like the poverty of a monk. The subject is so poor that it is almost absent– its will, its intention, is barely visible through the fog of the indistinguishable. Not only does it lack a trajectory, it lacks any point of initiation for a trajectory — no intending, no intended, no intention.

The Russian subject is the poor subject, a secret, mysterious force, the sphere of subtle being. This is real existence. It is hope that is not directed towards anything. It is Being itself. The Russian is too broad to be a subject. This meek, humble, directionless poverty is something confused, and hardly understands its own true wealth — that which, without being known, is already at the center of Being, at the center of Absolute Truth, at the center of the eternal light of the Good, in the punishment of the soul, where words are too exhausted to express the infinity and greatness of God.

***

The Russian Kitezhian, Oleg Fomin-Shakhov

The Great-Russian Mood[80]

Have you ever met a living bearer of Russian tradition? Not staged circle choir dances and not "*lubok*" style "Russian" folklore, but a real, "authentic" Russian? I have. His name was Oleg Fomin-Shakhov. Some know him as a poet, others as a philosopher, others as a historian of Russian tradition or as the founder of the Zlydota music group, and still others as a valiant Orthodox warrior and militant of the Pro-Life movement. I knew him as a genuine Russian Orthodox man.

We moderns ignore the past, laugh at our history, or simply reproduce it softly with a hushed tone. Have you noticed the zeal with which the peoples of the Caucasus dance the *lezginka*, how well they know their folk songs? How their feasts are always enveloped in sacred meanings (*supra*)? The Georgians for instance... but what about us? We know a couple of alleged folk songs, although we forget their words– we think that the song "Katyusha" is traditional, and at most we'll dip twice to "Kalinka" believing that this squat dance is Russia's national dance, we'll wear headscarves (tied with a knot instead of a pin) and put on fake theatrical *sarafan-*dresses over ripped jeans. We are prisoners of Modernity, and we — we ourselves alone — are the ones responsible for the withering of Russian tradition.

He Who Was Not a Prisoner of Modernity

But Oleg was not a prisoner of Modernity. Oleg was tradition — living tradition. This was manifest in everything he did. His mood was always "great," Great-Russian. It was hard not to notice this: he decisively occupied space, and wherever he was, he always wore a traditional Russian black hood (how shameful it is that I don't even remember exactly which Russian

---

80 The present text was a eulogy for Oleg Fomin-Shakhov (1976-2017) published in *Zavtra* on 26 October 2017.

tradition it's from), a cheerful and very sly smile, a hurdy-gurdy or harp and a very strong, loud voice.

In 2001, he founded the Zlydota music group. The name comes from the Silver Age, from a mysterious brotherhood in Pimen Karpov's novel, *The Flame*. Much of the group's lyrics were written in Old Church Slavonic or in Old Russian, and some songs were sung in verses from the writings of the Russian philosopher Vladimir Karpets (who developed the important doctrine of "social monarchism"). Zlydota concerts were always a rich and colorful spectacle. Every member of the group had their own image: the girls' heads were adorned with amazing patterned caps, and the stage was decorated with various canvases and fabrics. The group played on old instruments - the gusli, the lute, the hurdy-gurdy (where did Oleg even find all of this?!). All of it looked deeply authentic. There was no hint of a corny *lubok* style or anything "fake." I don't know any other group like Zlydota, and it is unlikely that any will appear. I don't know a single person who knew Russian tradition as well as Oleg: he could talk about the signs and symbols on any given church. I don't know a single person who was so Russian... precisely and nothing other than Russian... joyfully Russian.

Oleg died on 25 October, the day of the death of the Russian spirit-seer Yuri Vitalyevich Mamleev. I don't believe in coincidences. "*Tout se tient*," as a great philosopher once said. The world continues as before to plunge into hell, descending lower and lower into one circle and then another, into crises of all kinds. The human will be replaced by the cyborg, the "last humans" will come around and blink while declaring that they have "invented happiness" — this is precisely what will unfold before our very eyes.

Yet, somewhere far away, either above the world or below it, in the invisible city of Kitezh, there will be a banquet at which a real Russian gusli artist will sing about the end of time. At times, his song will be audible to us, too. We need only to listen closely...

***

Andrei Bely's Petersburg and Infernal Russia

The Infernal Russia of the Silver Age[81]

Greetings, dear participants of this seminar. Today, we will be descending into Russia. We will have to pull ourselves away from solar poetry à la Nikolai Gumilev in the spirit of:

Солнце свирепое, солнце грозящее,	Ferocious sun, menacing sun,
Бога, в пространствах идущего,	of God, walking in spaces,
Лицо сумасшедшее,	Crazed face,
Солнце, сожги настоящее	Sun, burn the present
Во имя грядущего,	in the name of the coming,
Но помилуй прошедшее!	but have mercy on the past!

These lines by Gumilev from 1907 could essentially be called a proto-manifesto of optimistic, imperial Eurasianism. At the same time, however, in the Silver Age, when we begin to study the field of myths and images, we also encounter a completely different Russia, an otherworldly, infernal, opposite Russia; a shapeshifter, a double. This is the Russia that we are talking about in today's seminar, which we will call "infernal."

I would like to talk about this infernal Russia within the framework of Andrei Bely's novel *Petersburg*, published in 1916.[82] It deals in part with the events of 1905. His Russia is a Russia of radical fissure, a Russia in which two paradigms clash. On the one hand, we still see the imperial Russia founded by Peter, the symbol of which is still the Bronze Horseman. The novel describes this Russia as a kind of Leviathan, an iron Empire with Machiavellian, cynical, cruel power. On the other hand, over the course of the novel we see the emergence of a new

---

81 The present text is based on a presentation at the third session of the online Plato Seminar organized by Alexander Dugin and Paideuma TV, "Political Platonism in Russian History," in 2020.

82 Andrei Bely, *Petersburg*, trans. Robert A. Maguire and John E. Malmstad (Bloomington: Indiana University Press, 2018).

paradigm that comes from the West and which, like imperial Russia, is founded on Western values. These values, however, are different. We see the advent of socialism, of new ideologies and visions. Socialism is presented here as completely unadapted to the Russian cultural code. Once it finds itself on Russian soil, it enters into complete contradiction, into dissonance. Socialism is not implanted like a transplanted stalk; it does not take root in the body, in the main stem of the Russian soul.

Thus, the Silver Age and the novel *Petersburg* harbor two significant principles. There is the principle of Western imperial Russia founded by Peter (the Petrine version of the state) and, on the other hand, the similarly Western form of socialism, which cross, fight each other, and constitute the main opposition throughout Bely's novel.

The Non-Russian Doubles of Apollo and Dionysus

In discussing the infernal Russia of the Silver Age, why do I refer to none other than Andrei Bely's novel? This is because Bely's *Petersburg*, with its morbidity and its war of two principles, both inauthentic to the Russian Logos, describes "infernal Russia" most fully. In such a Russia, that which is actually Russian does not reign — neither the Apollonian Russian (Orthodox-Byzantine) nor the Dionysian Russian (the folk and peasant, sacral-agricultural). Instead, the Russian state and the Russian people are ruled by their doubles.

In the novel — and this is often emphasized by scholars — a fine line of struggle is drawn between Apollonianism and Dionysianism. It bears noting that the Apollonian principle is represented in the novel by the rather unattractive character Apollon Apollonovich Abluekhov, a rather elderly senator who is a typical representative of a solid but alienated and dead bureaucratic system. He is a government official who wants nothing more than to move up the career ladder. Nothing remains of Apollonianism in him aside from how he sees Petersburg as an order of straight lines and avenues, and when he sees the islands he hates them in every possible way and wants to bind them to the mainland with bridges. His Apollonianism manifests itself exclusively in superficial, flat thoughts, conclusions, preferences, and desires which in fact have absolutely nothing to do with real Apollonianism. For instance, he desires to attach the island to the land so as to not see it, because the island reminds him of disorder, chaos, blurriness, and the possibility of disappearing from where one is at the moment. He likes clear geometric graphics: avenues drawn with a ruler, the facades of buildings measured down to the centimeter. Apollon Apollonovich Ableukhov sees the world through the perspective of parallelepipeds, squares, and other geometric shapes.

Bely contrasts the figure of Apollon Apollonovich Ableukhov to his son, Nikolai Apollonovich Ableukhov, whom the novel jokingly associates with the god Dionysus. When Nikolai Apollonovich, just ahead of committing a terrorist act against his own father, just before setting and activating a bomb in a sardine can, shares his doubts with his comrades from the terrorist party, Nikolai speaks of "Dionysus tormented." But what is properly Dionysian in this Dionysus? Is it really the Greek god who freely hovers over fields in free dance, overcomes all dualities, and is equally imperturbable in joy and suffering, in life and death? Is it really the one who laughs and distorts the Apollonian vertical by bending it into a wave or a spiral — the straight line here being the avenues, park squares, and palace parallelepipeds, the exact rectangular shapes of the Apollonian which are a caricature of the style of Ableukhov the father? Far from it. Ableukhov the son is also a parody of Dionysus, his dark double. He, of course, is no Dionysus, but rather a Titan. Although he is called "Dionysus," he completely lacks the divine, Olympian, mystical, inner axis thanks to which the ancient god was called the "midnight sun." Let us also recall that Nikolai Apollonovich is an ardent defender of Kantianism in the novel. There is very little of anything Dionysian here.

The semantic canvas of Andrei Bely's novel is a story of the interweaving and interaction of two clones, two copies, one might even say two doubles: the pseudo-Apollo father and the pseudo-Dionysus son. For Bely himself, this contrast is the code of Saint Petersburg and, more broadly, the model of infernal Russia.

Why is it infernal? Because there is nothing authentic, nothing Russian, nor genuine, nothing of the people, the folk. Everything is foreign. The Westernist state, imperial-bureaucratic Russia, and mechanical socialism are equally and absolutely uncharacteristic of the Russian spirit.

Remember that Bely wanted to call this trilogy *East and West*. Apparently, it was Blok who advised him to title the novel *Petersburg*. The first version of the title was supposed to emphasize that Saint Petersburg is the West in relation to the rest of Russia, to our inner East.

Whither Flies Petrovsky's Horse?

I would like to point out an interesting rumination by the young revolutionary Dudkin from this novel about Russia's fate. He notes that the Bronze Horseman's horse is rearing up and standing on two hooves, a symbolic scenario and symbol of Russia's opportunity to traverse four different paths of development. Firstly, the Petrovsky horse appears to Dudkin to be breaking away from the pedestal and thereby breaking away from the people to gallop into the dark abyss. The state disappears and recedes with its leap. Such is Russia torn from its foundation, the Russia of Peter and the successors to his cause. Here the soil of the spirit of the people recedes behind the feet of the ruling class. On the other hand, the socialism brought over from the West might also be symbolized by this leap, this break from traditions and Russian culture. In this case, the horse is carrying Russia away from its roots.

Yet, Dudkin has another, rather paradoxical and interesting interpretation: the horse might impulsively jump into the air and dissolve into the sky. This is a vertical image of a fully-fledged, solar, Apollonian Russia. Bely admits this image into his novel, but *Petersburg* is by no means this Russia. Yet Bely mentions it, he speaks of a fourth dimension, of the possibility of going out and overcoming, of taking off in flight and ascent, of a kind of transgressive experience. The Russian horse can leave this Westernist, non-Russian inferno. But Bely only thinly sketches this line and it is not the main point of the work taken as a whole.

On the other hand, Dudkin has yet another suggestion: perhaps this rambunctious horse climbed onto the pedestal by mistake and at some point will descend back to the ground to continue its natural, organic path on earth. The leap into the sky would be the heavenly option, while the descent to the horizon of the people would be the earthly one. These two interpretations can indeed be correlated with the Apollonian and Dionysian lines of the Russian Logos.

Nevertheless, the hope that the horse will take off in flight upwards is not realized in the novel. Bely's *Petersburg* remains an infernal Petersburg, in which two hybrids, two false principles, collide in mad conflict and cannot reach a resolution or form a new semantic element.

When you read Bely's novel, it makes a strong emotional impression. Without a doubt, it fits into the axis that Gogol had already set when he described his Petersburg — a heap of autonomous bureaucrats' noses roaming its avenues, its rectilinear and quadrilateral streets and squares, its crazed bureaucrats meticulously recording their delirium, and Akaky Akakiyevich investing all the wealth of the world in a government overcoat… the dark and hopeless dead ends of the fall of impoverished artists and doomed, dull, easy ladies. We see something similar in Dostoevsky's Petersburg, an atmosphere that is altogether conducive to the appearance of demons and beasts. However, if in Dostoevsky and Gogol (especially in Dostoevsky) there exists a parallel, meaningful, sacred axis around which the Russian man experiences the difficult shaping of their full-fledged spirit, an orientation, a hope to take off and soar, for the bronze horse to leap into the heavens– there is none of this in Andrei Bely.

Why does this axis not arise in Bely? Perhaps because he was no longer imbued with the spirit of Orthodoxy, because he left it and plunged into rather superficial neo-mystical teachings, primarily under the influence of the Russian Steinerians and Rudolf Steiner himself.

The "Molding" of Russia

Bely's *Petersburg* shows the process of Russia's "molding," a ceremony of its submersion into the underworld where Apollo no longer exists, devoid of the luminous supreme principle, where the state is represented by a simulacrum and a soulless, degenerate bureaucratic system, where patriarchy (first and foremost the relationship between father and son) has been undermined and represents an alienated formalism that gives way to rebellion. "Tormented Dionysus," who among the Greeks and in classical culture was a god who overcame dualities, is represented in the figure of the student and son conceived in a barbaric manner — as the novel accentuates, Nikolai Apollonovich was conceived out of his father's rape of his mother. It turns out that this Dionysus is a black double, a jester. As a jester, he becomes a red domino, a clown, a holy fool without Christ.

This is how Andrei Bely poignantly describes this Anti-Russia. If Vyacheslav Ivanov and the whole culture of the Silver Age had a serious attitude towards Apollo — he was still a god, even when they ironically toyed with him — then in Bely, Apollon Apollonovich Ableukhov is no longer the god, but his black copy.

In conclusion, I would like to cite a passage from the novel in which Nikolai Apollonovich, the pseudo-Dionysus, the black Dionysus, speaks about his father, the pseudo-Apollo, as he sees him: "And I understood that everything that exists is 'spawn.'

People as such do not exist: they are all 'spawned.' Apollon Apollonovich is also something 'spawned,' an unpleasant sum of blood and skin. Meat sweats and goes bad in the heat. There being no soul, I hate my own flesh."

What we see in Bely are not archetypes and Logoi, but their simulacra, their shadows in the realm of the infernal. It is difficult to come to a fully-fledged metaphysical and poetic topology starting here, because the entire fabric of *Petersburg* forms a semantic swamp, a city returning to its germs. This spiritual crisis of the Silver Age, this overlayering of substitutions, says a great deal about the last period of the Russian Empire and partly explains its subsequent collapse.

And yet, there is hope — if the Bronze Horseman's steed does somehow take off and soar into the inexplicable depths of the Russian sky.

***

The Political Subject of Populism and the Problem of "Unhappy Consciousness"

The West's Double Standards

I have a lively interest in the question of feminism and, from time to time, I attend events on the topic. I cannot help but notice how Western "advisors" impose the topic of gender on our society. Such an approach is clearly oriented towards destroying the family, yet this obsessive line is always camouflaged as "free discourse."

Western Postmodernists are very active. They advocate the destruction of the state and revolt against it — but only when it comes to our state, Russia. Here, they curse hierarchy and power. They stubbornly prefer not to notice their own oligarchy, monopoly, and closed elite groups. It's the same with feminism.

Western philosophical "grids" are actively imposed on our society, our state, but very selectively. Our values, pillars, and institutions are subjected to criticism first of all. It is hard not to notice the double standards here. But my talk is not about this. It is devoted rather to the political subject and the problem of "unhappy consciousness."

The Statesman as a Philosopher

When we try to understand who a politician should be, what a state should be, we cannot ignore Plato and his *Republic*, which is the pinnacle of not only Plato's political philosophy, but also the entirety of his teachings on metaphysics, the soul, ontology, and cosmology. The *Republic* is complex and multidimensional. The main question examined in it is: Who is the politician, the statesman? Who is the true political subject? The answer is given immediately: The true politician, the true subject of the Political, is the philosopher. It is always and exclusively a philosopher.

What makes a philosopher a philosopher? Everyone knows the myth of the cave that is set forth in the seventh book of Plato's *Republic*. The philosopher is the person who breaks off their chains, throws off the slave blocks, boldly stands up, and exits the situation in the cave — i.e. the state of submersion into matter, a status of a complete lack of awareness that remains at the level of contemplating shadows, indistinct objects, and images. After leaving the cave, the philosopher goes through several levels to finally reach the light of the world outside and beholds the hierarchical link of beautiful ideas and the highest of them all, the Idea of the One. A question arises here: What does this have to do with politics and political activity?

The Philosopher-Politician as a Doomed Creature

And here, what is most interesting begins. In fragment 519 of the seventh book, Socrates says:

> It is our task as founders, then, to compel the best natures to reach the study we said before is the most important, namely, to make the ascent and see the good. But when they've made it and looked sufficiently, we mustn't allow them to do what they're allowed to do today.
>
> What's that?
>
> To stay there and refuse to go down again to the prisoners in the cave and share their labors and honors, whether they are of less worth or of greater.[83]

Socrates means that, in ordinary society, as opposed to in the ideal state, philosophers would simply abandon political problems in order to attain the heights of speculation and contemplation of the One — after all, this is the highest aim of the philosopher. But in the ideal state, in Kallipolis, the philosophers cannot remain in the clouds. This is why Socrates stipulates that "We mustn't allow them to stay there." In the ideal state, the philosopher will be compelled to "go down again." At this point, the philosopher must transform from a contemplator, a beholder of the One and the Good, into a politician, be torn away from the euphoria

---

83 Plato, *Republic* 519c-e.

of contemplating the highest principle — which in Christianity will be interpreted to be God and in various other Neoplatonic models as the gods, ideas, archetypes, forms, and henads — and go down into society. Here is where real politics begins. This is how the state is established.

When the philosopher who has seen what is "beyond being" (ἐπέκεινα τῆς οὐσίας) in the world of archetypes and ideas and has seen how everything truly is, only to descend back down, at this point, as Glaucon rightly says to Socrates: "Are we to do them an injustice by making them lie a worse life when they could live a better one?"[84] He means that this person will be deeply unhappy. He has seen the highest values as they are, has had the honor to contemplate what is beyond everything, has seen the world above in a unique mystical experience, only for us to tear him away from this and cast him into the thick of people who are far from elevated, who are indifferent to everything true on the whole.

Here arises a quite paradoxical point: the political subject, the philosopher-king, will always be unhappy.

The Russian Wants Peace

To our mentality, this is very difficult to accept. Russian consciousness always wants harmony. We constantly try to glue and put everything together, to unify everything so that it is happy and good. Even our interpretation of Christianity is very soft, cordial, and kind.

We always miss the paradox that is otherwise crystal clear in Hegel. In his *Phenomenology of Spirit*, Hegel formulated a most important thought: true philosophical consciousness is always unhappy. It abides in dispersion, in absolute God-forsakenness and in the splintering world. The world is a space of terrible contradictions, terrible injustice and unhappiness. The subject does not coincide with the object, and this gap gives rise to the dialectic of tragic thought. Here lie the origins of philosophy.

---

84 Ibid.

Socrates talks about this in the fourth book of the *Republic* during the discussion on the philosopher. The philosopher-politicians are unhappy in the ordinary, mundane sense, as well-fed and materially satisfied farmers are happy. In some sense, they will always be unhappy, but the good of the state is built on the unhappiness of the philosopher-politicians. Such is the price that the politician pays for his state to live, prosper, and flourish.

The Ordinary Citizen is a Prisoner

Who are we, the ordinary citizens and representatives of consumer society, in this picture of the Political? We are the prisoners sitting in the cave, bound in fetters. We are the ones watching the shadows projected on the wall. What is this projection? It is the political show that we observe on TV everyday, on which something seems to be reflected, but no true reality is ever shown.

In any case, I recommend everyone — philosophers and politicians, beginners as well as those who are more experienced — to turn to the seventh book of Plato's *Republic* again and again. It would be best to learn it by heart (and preferably in ancient Greek). If you want to engage in politics or philosophy, be ready to live a life of unhappiness. I call this "eschatological optimism," but that is a separate topic.

Liberalism Appeals to the Unhappy Consciousness of the Idiot Layman

Let us now move on to the ideological level. Liberalism claims that the highest value is happiness. Everything needs to be balanced and done in such a way that all opposition — private and general, individual and collective, earthly and heavenly — comes into balance without conflict. This is the imperative even in everyday politics.

Recall Emmanuel Macron's pre-election program, in which he constantly appealed to feelings of happiness, peace, comfort, and plenitude. As opposed to what? As opposed to the unhappy consciousness of those in France who call themselves "populists."[85] In his election campaign, Macron constantly used the following phrases against his opponents: "they're nostalgic," "they're provoking conflict," "they aren't satisfied with peace and the world as it is," "they constantly want something else," "they're bad," "they hate everyone." What Macron criticizes about populism is in fact what, according to Plato, is the most valuable quality of the philosopher-politician. This is the lack of satisfaction with the world that is given to us, the nostalgia that is present in conservatism and makes up its main motive. This is what is most important in politics and this is precisely what is completely ignored by liberalism.

Contemporary conservatives, and we in particular, are fundamentally discontent with given reality.

Are Populists Stupid?

I've analyzed a number of typical statements by populists of both the right and left. Globalists and liberals virtually always base their criticism of populism on the allegation that it is eternally unsatisfied, incites hatred, and is rooted in "ignorance" and "stupidity."

Is this really the case? No. Populism is based on our unhappy consciousness, which is the guarantee of genuine politics and genuine philosophy. Liberalism is the ideology that presents a fake system, an artificial structure of happiness. It is liberalism that proposes imprisoning people in the cave of the "society of the spectacle" forever, so that they obediently behold the broadcasting of meaningless images on the wall and consume the propagandistic news of a World Government.

---

85 "Populism" is a generalizing and originally pejorative term used to describe all political forces in the West that protest the domination of liberalism and the reign of the liberal elites. Populists do not have any structured ideology. Their protests arise in reaction to liberal economics, policies, and strategies which they consider to be pernicious. Populists can be right-wing as well as left-wing, but most often they do not adhere to any single political platform. One example of populism would be the Yellow Vests movement in France.

Populism represents the genuine realization of the philosophical idea of leaving the cave and then descending back into it in order to enlighten the blind ones who remain there. Populists are not naive; on the contrary, they are the ones who are truly informed. Liberals criticize them for lacking a well-developed political philosophy, but they themselves prevent the populists from developing one by deliberately demonizing and repressing them.

The central idea of populism lies precisely in the people's unhappy consciousness, in dissatisfaction with the present, discontent with the given, in protesting the contemporary situation and revolting against the modern world. Populism spontaneously goes against the contemporary moment, and hence against liberalism. Let the populists have no complete concept, for, in the end, the truth itself is completely contradictory. Truth is more likely to manifest itself in mystical experience: it is something completely indescribable. What is expressible in the word, in cataphatic discourse, will always contain dissonance, discrepancy, and discord.

The Choice of the Subject

I hope that I've managed to offer some images useful in describing the closed (by no means open!) space that liberalism cultivates in its aspiration to keep society inside of its fake system as it strictly forbids us from accessing the real world outside the cave.

In contrast and opposition to liberalism, we have populism, and this opposition correlates with the philosophical model of Plato's cave, where the philosopher first ascends to the highest level of pure contemplation before making the sacrifice of going back down. Populism is the prerequisite for a real political philosophy with a fully-fledged subject. It represents a desperate attempt to leave the closed society of totalitarian liberals behind and break their obsessive dictatorship, which strives to force the diversity of human choice into a single matrix.

Philosophers are always and everywhere the ideal political subject. Philosophers are also fundamentally unhappy people. If we really want to bring about a Russian renaissance, we must understand that we are making a conscious choice to be unhappy, to take on a difficult and tragic lot, a fatal destiny, dissension, and an unattainable dream. Genuine politicians and genuine thinkers never find true harmony.

It is with the recognition that the status quo is deeply abnormal, unbearable, and unacceptable, and that it is necessary to immediately and desperately seek a way out, that the formation of a fully-fledged political perspective and position begins. This is also where philosophy begins.

We must accept dissent as a given. Such a tragic state is surmountable through the Christian religion, in deep Orthodox experience, perhaps in Hesychastic prayer. It is also surmountable through active deeds that transform the world, through the will to correct and decorate it, to turn it into something meaningful and just, and to reach towards the primordial heavenly archetypes, towards what God originally wanted from us, but from which we have shrunk back.

***

PART III:
NEOPLATONISM AND THE IDEAL *POLIS*

The Political Philosophy of Proclus Diadochus

Introduction: The Political Theology of Neoplatonism[86]

In the traditional history of philosophy, Neoplatonic political philosophy has always been held back from full recognition as a result of a focus on Neoplatonism's metaphysical aspects. Such Neoplatonic concepts as "abiding" (μονή), "emanation" (πρόοδος), "return" (ἐπιστροφή), and others have been examined in historical-philosophical works in separation from the sphere of the Political.[87] Thus, the Political has been interpreted as merely a stage in the ascent to the Good (τὸ ἀγαθόν), as an exclusively ethical-social stage embedded in Neoplatonism's strict hierarchical model, rather than as the independent pole of the philosophical model. Such a view of the Neoplatonic philosophical heritage seems to us to be inadequate.

Through Proclus' works, we wish to show how the Political is understood within Neoplatonism as an important and substantive phenomenon incorporated into the general philosophical, metaphysical, ontological, gnoseological, and cosmological context.

If political philosophy was expressed explicitly in classical Platonism and by Plato himself (in the dialogues *Republic*, *Statesman*, *Laws*, etc.), then in Neoplatonism, especially in Proclus, we can discern political philosophy only indirectly and largely through commentaries on Plato's dialogues. This

---

86 The present text was Daria Platonova Dugina's Master's thesis defended at the Faculty of Philosophy of Moscow State University in 2015. Portions of it appeared in various journal publications and conference papers.

87 Carl Schmitt's term "the Political" (*das Politische*) accentuates that the matter at hand is not the technical organization of the process of ruling and governance, but a metaphysical phenomenon possessing its own inner metaphysical structure, autonomous ontology, and "theology," hence Schmitt's term "political theology." See Carl Schmitt, *The Concept of the Political*, trans. George Schwab (Chicago: University of Chicago Press, 2007).

is connected with, among other things, the historical political-religious context of the society in which the late Neoplatonists, including Proclus himself, operated.

The Implicitness of the Political

At present, the political ideas of the Neoplatonists have not been sufficiently studied. Moreover, the very fact of the existence of Neoplatonic political philosophy (in the very least among the late Hellenic Neoplatonists) has not been demonstrated and generally has not even been thematized in historical-philosophical scholarship. However, Neoplatonic systems of political philosophy were widely developed in the Islamic context (from al-Farabi to Shiite political gnosis[88]), and in Christian Neoplatonism among Western authors (particularly in Blessed Augustine), which significantly influenced the political structure of Medieval Europe. In our time, all over the world and in Russia in particular, there is an ongoing search for a new political model, and the experience of the Neoplatonists might very well turn out to be one of the sources for this new political construct or, on the contrary, an object of Postmodernist deconstruction. In both cases, Neoplatonic political philosophy should be thematized and studied.

We will attempt to reconstruct in the most general terms and proportions Proclus' political philosophy as implicitly present in his works. We will start from the basic hypothesis that there is a homology between psychological (pertaining to the soul, ψῡχή), cosmological (ontological), and political structures.

Our task is to show that Proclus did indeed have a political philosophy, albeit not explicitly expressed, and to reconstruct it on the basis of Proclus' remarks on the state which we find in his commentaries on Plato's *Republic* and *Timaeus*.

---

[88] See Henry Corbin, *History of Islamic Philosophy*, trans. Liadain Sherrard and Philip Sherrard (London: Routledge, 2004)

The present topic has not enjoyed any detailed development at the present moment. Scholarly works specifically dedicated to Proclus' political philosophy are virtually absent in Russian. As for specialist studies among foreign sources, we can mention only *Platonopolis: Platonic Political Philosophy in Late Antiquity* by the English specialist on Neoplatonic philosophy, Dominic O'Meara[89], J. M. Schott's article "Founding Platonopolis: The Platonic Politeia in Eusebius, Porphyry, and Iamblichus,"[90] separate chapters in Lucas Siorvanes' *Proclus: Neo-Platonic Philosophy and Science*[91], and André-Jean Festugière's French translations and commentaries on Proclus' main works, especially the five-volume *Commentaries on the Timaeus*[92] and the three-volume *Commentaries on the Republic*.[93]

---

89 Dominic J. O'Meara, *Platonopolis: Platonic Political Philosophy in Late Antiquity* (Oxford: Clarendon Press, 2003).

90 J.M. Schott, "Founding Platonopolis: The Platonic Politeía in Eusebius, Porphyry, and Iamblichus", *Journal of Early Christian Studies* 11:4 (2003).

91 Lucas Siorvanes, *Proclus: Neo-Platonic Philosophy and Science* (Edinburgh: Edinburgh University Press, 1996).

92 Proclus, *Commentaires sur le Timée. Tome 1, Livre I*, trans. André-Jean Festugière (Paris: J. Vrin-CNRS, 1966); idem., *Commentaires sur le Timée. Tome 2, Livre II*, trans. André-Jean Festugière (Paris: J. Vrin-CNRS, 1967); idem., *Commentaires sur le Timée. Tome 3, Livre III*, trans. André-Jean Festugière (Paris: J. Vrin-CNRS, 1967); idem, *Commentaires sur le Timée. Tome 4, Livre IV*, trans. André-Jean Festugière (Paris: J. Vrin-CNRS, 1968); idem., *Commentaires sur le Timée. Tome 5, Livre V*, tr. André-Jean Festugière (Paris: J. Vrin-CNRS, 1969).

93 Proclus, *Commentaires sur la République. Tome 1, Livres 1-3*, trans. André-Jean Festugière (Paris: J. Vrin-CNRS, 1970); idem., *Commentaires sur la République. Tome 2, Livres 4-9*, trans. André-Jean Festugière (Paris: J. Vrin-CNRS, 1970); idem., *Commentaires sur la République. Tome 3, Livre 10*, trans. André-Jean Festugière (Paris: J. Vrin-CNRS, 1970).

The Historical and Philosophical Contexts of the Formation of Proclus' Political Philosophy

Proclus Diadochus as a Commentator on Plato: Peculiarities of the Genre

"Interpreting Plato is Neoplatonism" - Karl Prechter

Proclus Diadochus (412-485 C.E.) was the scholarch of the Athenian school of Neoplatonism, one of the most prolific thinkers of late antiquity, and a philosopher whose works expounded the main Platonic ideas that had been developed over the course of centuries. His writings synthesize religious Platonism and metaphysical Platonism, to some extent constituting a synthesis of all preceding Platonisms — classical (Plato and the Academy), "middle" (voluminously described in John Dillon's book[94]), and Neoplatonism (Plotinus, Porphyry, Iamblichus, etc.). Proclus was the third scholarch of the Athenian school of Neoplatonism (following Plutarch of Athens and Syrianus, Proclus' teacher), which existed until 539 (when it was closed by Emperor Justinian, who issued edicts against pagans, Jews, Arians, numerous sects, and also condemned the teachings of the Christian Platonist Origen).

According to the scholar of Neoplatonism Henri-Dominique Saffrey, "the curriculum in the Neoplatonic Athenian school was organized in the following order: for two years, Aristotle's dialogues were read, then Plato's dialogues were studied, then the connection between the Orphic writings or the *Chaldean Oracles*, which were considered holy scripture, and Platonic theology was studied."[95] In the 5th century, the Athenian school was the main intellectual center of the Empire (and it was held to be such even in comparison to the Alexandrian school). The majority of the teachers who gathered at the Mouseion

---
94 John Dillon, *The Middle Platonists: 80 B.C. to A.D. 220* (Ithaca: Cornell University Press, 1996).

95 *Dictionnaire des philosophes* (Paris: Albin Michel, 1998), 123-127.

of Alexandria had been educated in Athens. Among the main features of the Athenian school of Neoplatonism, we can distinguish:

1. An aspiration to synthesize various theological currents of thought (Orphism, Pythagoreanism, Platonism, the *Chaldean Oracles*, etc.). Proclus proclaimed the principle of "harmonizing theological traditions between each other."[96] Saffrey has written extensively of this peculiarity of the Neoplatonic Athenian school: "Proclus' Platonic theology is a beautiful body, the skeleton of which consists of the poetic heritage of Homer and Hesiod, the myths, oracles, and sayings about the divine, as well as the works of Plato, Aristotle, and Pythagoras."[97]

2. An aspiration to describe and interpret religious and traditional rites as broadly as possible, since they correspond to the explicit will of the gods (unlike Proclus, Plotinus and Porphyry considered religious practice to be unworthy of examination, since they believed it was possible to comprehend God or achieve the divine level directly thanks to the spiritual ascent of thought).[98]

The scholar of Neoplatonism Ilsetraut Hadot has rightly pointed out that "there did not exist any separate Alexandrian Neoplatonic school, since all of its main doctrines were in essence the doctrines of the Athenian school."[99] Thus, the Athenian school dominated the philosophical space of the time.

96 Proclus, *Théologie platonicienne*, trans./ed. H.D. Saffrey and L.G. Westerink (Paris: Les Belles Lettres, 1968), 5.

97 H.D. Saffrey, *Le Néoplatonisme après Plotin* (Paris: J. Vrin, 2000), 184.

98 "Carried off, as it were, by the wave of the Spirit itself, lifted up high by it, as if it were swollen, 'he suddenly saw, without seeing how.' But the spectacle, filling the eyes with light, did not cause some other object to be seen by its means; rather, what was seen was light itself. It is not that there were two things within it: on the one hand a visible object, and on the other its light, nor was there the Spirit and then what is thought by the Spirit; there is only a dazzling light, which engenders all these things later on." - Plotinus, quoted in Pierre Hadot, *Plotinus, or The Simplicity of Vision*, trans. Michael Chase (Chicago: University of Chicago Press, 1998), 62.

99 Ilsetraut Hadot, *Le problème du néoplatonisme alexandrin. Hiéroclès et Simplicius* (Paris: Études Augustiniennes, 1978).

One of the important genre-specific traits of the Athenian school was the compilation of philosophical works in the form of commentaries on the works of previous philosophers, poets, and theologians (first and foremost, of course, Plato). In its composition, the classic Neoplatonic commentary consisted of an introduction that discussed the subject of the dialogue to be commented on and its genre, style, and place among the author's other works, to which a brief retelling of the dialogue was often appended. An important place was allotted to analyzing the circumstances of the dialogue, the significance of the characters involved, and their symbolic meaning. Further, the text was divided into "lemmas," or phrases to be interpreted. The commentary on one lemma sometimes took up a whole lecture. First, a general interpretation of the fragment's meaning was undertaken, then a more detailed examination was carried out to clarify the significance of individual terms within the phrase. According to Prechter, Proclus did not introduce any innovations into the order of the commentary; he completely imitated the commentaries of Iamblichus and Syrianus.[100]

However, Proclus did not always follow the rules of Iamblichus' commentary. In his commentary on the *Timaeus*, for example, he would analyze several phrases over the course of multiple lectures while omitting others. Throughout his commentaries on Plato's dialogues, one can trace the substantive development of the topics that interested him. Proclus used Plato's dialogues as an invitation to think. His commentaries are fully-fledged philosophical works in which lemmas from Plato's dialogues are only the starting point of a philosophical path. The Dutch scholar of Neoplatonism Leendert Gerrit Westerink has noted that the essential feature of Proclus' commentaries is their "triadic character."[101] In Westerink's opinion, Proclus strove to break up Plato's works as much as possible so that the philosophical doctrines of Platonism might be better

---

[100] Karl Prechter (ed.), *Die Philosophie des Altertums* (Leipzig, 1926).

[101] L.G. Westerink (ed.), *The Greek Commentaries on Plato's Phaedo*, Vol. I [*Olympiodorus*] (Amsterdam: North-Holland, 1976).

integrated into the complex, hierarchical model of Neoplatonic metaphysics.

Proclus' philosophical hermeneutics were an absolutely unique event in the history of late ancient philosophy. His works were the culmination of the exegetical tradition of Neoplatonism. His commentaries proceeded from Plato's original works, but took into account the development of his ideas in the most detailed way, including the critiques of Aristotle and the Stoic philosophers. To this was added the tradition of middle Platonism, where special emphasis was placed on religious and theistic issues (as in Numenius and Philo of Alexandria).[102] Plotinus thematized the apophatic One for exegesis. Porphyry drew attention to the doctrine of political virtues and those virtues which appeal to the intellect. Iamblichus introduced a differentiation into Plotinus' hierarchy of the main ontological and eidetic series represented by the gods, angels, demons, heroes, etc.[103] If in Plotinus we see the main triad of principles as the One, the Intellect, and the Soul, then in Iamblichus there arise multileveled eidetic series which separate humans from the World Soul and the speculative realms of the Intellect. To Iamblichus belongs the practice of commentating on Plato's dialogue in an esoteric vein.

---

102 The central idea proclaimed in the Middle Platonists' ethical teachings was to become like the divine.

103 Iamblichus also systematized the method of commentary on Plato's dialogues by introducing a division into different types of interpretations: ethical, logical, cosmological, physical, and theological. Iamblichus' method of commentary laid the foundation for Proclus' approach. Out of the 12 Platonic dialogues, he distinguished two cycles (the so-called "Canon of Iamblichus"): the first included dialogues treating ethical, logical, and physical questions, and the second included the most complex and difficult Platonic dialogues which were studied at the last stages of education in Neoplatonic schools (such as the *Timaeus* and the *Parmenides*, dialogues concerning theological and cosmological issues). Iamblichus' influence on the Athenian school of Neoplatonism was extraordinarily large, to the point that this art of interpretation would be adopted by later Byzantine authors (such as Michael Psellos).

The Political and Religious Context of the Formation of Proclus' Philosophy

In order to accurately reconstruct Proclus' political philosophy, it is necessary to pay attention to the political and religious context in which he lived, thought, and worked. From the political point of view, Proclus' time was very eventful: the philosopher witnessed the destruction of the Western borders of the Roman Empire, the great migration of peoples, the invasion of the Huns, the fall of Rome first to the Visigoths (410) and then the Vandals (455), and then the end of the Western Empire (476). One of the chosen attendees of Proclus' school, Anthemius, was a patrician from Byzantium who became the Western Emperor for a short period before being killed.

Proclus' time was one of large-scale shifts: the closing of the pagan temples (in 395, 399, and 435 AD), the liquidation of pagan religion (pagan rituals were partially banned under the Eastern Roman Emperors), and the final (at times forced) transition to Christianity. Christians killed Hypatia (the mentor of a whole constellation of Platonists) and increasingly persecuted pagans. Phidias' famous statue of Athena was taken out of the Parthenon, an act which in Proclus' milieu was seen as an act of blasphemy.

The question of Proclus' opinion of the Christian religion still does not have an unambiguous answer. Some scholars believe that Proclus was not passive towards the ongoing polemics with Christians and allege that he wrote a treatise entitled *Arguments against the Christians* in 18 books. This work has not come down to us, and its mention is extremely rare in the texts of various philosophers, including Proclus' contemporaries, which makes its existence rather dubious. It is known for certain that at some point the conflict between Christians and the academy became so tense that Proclus was forced to leave Athens to Lydia for a year.

Proclus' time was the period of the decline of great late ancient Greek culture, a point of bifurcation marked by a transition to an absolutely new type of Empire founded on a new religious doctrine. While being a period of decline of late ancient pagan culture, this time also saw the birth and formation of the new Christian theology, ideology, and culture that would dominate for a thousand years across medieval Europe. Without a doubt, many Neoplatonic and pagan ideas smoothly underwent transformation and passed into Christian mysticism (the Areopagitic corpus is especially noteworthy and resembles a Christian exposition of Proclus' doctrine). The overtly pagan side of Neoplatonic philosophy was banned in 529, when Emperor Justinian issued an edict against pagans, Jews, and Arians, as a result of which the Athenian Neoplatonic school was closed and the remaining Platonists fled to Persia, later to settle in Haran on the border with Byzantium.

The context of the formation of Proclus' political philosophy therefore differed substantially from that of Plato. Both philosophers lived in Athens, but in completely different conditions. Plato worked during the period of Athenian democracy. He did not approve of the political system of the Athenian *polis*, as he advocated a "philosophical monarchy" under the auspices of a philosopher-king and caste of guardians. Plato was in the opposition of the political system of his day, and his political ideal contradicted the concrete reality of the Athenian polis.

In his lecture course delivered in the 1871-72 and 1873-74 winter semesters at the University of Basil, *Introduction to the Study of Plato's Dialogues*, Friedrich Nietzsche pointed to the uniqueness of Plato's political doctrine.[104] In his opinion, there is a fundamental difference between Socratic man and Platonic man. Socratic man obeys the gods, is well versed in his craft, whether agriculture or medicine, and honestly fulfills his duty towards the state. We see in this type of behavior – in submission to the gods and unconditionally fulfilling one's duties – a model of strict adherence to the tradition established

---

104 Friedrich Nietzsche, *Introduction à l'étude des dialogues de Platon* (Paris: De l'Éclat, 1991).

in society. In such an understanding of man's duties, there is no sign of the transcendent vertical that will become central to Plato. As Nietzsche said: "Socrates was a good citizen. Plato was a bad one, as R. Niebuhr has dared to point out. This suggests that Plato fought to the death against the established political circumstances and was a radical revolutionary."[105] The introduction of an ontological dimension into politics (in addition to the religious one that already existed at the time) was Platonism's revolutionary revelation.

Plato's student, Aristotle, adhered to a similar political philosophy and was the mentor of the Empire-builder Alexander the Great. In the Judeo-Christian teaching on the Four Kingdoms, which is based on commentaries on the Book of the Prophet Daniel (8:22) and the vision of Nebuchadnezzar, Alexander's Empire was considered to have been the Third Empire.[106] The first was the Babylonian, the second the Persian, and the fourth and last would be the Roman Empire. Each subsequent empire corresponded to a lesser kind of metal: the first kingdom corresponded to gold, the second to silver, the third to bronze, and the fourth to iron. Alexander's Empire, founded in accordance with Aristotle's precepts, was the "Bronze Empire."

Alexander the Macedonian's great achievement was to spread a single code of laws throughout the whole Greek Empire, including the Middle East and Egypt, culminating in the deification of the figure of the Emperor. The idea that the Emperor or Monarch is the inspiration of the law and the representative of the Good in the state was held by some Neo-Pythagoreans. Alexander was identified with the new world order in which all people were free citizens, cosmopolitans, and residents of one city, the cosmopolis, rather than separate city-states. For this reason, Alexander allowed for Greeks, Persians, Syrians, and Egyptians to mix. Before then, the Cynics had

---

105 Ibid., 84.

106 H.H. Rowley, *Darius the Mede and the Four World Empires in the Book of Daniel: A Historical Study of Contemporary Theories* (Cardiff : University of Wales Press Board, 1935).

already proclaimed the principle that people are not simply part of society, but part of universal nature, the individual being at once independent, autocratic (αὐταρκες), and complicit in the cosmic. This model of universal cosmopolitanism is entirely resonant with Platonic political philosophy.

After the collapse of Alexander's Empire, Rome, the Fourth Empire, began its historic ascent. The political philosophers of Rome, such as Cicero, drew heavily on Platonism, Plato himself, and the teachings of Aristotle.[107] Cicero believed that the Roman Empire embodied the synthesis of Aristotle's three positive models, i.e., monarchy, aristocracy, and polity, as opposed to the three worse types: tyranny, oligarchy, and democracy. Thus, both the third and fourth kingdoms were in one way or another conceptualized within the context of Platonic philosophy (both directly and through Aristotle).

Neoplatonism proper took shape in the context of the Roman Empire (the Fourth Empire). Plotinus lived and taught in Rome and tried to influence Roman politics in a Platonic way through Emperor Publius Gallienus, and especially his wife, Cornelia Solonina. His failed project for a Platonopolis can be seen as a blueprint for the model state. Between Plotinus, who taught in pagan Rome, and Proclus, who lived in Athens in the era of the Byzantine Empire after Christianity turned into the Empire's state religion, an important shift took place in the dominant political philosophy: the Christianization of the Empire. The Christians (from Tertullian to John Chrysostom) thought of the Roman Empire as the Fourth Empire, the chosen one, because Jesus Christ had been born in it. The Christianization of the Empire rendered its Emperor the "withholder" or "restrainer" (ὁ κατέχων), a term from the Second Epistle of St. Apostle Paul to the Thessalonians (2:7): "For the secret power of lawlessness is already at work; but the one who now holds it back will continue to do so till he is taken out of the way." Following Tertullian, John Chrysostom, as well as the whole Eastern tradition, interpreted this mysterious position to be an indication that the Roman

---

107 See Cicero's dialogues *On the Republic* and *On the Laws*.

Emperor was the condition that prevented the "secret power of lawlessness," that is the Antichrist, the "lawless one," the "son of perdition," from coming into the world. From this follows the Christian understanding of Empire as the "katechon." St. John Chrysostom wrote:

> What then is it that withholdeth, that is, hindereth him from being revealed? Some indeed say, the grace of the Spirit, but others the Roman empire, to whom I most of all accede. Wherefore? Because if he meant to say the Spirit, he would not have spoken obscurely, but plainly, that even now the grace of the Spirit, that is the gifts, withhold him. And otherwise he ought now to have come, if he was about to come when the gifts ceased; for they have long since ceased. But because he said this of the Roman empire, he naturally glanced at it, and speaks covertly and darkly. For he did not wish to bring upon himself superfluous enmities, and useless dangers. For if he had said that after a little while the Roman empire would be dissolved, they would immediately have even overwhelmed him, as a pestilent person, and all the faithful, as living and warring to this end. And he did not say that it will be quickly, although he is always saying it—but what? "that he may be revealed in his own season," he says, "For the mystery of lawlessness doth already work." He speaks here of Nero, as if he were the type of Antichrist. For he too wished to be thought a god. And he has well said, "the mystery"; that is, it worketh not openly, as the other, nor without shame. For if there was found a man before that time, he means, who was not much behind Antichrist in wickedness, what wonder, if there shall now be one? But he did not also wish to point him out plainly: and this not from cowardice, but instructing us not to bring upon ourselves unnecessary enmities, when there is nothing to call for it. So indeed he also says here. "Only there is one that restraineth now, until he be taken out of the way," that is, when the Roman empire is taken out of the way, then he shall come. And naturally. For as long as the fear of this empire lasts, no one will willingly exalt himself, but when that is dissolved, he will attack the anarchy, and endeavor to seize upon the government both of man and of God. For as the kingdoms before this were destroyed, for example, that of the Medes by the Babylonians, that of the Babylonians by the Persians, that of the Persians by the Macedonians, that of the Macedonians by the Romans: so will this also be by the Antichrist, and he by Christ, and it will no longer withhold.[108]

---

[108] Saint John Chrysostom, "Homily IV. 2 Thessalonians ii. 6-9", trans. Philip Schaff, *Christian Classics Ethereal Library*.

Herein lies the political theology of Empire: the Emperor is the "withholder" or "restrainer" (ὁ κατέχων), the vertical of the immanent political structure, and the Empire, the Kingdom, is also the "withholding" (τὸ κατέχον), a special space under his sacred power where complete apostasy cannot come to fruition. In this theology of Empire, the transcendent vertical in politics was believed to be none other than the Emperor, whose power was absolutely transcendent for the "Earthly City." Thus, the figure of the Emperor was also sacralized (as in Plato), but was placed within the historical context, for the figure of the "withholder" was seen as the one preventing the coming of the Antichrist, the "son of perdition." In the Christian context, the philosopher-king became the Orthodox Basileus. Here we see Platonism refracted through the context of Christian eschatology. The notion of history as eternity is replaced by linear time.

Proclus was a pagan Neoplatonist who strictly followed Plato and Plotinus and, as far as we can tell, ignored Christianity.[109] He taught in Athens, which was no longer the pagan polis, but simply part of the pagan Roman Empire and then a domain of Christian Byzantium. This created the important context for Proclus' political philosophy: he acted as a non-Christian Platonist within the Christian Empire when the Roman idea and the Platonism linked to it (the figure of the philosopher-king) were refracted through Christian historicism and the idea of the Emperor as the katechon withholding the coming of the Antichrist in the framework of linear history.

In connection with this political situation, Proclus could not express his political philosophy explicitly and openly, much less try to directly implement it. Nevertheless, Proclus' student, Marinus, left us the following testimony on Proclus' political engagements:

---

109 We are not in possession of sufficient material to determine Proclus' final position on Christianity due to the fact that not all of his writings have come down to us. We can only attempt to reconstruct his attitude towards Christianity on the basis of his metaphysical perspective.

Nevertheless, sometimes he undertook to give political advice. He would attend the public meetings where they deliberated on the town interests, proposed resolutions of a great practical wisdom, conferred with the magistrates on matters appertaining to justice, and not only gave them counsel, but, with a philosopher's boldness, would partly constrain them to administer justice generally.[110]

The last opportunity in the full sense for the pagan Neoplatonists to put their political philosophy into practice was the short reign of Emperor Julian the Apostate, himself a Neoplatonist and a pagan educated in the Pergamon school of Neoplatonism. Julian the Apostate attempted to reorganize the Empire in accordance with the principles of the pagan version of political Platonism, but after his death this prospect became unrealistic. Proclus' political views would have been naturally consonant with Julian the Apostate's ideas, but in his time it was no longer possible to express them openly.

In the circumstances of the spread of the new Christian religion, Proclus was a figure who stood in defense of the old foundations — he was a revolutionary conservative. In his article "Proclus' Anti-Christian Grievance: Theological Ignorance," Philippe Hofmann says of this intentional "ignoring" of Christianity: "[The Neoplatonists] considered Christians to be the uneducated crowd, πολλοί, subject to their own passions and ignorant of true being."[111]

In Damascius' work *The Life of Isidore*, we can find a philosophy of history in which there are three human epochs, each characterized by the part of the soul that dominates in the them and by their ruling political regime (which represents a reproduction of Plato's interpretation of political cycles).[112]

---

110 Marinus of Samaria, *The Life of Proclus, or Concerning Happiness*, trans. Kenneth S. Guthrie (Phanes Press, 1986). See also the account of Diogenes Laertius.

111 Philippe Hoffmann, "*Un grief antichrétien chez Proclus: l'ignorance en théologie*" in Arnaud Perrot (ed.), *Les chrétiens et l'hellénisme: identités religieuses et culture grecque dans l'Antiquité tardive* (Paris: Rue d'Ulm, Presses de l'École normale supérieure, 2012), 162.

112 See Damascius, *La vie d'Isidore ou Histoire de la philosophie / Commentaire sur le Parménide. Proclus le Philosophe. Suivi d'une traduction de La Vie d'Isidore ou Histoire de la philosophie de Damascius*, 3. vols. (Paris: E. Leroux: 1900-1903).

Damascius sees the "Golden Age" in the age of Hesiod, who also called this era one of "life under the auspices and governance of Kronos," a mystical time dominated by the intellect. This was followed by the age of wars, battles, and conquests. Finally, the Christian Empire arises, at which point passions (ἐπιθυμία) and softness (τρυφή) prevail in the midst of cowardice, theft, greed, and servility. This is the life led by people today, who are submersed in the world of becoming.[113]

Damascius' appraisal of his time, when he was a disciple and then the heir of Proclus at the head of the Athenian Academy, was most likely shared by Proclus himself. The Neoplatonic vision of the world was based on eternity, whereas the Christian view was based on history. The acuteness of the polemic between the Christian Neoplatonists and pagan Neoplatonists can be felt in the case of the Christian philosopher John Philoponus' treatise which criticized Proclus himself and the Neoplatonic idea of the eternity of the world.[114] Proclus was a dissident in a world dominated by Christians. Consequently, he could not express his political views directly. Hence, Proclus' political philosophy is implicit, and it must be reconstructed through unraveling the theses contained in his commentaries on Plato in a hidden, veiled form.

The Peculiarity of the (Neo-)Platonic Approach to Politics: Is There a Political Philosophy in the Neoplatonic Tradition?

"For the state is man in large form and man is the state in small form."
— Nietzsche

Let us recall Nietzsche's remark that Plato was a radical revolutionary who went beyond the classical Greek understanding of the ideal citizen: the philosopher rises above religiosity and directly contemplates the idea of the Good. This

---

113 Hoffmann, "*Un grief antichrétien chez Proclus*".
114 See Philoponus, *Against Proclus' On the Eternity of the World* (Ithaca: Cornell University Press, 2005).

rather closely echoes the model of Proclus' Platonic theology, in which the gods occupy a lower position in the world hierarchy. Let us recall that in Festugière's systematization, the world hierarchy looks like the following:

- Beyond being (in which there are two principles: limit and the limitless);
- The intelligible (being, life, the intellect);
- The intermediate (intelligible-thinking: the heavenly, the celestial);
- The thinking (Kronos, Rhea, Zeus);
- The gods (divine leaders who are indifferent and intracosmic).

Plotinus puts the forms above the gods. The gods are merely contemplators of the absolutely ideal forms (and this is how theurgy is possible: man becomes a god in undergoing mystical experience and becoming a philosopher). Plotinus writes:

> Carried off, as it were, by the wave of the Spirit itself, lifted up high by it, as if it were swollen, 'he suddenly saw, without seeing how.' But the spectacle, filling the eyes with light, did not cause some other object to be seen by its means; rather, what was seen was light itself. It is not that there were two things within it: on the one hand a visible object, and on the other its light, nor was there the Spirit and then what is thought by the Spirit; there is only a dazzling light, which engenders all these things later on.[115]

In the *Timaeus*, the Demiurge-God creates the world in accordance with the models of the world of ideas and occupies an intermediate position between the sensual world and the intelligible world. The philosopher operates in the same way and maintains justice in the state. For ancient Greek society, this was a rather revolutionary concept. Putting another essence above and surpassing the gods was an instance of supra-religious, philosophical thinking (and let us also recall the charge incorrectly brought against Socrates — he was accused

---

115 Plotinus *Ennead* VI. 7, 36, 17, quoted in Pierre Hadot, *Plotinus, or The Simplicity of Vision*, 62.

of not believing in the gods, because he did not worship the gods of one given *polis*!).

Plato's *Republic* constructed a non-classical, psychological and political philosophy. The types of souls are compared to the types of state systems, from which different conceptions of happiness unfold. The aim of every person — both ruler and subject — is to build a just state that is consistent with the world's ontological hierarchy. It is precisely this conceptualization of interpreting politics and the soul as the manifestation of an ontological axis that Proclus Diadochus developed in his commentaries on Plato's dialogues.

If it is easy to speak of Plato's political philosophy, then it is much more difficult and complex a matter to speak of a political philosophy in the Neoplatonic tradition. Neoplatonism is habitually perceived as a metaphysics aimed at the deification of man (θέωσις), which is taken to be separate from the political sphere. However, this view of Neoplatonic philosophy is incomplete. In Proclus, who proceeded from the metaphysical function of the philosopher in Plato, the process of deification implies and includes the Political. Deification is also carried out through the political sphere. In the seventh book of the *Republic*, in the myth of the cave, Plato described the philosopher who makes his way out of the world of copies, ascends to the world of ideas, and then returns back into the cave. Thus, the process of deification has two directions: the philosopher turns his gaze towards the ideas, overcomes the world of illusions, and elevates himself to the level of the contemplation of the ideas and then the idea of the Good; however, this process does not end with beholding the idea of the Good as the final state, for the philosopher then goes back into the cave. What is this descent of the philosopher, the one who has already reached the level of contemplating the ideas, back down into the untrue world of shadows, copies, and becoming? Is this not the philosopher-ruler sacrificing himself for the people, for his people? Does this descent have an ontological apologia?

One scholar of Plato's *Republic*, Georgia Mouroutsou, suggests[116] that this descent has a double meaning (which refers to Schleiermacher's reading of Platonism):

(1) The exoteric interpretation explains the descent into the cave in terms of how the law obliges the philosopher who has reached the Good through the power of contemplation to create justice within the state and enlighten citizens (the philosopher sacrifices himself for the sake of the people).

(2) The esoteric meaning of the philosopher's descent back into the lower world (the realm of becoming) echoes the demiurge's descent and reflects the emanation of the world intellect.

The latter interpretation is widespread within the Neoplatonic tradition. The philosopher's role consists of embodying in public life, in the structures of the states, in the rules of community life, and in the norms of education (παιδεία), that which he eidetically contemplates. In the *Timaeus*, the creation of the world is explicated as the Good (overflowing with "its goodness") sharing its content with the world. Similarly, like the Good itself, the philosopher who contemplates the idea of the Good pours out goodness into the world, and in this gesture of emanation he creates order and justice within the soul and within the state. We read in the *Republic*:

> And if you interpret the upward journey and the study of things above as the upward journey of the soul to the intelligible realm, you'll grasp what I hope to convey, since that is what you wanted to hear about. Whether it's true or not, only the god knows. But this is how I see it: In the knowable realm, the form of the good is the last thing to be seen, and it is reached only with difficulty. Once one has seen it, however, one must conclude that it is the cause of all that is correct and beautiful in anything, that it produces both light and its source in the visible realm, and that in the intelligible realm

---

116 Georgia Mouroutsou, "The Allegory of the Cave: The Necessity of the Philosopher's Descent", *Plato: The Internet Journal of the International Plato Society* 11 (2011).

it controls and provides truth and understanding, so that anyone who is to act sensible in private or public must see it.[117]

It bears noting that the return — the descent back into the cave — is not a one-time event, but a constantly repeating process (like ruling). It is the infinite emanation of the Good into something other, of the One into many. This manifestation of the Good is determinable through the creation of laws and the education of citizens. Thus, in the myth of the cave, it is important to distinguish the moment of the ruler's descent into the cave, κάθοδος. Viewing the shadows after contemplating the idea of the Good will differ from their perception by the prisoners who have spent their entire life in the lower horizon of the cave (the level of ignorance).

The idea that deification and the special kenotic mission of the philosopher in Plato's *Republic* in its Neoplatonic interpretation is paradigmatic of Proclus' and other later Neoplatonists' political philosophy was first expressed by Dominic O'Meara.[118] Acknowledging that the "conventional view" in the critical literature on Platonism is that the Neoplatonists "had no political philosophy," O'Meara expressed the conviction that such a position is incorrect. Instead of contrasting the ideal of deification and theurgy to political philosophy, as scholars often do, he proposed to interpret θέωσις in political terms.

Thus, the key to Proclus' implicit philosophy of politics is the "philosopher's descent," κάθοδος, which, on the one hand, repeats the demiurgic gesture, and on the other is the process of the Principle's emanation and procession, πρόοδος. The philosopher who descends from the heights of contemplation is the source of legal, religious, historical, and political reforms. What gives him legitimacy in the realm of the Political is the deification, contemplation, "ascent" (ἄνοδος), and return (ἐπιστροφή) that he has accomplished. The philosopher, whose soul has become divine, receives the political ideal from the

---

117 Plato, *Republic* 517b-c.

118 O'Meara, *Platonopolis*.

source itself, and he is obliged to carry his knowledge and its light to the rest of humankind.

The Neoplatonists' philosopher-king is not gender-specific. A woman philosopher might also find herself in this role. O'Meara considers the prototypes of such philosopher-ruler women exalted by the Neoplatonists to have been Hypatia, Asclepigenia, Sosipatra, Marcella, or Aedesia. Sosipatra, who represented theurgical charisma and was the head of the Pergamon school, took on the image of such a queen. Her teaching was a prototype for raising disciples up the ladder of virtues to the One itself. Hypatia of Alexandria, the queen of astronomy, represented an analogous figure in her Alexandrian school. Moreover, Hypatia was well-known for having advised city politicians on the best way to govern. Her descent into the cave of men from the heights of contemplation cost her a tragic death. Yet, Plato himself, in the case of Socrates' execution, clearly foresaw the possibility of such an outcome for the philosopher who descends into the Political. It is telling that the Christian Platonists saw in this the archetype of the tragic execution of Christ.[119]

Plato set up a similar descent for himself when he set off to create the ideal state for the ruler of Syracuse, Dionysius, and was treacherously sold into slavery by the satiated tyrant. The Neoplatonic figure of the philosopher-queen, based on the equality of women presumed in Plato's *Republic*, is a particular instance of the general idea of a connection between theurgy and the domain of the Political. For us, it is of importance that Plato's image of the philosopher's ascent out of the cave and descent back into it has a rigorous, parallel interpretation in the sphere of the Political and theurgy. This lies at the core of Plato's political philosophy, and this could not but have been thought through and developed by the Neoplatonists. It is another matter that Proclus, finding himself in the circumstances

---

[119] M. Dzielska, Review of Dominic J. O'Meara, *Platonopolis: Platonic Political Philosophy in Late Antiquity*, Plato 5 (2005).

of a Christian society, did not have the opportunity to fully and openly develop this topic, or that his purely political treatises have not come down to us. The case of Hypatia shows us that Proclus' caution was clearly not without reason. However, knowing that the ascent and descent was originally interpreted metaphysically, gnoseologically, as well as politically, we can by all means consider everything that Proclus said about theurgy in a political vein. The deification of the contemplator and theurgist's soul made them a true statesman, and society might or might not accept this. It is on this point that Socrates' fate becomes clear, as do Plato's problems with the tyrant Dionysius, as well as the tragic death of Christ, on whose cross was written "INRI" — "Jesus the Nazarene, King of the Jews." Jesus was the King who descended from the heavens to the people and then ascended back to the heavens. In the context of the pagan Neoplatonism of Proclus, who was in fact not necessarily anti-Christian, this idea of truly legitimate political governance necessarily had to have been present and built on exactly the same principle: only the one who has "descended" has the right to rule. Yet, in order to descend (at the very least in the case of the human being), one must first ascend. Therefore, theurgy and θέωσις, while not in themselves political operations, implicitly encompass the Political; moreover, the Political becomes Platonically legitimate only through them.

Our further study can be built upon taking this into account: if θέωσις and the Neoplatonists' (and in our case Proclus') theurgy encompassed a political dimension embodied in the moment of the philosopher's "descent" into the cave, then there are grounds to speak of a Neoplatonic political philosophy, and we are left with examining the structure of this political philosophy in its general outlines.

Homologies and Hierarchies

> Hence both amount to the same thing, and justice in the soul, constitution in the state, and orderliness in the cosmos are the same thing; one should not make trouble for oneself by dividing from one another things that are joined by nature.[120]

Proclus' Commentaries on Plato's Republic: Triadic Symbolism, Castes, and the Hierarchy of Demiurgic Systems

Writing philosophical works in the genre of commentary was one of the distinct traits of the Athenian school of Neoplatonism. As noted earlier, these commentaries were not simply explanations appended to Plato's texts, but fully-fledged philosophical works in which certain ideas of Plato's were taken as starting points for thinking. Platonic philosophy underwent formidable development in these commentaries: hierarchies became more complex and detailed, the similarities between ontological, cosmological, psychic, and political structures were analyzed in more nuance, and concepts which were only sketched out in Plato were concretized.

It bears paying special attention to two of Proclus' commentaries: on the *Republic* and on the *Timaeus*. These commentaries most fully express Proclus' understanding of the Political. We consider these commentaries to be the most important sources for the reconstruction of Proclus' political philosophy. In accordance with the traditional rules for interpreting Plato's dialogues, Proclus began his commentaries on the *Republic* and *Timaeus* with an introduction in which he defined the subject (σκοπός) or intention (πρόθησις) of the dialogue, described its composition (οἰκονομία), its genre or

---

[120] Proclus, *Commentary on Plato's Timaeus - Volume I, Book I: Proclus on the Socratic State and Atlantis*, trans. Harold Tarrant (Cambridge: Cambridge University Press, 2007), 126.

style (εἶδος, χαρακτήρ), and the circumstances in which the dialogue took place, i.e., its topography, time, and participants.

In defining the subject of the dialogue, Proclus distinguished several points of view on Plato's *Republic* then in currency in the philosophical tradition:

(1) Some are inclined to see the dialogue's subject as the notion of justice, in which case the examination of political regimes or the soul are additions to the discussion on justice, i.e., merely examples for better articulating the essence of the notion of justice.

(2) Others see the subject of the dialogue as the analysis of political regimes, while the examination of the question of justice in the first book is, in their opinion, only an introduction to the further study of the Political.

Thus, we are confronted with a certain difficulty in determining the subject of the dialogue: does the dialogue have the aim of describing the manifestation of justice in the political sphere or in the soul? Proclus believes that these two determinations of the subject of the dialogue are incomplete on their own, as he argues that both aims share a common paradigm: "These two aims are in fact the same as each other, since what is justice in a single soul is a constitution of this kind in the well-ordered state as a whole."[121] Defining the main plot of the dialogue, Proclus remarks that "the text's purpose concerns both the constitution [of political regime] and justice properly defined. These are not, however, two aims (*skopos*), for that would not be possible."[122] Thus, we cannot say that the main aim of the dialogue is solely an attempt to define justice or describe the best political regime. Upon acknowledging that the Political and justice are interrelated, we also note that the dialogue deals in detail with the manifestation of justice in the sphere of the soul. Justice and the state are not independent phenomena. Justice

---

121 Proclus, *Commentary on Plato's Republic - Volume I, Essays 1-6*, trans./eds. Dirk Baltzly, John F. Finamore and Graeme Miles (Cambridge: Cambridge University Press, 2018), 59.

122 Ibid.

manifests itself both in the Political and in the sphere of the soul (or in the cosmic sphere).

After clarifying this condition, the following question arises: What is primary — the soul (ψυχή) or the state (πολιτεία)? Is there a hierarchical relationship between these two entities? An answer to this question can be found in Plato's *Republic* itself, when Plato introduces the hypothesis of a homology (ὁμολογία) between the soul and the state, or between the sphere of the soul and the political sphere. This compels us to think carefully about what Plato had in mind with such a homology and what the Neoplatonists had in mind in continuing his tradition. In the later philosophy of the modern era (New Time), the (real) model is most often a thing or an object, and in this case ontology and gnoseology are arranged hierarchically: for objectivists (empiricists, realists, positivists, materialists), knowledge is understood as a reflection of external reality, whereas subjectivists (idealists) interpret reality to be a projection of consciousness. The most diverse relations in the sphere of ontology and gnoseology are then built on this dualism. However, applying such a method (either one of the two — the objectivist or the subjectivist) to Neoplatonism would be anachronistic, for here neither the state, nor the soul, nor their concepts are primary. In Plato and the Neoplatonists, ideas and paradigms are endowed with ontological primacy, while the intellect, the soul, as well as the political and cosmic spheres represent reflections, copies, icons, or the results of *eikasia* (εἰκασία). Accordingly, in view of the model form, any types of copies — whether the political, the soul, the cosmic — have an equal nature, an equal degree of removal from the model. They are considered not in terms of comparison with one another, but through comparison with their eidetic archetype. In this case, the answer to the question of the primacy of the Political over the soul or vice versa becomes obvious: the Political does not copy the soul or vice versa; instead, they are homologous to each other in their being secondary to their common form or *eidos*.

Recognizing this homology is the foundation of Proclus' hermeneutic method. For him, the state, the world, the intellect, nature, theology, and theurgy are eidetic chains of the manifestation of ideas. Therefore, what is true for justice in the domain of the Political (for example, hierarchical structure, putting philosopher-guardians at the head of the state, etc.) simultaneously applies to the organization of theology, i.e., the hierarchies of gods, daimons, souls, etc., as well as the qualities of the soul and virtues. The presence of a form (the paradigm, the idea) ensures the unity of the structure for all orders of copies. This enables us to reliably extract Proclus' political philosophy out of his overall corpus, in which politics proper is devoted little space. Like Plato, Proclus necessarily has the Political in mind, but unlike Plato, he thematizes the Political much less often. Nevertheless, any treatment of Proclus' Platonic concepts almost always implicitly encompasses interpreting the analogies in the domain of the Political.

The overarching homology does not, however, negate the fact that a certain hierarchy exists among copies themselves. The question of the hierarchization of copies was resolved by various commentators on Plato in different ways. For some of them, phenomena pertaining to the soul are closer to the paradigm, to the form, while for others phenomena of the state level, and for others the cosmic, are closest. The construction of such a hierarchy is a space of freedom for interpreting and hierarchizing virtues. For Marinus, for instance, Proclus' life represented the ascent up the hierarchical ladder of virtues: from the natural, ethical, and social to the theocratic (theurgic) through the purifying and contemplative. Political virtues are usually seen as on the middle level, i.e., between the gymnastic and theological.[123] The politician is higher than the gymnast, but lower than the theurgist.

The above-cited passage in which Proclus deliberates on the subject of the Republic shows his aspiration to underscore that the hierarchization of interpretations is always secondary

---

123 Marinus, *The Life of Proclus, or Concerning Happiness.*

in relation to the basic onto-gnoseological structure of Platonism as a contemplative method. Therefore, the construction of any system of hierarchies over the course of interpretation and commentary turns out to be secondary to the construction of a general metaphysical topology reflecting the relationship between form and copies. Even if Proclus himself situationally paid more attention to spiritual, contemplative, theurgical, and theological interpretations over the course of his commentary, this does not at all mean that political interpretation is excluded or secondary. Perhaps under different political and religious circumstances from those we described as the political situation of Proclus' time and life within the context of Christian society, Proclus would have focused more on political hermeneutics, and in so doing he would not violate the general structure of and fidelity to Platonic methodology. However, in the situation he was given, he was compelled to speak of politics in less detail.

Proclus' interpretation of the *Republic*, in which Plato himself's topic is the optimal structure of the state (the *polis*), is a semantic polyphony which implicitly contains whole chains of new homologies. To each of the elements of the dialogue which Proclus interprets in terms of the soul or cosmology, there corresponds a political equivalent that is at times explicitly designated and at other times only implied. Therefore, the commentaries on Plato's dialogue which thematize *politeia* are for Proclus a change in register for the majority of his commentaries busy with examining the ontological and theological dimensions. By virtue of homology, Proclus can always act in accordance with the given circumstances and freely develop a hermeneutic scheme that can unfold in any direction.

According to Plato, the three classes in the state correspond to the tripartite division of the soul. Therefore, justice is understood in the *Republic* to be at once the best arrangement of the soul and the best structure of the state. Proclus comments: "the consideration of arrangement of cities (*politeia*) comes into the discussions for the sake of [understanding] justice, so that we might be able to see in large letters what it is not easy to see in small ones."¹²⁴ As follows, the discussion on justice in the soul and in the state structure differs only in scale, not in substance. Proclus borrows the image of large and small letters from the 368th passage of the second book of the *Republic*:

> [W]e should adopt the method of investigation that we'd use if, lacking keen eyesight, we were told to read small letters from a distance and then noticed that the same letters existed elsewhere in a larger size and on a larger surface. We'd consider it a godsend, I think, to be allowed to read the larger ones first and then to examine the smaller ones, to see whether they really are the same.¹²⁵

And further: "I'll tell you. We say, don't we, that there is the justice of a single man and also the justice of a whole city."¹²⁶ Plato then concludes in the 369th passage: "Perhaps, then, there is more justice in the larger thing, and it will be easier to learn what it is. So, if you're willing, let's first find out what sort of thing justice is in a city and afterwards look for it in the individual observing the ways in which the smaller is similar to the larger."¹²⁷ This hypothetical approach adopted by Socrates for the sake of clarifying the notion of justice between the soul and the Political is based on a presumption of identity between the inner structure of the soul and the state. In the second book, the analogy between the soul and the state is presented as a hypothesis, whereas in the fourth book Socrates takes it to be an axiom that there is a strict parallel between the soul and the state (434e-435a). Three parts are singled out within the soul which resemble the parts of the state: the rational principle (the charioteer from the *Phaedrus*), the inspirited part (the white horse from the *Phaedrus*), and the lustful element (the black horse in the *Phaedrus*) in the soul are akin to the qualities of the three estates of the state: the rulers (the philosophers and guardians), the warriors (the auxiliaries), and the farmers (435c). Socrates resorts to the soul-state analogy in both

---

124 Proclus, *Commentary on Plato's Republic*, 56.
125 Plato, *Republic* 368d.
126 Ibid., 368e.
127 Ibid., 368e-369a.

directions: the soul is to be understood through the example of the state, and the state through the parts of the soul.

In Plato, the virtues (ἀρεταί) of the state (*Republic* 428) and the virtues of the soul are identical: wisdom (428b-429a), courage (429a-430c), prudence (430e-432b), and justice (432b-434d). Wisdom is defined as the art of always being on guard and is attributed to be a quality of the rulers/philosophers, while courage as keeping awareness and mindfulness of danger corresponds to the class of warriors, the guardians of the state's borders. At 441 Socrates recognizes the identity of the virtues of the soul and the virtues of the state. This structure of virtues concerns both the structure of the soul and the structure of the state:

> We are pretty much agreed that the same number and the same kinds of classes as are in the city are also in the soul of each individual.
>
> That's true.
>
> Therefore, it necessarily follows that the individual is wise in the same way and in the same part of himself as the city.
>
> That's right.
>
> And isn't the individual courageous in the same way and in the same part of himself as the city? And isn't everything else that has to do with virtue the same in both?
>
> Necessarily...
>
> Then we must also remember that each one of us in whom each part is doing its own work will himself be just and do his own.[128]

Proclus develops this triadic model further and projects it onto the tripartite structure of the Intellect, onto the types of gods, daimons, heroes, and the soul, as well as onto the other eidetic hierarchies elaborated by Iamblichus.

The very model of a tripartite caste division of the state is classically typical of Indo-European peoples. This model was distinguished and formulated in the "trifunctional theory" of the French sociologist, mythologist, and comparative philologist Georges Dumézil, who meticulously studied the myths and

---

128 Plato, *Republic* 441c-e.

legends of Indo-European peoples (particularly Ossetian culture, Indian and Iranian society, etc.). Dumézil distinguished three estates in Indo-European society, each of which fulfills its own function: priests (Brahmins), warriors (Kshatriyas), and farmers (Vaishyas; in Indian society yet another caste is distinguished: the Shudras, or servants).[129] Despite the fact that Dumézil believed that this model was barely expressed in Greece and that he did not conduct a detailed analysis of Greek society, we are inclined to argue that that the paradigmatic understanding of trifunctionality (a pan-Indo-European form) is vividly manifest in Plato's political thought. In addition to the ordinary socio-political division of functions, the philosopher also cited metaphysical criteria for the arrangement of hierarchy within the state. Proclus, in turn, noted the special significance of dividing the state into three estates which, in the metaphysical dimension, as we have already indicated above, are akin to the tripartite division of the soul. The castes of Plato's ideal state correspond to the three functions in Dumézil's model:

- The guardian-philosophers are analogous to the Indo-European priests or sacred kings (their rule is monarchical and aristocratic, which Plato and Proclus after him held to be the best regime);
- The auxiliaries or warriors correspond to the Kshatriya-warriors;
- The ordinary folk are strictly identical to the Vaishyas, or peasants, artisans, and traders.

Proclus interpreted the tripartite structure of Plato's caste society even further, up to the point of systematizing the ethnic character of the peoples of the Mediterranean. The commentator noted:

> First he shows that those very differences in way of life between people – whether one considers them merely in the differences in social orders in a single city-state or whether one considers differences in entire nations (*ethnos*) – derive from no other source

---

129 Georges Dumézil, *L'Idéologie des trois fonctions dans les épopées des peuples indo-européens* (Paris: Gallimard, 1968).

than differences in the life of the soul. As he says [people are] 'not sprung from oak or rock' (544d). That is to say, they are not the result of the lowest level of nature (for which the oak is an image) nor as a result of the lifeless and three- dimensional body insofar as it is body (for this is what the rock illustrates). Speaking at the level of the nation generally, he says that Greeks are more receptive to intelligence, while Thracians have more of the spirited part of the soul, and Phoenicians are more commercially inclined. In each of these cases, the entire nation is like that as a result of the soul since some of them are ruled by reason, while the others are ruled by spirited or appetitive parts of the soul. For whichever part each lives [most fully], that is what they are, even if, as they live, they possess all of the parts, [nonetheless] their character is determined by what occurs to them most readily, and the whole nation is called rational (*logoeidês*) or spirited (*thymoeidês*) with reference to the part of the soul which lives in it most fully. They [sc. whole nations] therefore either possess these differences as a result of the body or as a result of the soul. But it is not as a result of the body, for while they might be hot or cold and white or black as a result of the body, they are not intelligent or courageous or moderate or the opposite of these [virtues]. Therefore it would be as a result of the soul that they possess differences in these [characteristics]. This is the first point that he showed.[130]

Thus, Proclus correlated not only the three castes within one society with the qualities of the soul, but also the three main peoples of the Mediterranean, among which the philosopher held the Hellenes to be the embodiment of intellect (the charioteer from the *Phaedrus*), the Thracians the warrior element, and the Phoenicians natural born artisans and merchants, the lustful principle predominating within their soul.

In accordance with this triadic model of interpretation, Proclus also speaks of three types of political governance which he associates with three kinds of demiurgy: those of Zeus, Dionysus, and Adonis. Proclus writes:

> For every statesman (*politikos*) wishes to imitate some Demiurge: the statesman who establishes all property in common wishes to imitate

---

[130] Proclus, *Commentary on Plato's Republic - Volume II, Essays 7-15*, trans./eds. Dirk Baltzly, John F. Finamore and Graeme Miles (Cambridge: Cambridge University Press, 2022), 51-52.

the Demiurge of the universe (*ta hola*), the one who apportions and divides wishes to imitate the Demiurge who divides parts from wholes, and the one who sets right the twisted form [of government] wishes to imitate the Demiurge who weaves anew what comes into being and perishes.[131]

Here we once again see a homology between the structure of the universe (the three demiurges governing the spiritual, psychic, and corporeal worlds) and the three political functions: the creation of the state (Zeus' demiurgy), the maintenance of the state (Dionysus' demiurgy), and the assurance of material well-being (Adonis' demiurgy).

Proclus believes that the ideal statesman is he who imitates the demiurgy of Zeus, i.e., the creator of the state, the establisher of laws and norms. In this sense, he speaks of the production of structures (σύστασις) and of a structured, ordered world. This structure is partially broken or is weakened upon the transition to the level of becoming, whereby we enter the demiurgy of Dionysus, which consists in restarting the repeatedly violated unity. The statesman of this type corresponding to Dionysus' demiurgy does not create a *polis* or establish laws, but maintains the order previously established by the gods and heroes. Entering the realm of becoming (the demiurgy of Dionysus), the political system is subject to entropy, its structure is distorted and blurred, and the statesman of this second level has the mission of maintaining the eidetic vertical structure. Finally, there are the bearers of the third demiurgy, which is correlated with Adonis and the corporeal world, the main function of which is to care for the material well-being of citizens, their satiety and health. As long as these three types of statesmen fulfill their functions, the state is preserved, but at different stages predominate different rulers (rulers of Zeus' type at the first, of Dionysus' type on the second, and of Adonis' type on the third). When politicians cannot cope even with the third task, the state collapses. According to Proclus, this is necessarily followed by a new demiurgy of Zeus.

---

131 Ibid., 210.

Continuing the analogy of demiurgy, one can imagine the statesman who corresponds to Proclus' demiurgy of Zeus in creating the polis ("politeia"), thereby constituting time and space. It is no coincidence that Proclus insists that time has no source and that, according to Plato, it is a "moving image of eternity." The ruler creates his time, his era, and his dynasty, which are also reflections of the celestial idea reproduced on different levels. This is a kind of "political time" measured in parallel to the time of the cosmos, the year, or religious (liturgical) time. This is the origin of the tradition of naming eras after rulers, Emperors, and kings. This connection with time is not accidental: the time of every ruler, their epoch or dynasty, is constituted as part of the demiurgy of Zeus. At the same time, "political space" is organized and embodied in the territory of the state. The landscape and borders of this state, as well as the spiritual qualities of the people inhabiting it, compose a political *"khora"* (χώρα), that is not purely a physical space, but a locality encompassing the specifics of the landscape and the temperament of the population, which the Neoplatonists interpreted in symbolic terms.

On the level of the second demiurgy (the demiurgy of Dionysus), time and space are not created but are only maintained in an orderly state. The ruler of the second level defends and reinforces the territories bequeathed to him, like the gods ruling over sacred places, and in the same manner he consecrates political time through implementing laws, upholding order, and organizing the education of the guardians and the political and intellectual elites. This second time and second space are also political, but they pertain to the realm of becoming, i.e., to birth and disappearance. Political rhythm, not constancy, dominates here in a state of periodic ordering of the political whole that is subject to natural entropy.

On the level of the third demiurgy (the demiurgy of Adonis), we pass to the third form of political time and political space. This time, we are closer to what we are used to dealing with in the present era. This is natural time, the time of changing seasons, and the physical space in which the state is located. In Aristotle's view, this is the economic, or more precisely the oikonomic sphere. Caring for the physical well-being of citizens, athletics (the Olympics), medical care, nutrition, and the provision of needed material good and products — all of this is the task of the state economist, who deals with the economic time and economic space that is the zone of responsibility of the third demiurgy of Adonis.

In the optimal case, this structure is seen synchronously, and all three levels of *political* time and space co-exist in hierarchical order. Insofar as a regime deteriorates, there is a shift from the political space and time of Zeus to that of Dionysus and then to that of Adonis. The same phases can be traced in terms of the logic of the degradation of politeia treated in Plato's *Republic* and examined by Proclus. The best regimes, aristocracy and monarchy, correspond to the demiurgy of Zeus and his political time and space. Timocracy, the rule of the military, already marks a shift down to the demiurgy of Dionysus, and in oligarchy we already see materialization and an increase in the role of the economic factor, until the chaotic processes of matter take over and in the democratic regime both time and space dissolve into fragments that have lost their integrity (hence the increased significance of time and space). In practice, this is expressed in territorial fragmentation and in the absence of systematic social organization. The ultimate degradation of demiurgy is the tyranny that follows democracy, in which there is essentially a coup against the normative political structure of society. We can speak of the tyrant's time and tyrannical space as a parody of the tripartite hierarchy of demiurgies.

In his commentary on the discourse of the Muses in the *Republic*, Proclus offers his interpretation of the order of the degradation of political systems described by Plato. He draws attention to the symbolism of the bee which, according to him, being an initiate of the Muses, instructs people that the best political regime is monarchy. Proclus writes:

> He [Plato] seems to me to be responding to those who lay claim to political knowledge that the change of constitutions from the higher to the next lowest does not come about by necessity. (For the decline would have then also come about from an aristocracy into a tyranny, not only into the others, since the ruling [constitution] would have been compelled by some tyrannical force from without that had risen up against the ruler and had changed the character of the constitution into its linked unlawful form of rule; this is because it is impossible for such an uprising to occur in such a city, since its rulers are so divine and the auxiliary class was brought up with the same education, but some forced uprising might occur from without). Rather he seems to me to demonstrate that the decline of human life is as orderly as it can be, arising through intermediate and similar stages because the similarities that proceed in small increments produce a smooth change.[132]

Thus, Proclus wants to show that Plato's account of the transformation of political regimes from monarchy and aristocracy through timocracy, oligarchy, and democracy down to tyranny is analogous to the cosmic descent of emanation and is a particular case of the overall cosmic demiurgy. Proclus therefore conceives of the deterioration of the quality of a political regime not as the consequence of external influence, but as a kind of natural process of the hardening of the ontological cosmological states caused by the natural decline of the entire system within ontology as a whole, starting with the most important part, the education (παιδεία) of the guardian-philosophers. Of importance in this passage is how Proclus rules out the possibility of a sharp transition from the best regime, aristocracy, to the worst, tyranny. Proclus then asserts that "everything that is destroyed is destroyed by its own evil."[133]

This means that there exists a continuity between the points in the degradation of state type. The systematic degradation of political models is supposed to occur gradually, since, as Proclus argues, "the destruction of the whole city would occur from outside, but change could not occur from such a life as that of those who remain citizens, since they would all choose to perish

---
132 Proclus, *Commentary on Plato's Republic - Volume II*, 202-203.
133 Ibid.

completely rather than to decline into a shameful life."[134] In order for the cycle of political degradation to proceed from monarchy to democracy to tyranny, it must be gradual and imperceptible, with society descending no more than one step down in each instance.

The cause of the decline of the best regime, according to Plato as well as Proclus, is disagreement among its leaders (the ruling guardians and philosophers). Proclus writes:

> But he [Socrates] says that the change from the best constitution will have as its cause the discord among the rulers, not at all among the lower ranks in it. This is because [the city] is an image of the universe, and the rulers are similar to the gods who are the causes of all things, and the auxiliaries to the daemons who are the followers of the gods, who watch over the immoveable order of the cosmos and suppress the disturbance coming from the worse.[135]

This is to say that the best regime only deteriorates once dissension arises among the philosophers themselves. Thus, Proclus designates the process of political degradation to be of a non-random and non-catastrophic character. Rather, Proclus sees the cause for degradation as well as the cause for the shift from paganism to Christianity in the very logic of cosmic manifestation itself, that is, in the expression of the will of the gods, for in the very structure of the manifestation, beginning with the overflowing of the chalice of the One (ἕν) and including the last natural demiurgy, that of Adonis, we are dealing with a passage from best to worst.

Taking into consideration this interpretation of the cosmos as a consistent, descending emanation from the intellect to the soul and from the soul to the body, along with the analogues of such in the macrocosm, there is a certain predestination and logical regularity in the process of the degradation of the Political from monarchy through timocracy, oligarchy, and democracy to tyranny. Proceeding from this analysis, we can assume that Proclus considered the Christian Empire to be a tyranny and,

---

134 Ibid.
135 Ibid., 203-204.

as follows, its existence was justified even if he did not agree to call "the best" what he saw with his own eyes as "the least good."

It may be supposed that the hermeneutics of the Platonic topic of the degradation of political systems had yet another dimension, one which Proclus did not describe explicitly. We have in mind the political interpretation of the "return" (ἐπιστροφή) in the form of a project for a Neoplatonist conservative revolution, the archetype of which, for the Neoplatonists, could have been the reign of Julian the Apostate. Having reached the extreme limits of political degradation, having touched the bottom of the descending emanation (πρόοδος), i.e., tyranny, the Political must then begin its ascent, its return to new heights under the leadership of the divine contemplators of that fully-fledged sacred monarchy which the Muse-initiated bees taught to people.

Proclus' Political Philosophy in the Commentary on the *Timaeus*: Cosmos and Politics

Proclus compiled his commentary on the *Timaeus* at the age of 28. If we examine Proclus' works chronologically, then this commentary was one of his first productions, yet on the philosophical scale it is one of his most interesting and complex works. In the philosophical schools of late antiquity, the *Timaeus* dialogue was always read and commented on during the final stages of one's studies and was considered to be the pinnacle of Platonic metaphysics. To study the beginning and cause of the world, to in some sense write a history of creation, and to study the human soul's nature and its connection with the world and God — such is the purpose and plan of the *Timaeus*. This dialogue contains all of Plato's metaphysics. Five books of Proclus' commentaries on the *Timaeus* have survived. According to Marinus, Proclus began working on the commentary during his studies under Syrianus; hence, at the heart of the commentary are Syrianus' lectures written down in abstract with Proclus' appended clarifications. Harold Tarrant and Dirk Baltzly have remarked that this commentary is especially unique among

Proclus' works insofar as it was recorded by ear as a summary of his teacher's lectures.

The *Timaeus* dialogue itself is divided into three parts: the first deals with the doctrine of the origin of the cosmos, the second with the doctrine of necessity, and the third with the doctrine of the unity of the intellect and necessity in the final creation of the cosmos. The first part of the first book of Proclus' commentary on the *Timaeus* is dedicated to retelling the main ideas of the *Republic*, and the second to a detailed examination of the myth of Atlantis, which takes on not only a historical character, but also a metaphysical-ontological dimension. The second book is devoted to analyzing the cosmos as a whole, and the third to the cosmos as body and as soul. The fourth investigates time, the heavenly bodies, and the cosmos' saturation with life. The fifth book examines the genealogies of the gods, the demiurgic creation, the relation between the demiurge and souls, the problem of the predestination of the soul, the structure of the soul, and the duties of the intracosmic gods.

Proclus compares the *Timaeus* to a cosmological map of Platonic philosophy. In the *Republic*, Plato examined the intracosmic world, transitioning in the sixth and seventh books to the relation between the One or the idea of the Good and the intracosmic world. The *Timaeus* analyzes the intermediate causes of the intracosmic world, i.e., the demiurge, while the *Parmenides* deals with the highest, apophatic principle and the dialectic of the passage from the One to the many. Thus, we can see a certain hierarchy along which the dialogues are structured in connection with the subject of their consideration (and this corresponds to the study curriculum in the Academy): The *Republic* presents the intracosmic, i.e., the political and the psychic; the *Timaeus* examines the intermediate causes of the intracosmic, i.e., "a god"; and the *Parmenides* is the height of Platonic metaphysics dealing with the supreme apophatic principle, i.e., "God simply." Proclus writes in his commentary on the *Parmenides*:

Timaeus traces all things back to the Demiurge. Parmenides traces them to the One, and there is an analogous relation between the Demiurge and the contents of the cosmos, and the One and all things whatsoever, [the Demiurge being a kind of one] but not One in the absolute sense; for he is a god, not God, and the god that is the One is not a god, but God simply. So the Demiurge is a god, since demiurgy is a property of a god, and there are other divine properties that are not demiurgic.[136]

In the *Timaeus*, the discussion of the cosmological structure of the world and the demiurge's creation of the world is preceded by a recapitulation of the *Republic*. Proclus believes that this retelling is symbolic, and he identifies three possible reasons for this interpretation: (1) the ethical interpretation (most likely belonging to Porphyry), (2) the physical interpretation (Iamblichus), and (3) the theological interpretation (Syrianus). The ethical explanation lies in that only people who have learned the truth of the ideal structure of the state can proceed to the higher level of considering the order of the world. Iamblichus' physical explanation holds that the retelling of the *Republic* is a kind of introduction presented in order to reawaken the interlocutors' thinking (the state is an image of the structure of the world, like the myth of Atlantis) — and this idea of a gradual transition from less to more complex is similar to the Pythagorean tradition of teaching. The theological explanation to which Proclus' teacher Syrianus and Proclus himself adhered consists in the thesis that the state exists in three forms: as an idea first in the intelligible world, then in the cosmos, and then as an arrangement of human life (corresponding to the analysis of the state in the second, third, and fourth books of the *Republic*). Proclus writes:

> In other words, the state exists first in the intelligible realm, then in the heavens, and then, lastly, in human life. Therefore, if it is higher than the creation of nature, it is natural for it to be positioned before the discourse of Timaeus, and if it is lower than it (insofar as it is an

---

136 Proclus, *Commentary on Plato's Parmenides*, trans. Glenn R. Morrow and John M. Dillon (Princeton: Princeton University Press, 1987), 37.

ethical cosmos, whereas nature is integral and all-perfect), then we would naturally want to rise from the lower to the higher.[137]

The participants of the dialogue themselves are charged with metaphysical significance. In the dramatic opening of the dialogue, Proclus is inclined to see a symbolic representation of the structure of the universe. The number of interlocutors is therefore no coincidence: Timaeus is akin to the world demiurge, and Socrates, Critias, and Hermocrates listen to his story like the junior demiurgic gods. At the very outset of the dialogue, Socrates asks his interlocutors: "One, two, three... Where's number four, Timaeus? The four of you were my guests yesterday and today I'm to be yours."[138] Keeping to the interpretation of his teacher Syrianus, Proclus explains the absence of the fourth person, i.e., the one who would represent matter, as the weakness and inability of the "fourth element" to perceive lofty speeches about the world whose metaphysical force goes beyond discourse on the state.

Proclus bases his political doctrine on Plato's hypothesis on the identity of the inner structure of the soul and the state, complementing this model with the metaphysical hierarchy presented in the *Parmenides*. The division of estates, in Proclus' opinion, represents the demiurgic division of the cosmos in accordance with a strict order. For this Neoplatonist, the analogy between the state and the cosmos is absolutely natural.

- The state is divided into:

    (1) servant castes
    (2) warriors
    (3) guardians

- The soul is divided into:

    (1) the lusting part that provides for the needs of the body

---

137 Translated from the Russian edition: Prokl, *Kommentarii k "Parmenidu"*, trans. L.Y. Lukomsky (Saint Petersburg: Mir, 2006), 70.

138 Plato, *Timaeus* 17a.

- (2) the spirited part that "has been given the job of repressing all that is injurious to the animal, acting as bodyguard to what rules in us"[139]
- (3) the rational part that loves wisdom and reigns over life

♦ The totality of souls is divided into:
- (1) Souls serving in the realm of becoming
- (2) Souls contributing to the quasi-cosmic crafts of the gods
- (3) Souls ascending to the intelligible

♦ Intracosmic things are divided into:
- (1) Mortal kinds
- (2) Tribes of daimons
- (3) The ranks of celestial gods

♦ There is an analogy with patron gods:
- (1) Selene (the Moon) / Aphrodite (Venus) / Hermes (Mercury) = becoming
- (2) Ares (Mars) = warriors
- (3) Kronos (Saturn) / Helios (the Sun)

The political division of the Platonic state fully corresponds to the demiurge's division of the world into pairs of two, three, and seven:

- ♦ 2 = The two lower/higher estates. In the *Timaeus*, Plato combines the second estate of auxiliaries and the first of guardian-philosophers into one, which he calls the "warriors." They are united on the grounds that both the guardians and the auxiliaries wage war to establish justice in the state/soul/cosmos — the first by the intellect and the second with their hands.
- ♦ 3 = The three estates distinguished by Plato in the *Republic* as well as the tripartite division of the soul and the division of the totality of souls (see the above division).

---

139 Proclus, *Commentary on Plato's Timaeus - Volume I*, Book I, 128.

- 7 = the division into seven planetary spheres, the division of the state into seven parts and main occupations of citizens, each of which has a patron Olympian deity.

The division of duties within the ideal state is justified by two reasons, one literal and one theological and metaphysical. The literal reason is that for the sake of the state's well-being, everyone must engage in what their nature predestines them to do. The metaphysical reason appeals to the principle of "everything in all, but in each in a particular way." Citizens ought to follow the divine world order in accordance with which each god has their own domain of rule and lot (κλῆρος), i.e., a part of the world entrusted by the cosmic demiurge to the care of one or another demiurgic god.

Relations between men and women in the ideal state correspond to the ontological pair of "limit" and "limitless," or πέρας and ἄπειρον. Both principles are part of all that exists and contribute to the common cause. Proclus saw Plato's community of wives and husbands as an allusion to the sacred marriages of the gods.

Proclus' Symbolism of Space: The Sacred and the Political

Throughout his commentaries on Plato's dialogues, Proclus often drew attention to so-called philosophical geography. In his commentaries on the *Republic* and *Parmenides*, Proclus compared the cities in which the dialogues unfolded or from which the participants came with the ontological levels of the manifestation of the One. In his commentary on the *Parmenides*, Proclus correlated the three groups of philosophers from all over Greece who gathered in Athens for the Panathenaia festival:

(1) From the West (from Magna Graecia) came the philosophers of the Eleatic school: Parmenides and Zeno;

(2) Pythodorus and Antiphon were Athenians

(3) "The guests from Clazomenae"

(1) The philosophers of the Eleatic school correspond to the supreme noetic triad of "Being-Life-Intellect"

(2) The Athenians are likened to the ranks of angels and daemons who transmit the higher knowledge to the "guests from Clazomenae"

(3) The "guests from Clazomenae" are identified with lower entities bound to the elements, matter, and nature.

In this arrangement of the dialogue's participants, Socrates occupies an intermediate position between the supreme noetic tradition with its teaching on the One and the Athenians (the angelic-daemonic level), and he plays the role of the "demiurgic intellect" (in Proclus' opinion, Socrates played a similar role in the *Timaeus* as a "junior member of the triad of demiurgic gods"). Proclus writes:

> In this case the plot involves bringing to Athens the men from Italy to impart to the Athenians their traditional doctrines, and bringing the men from Ionia, that they may share in the Italian teachings. Clazomenae is in Ionia and Elea in Italy. Just as all events in nature share in intelligible through the mediation of the forms in souls, so this setting shows how the Italian philosophy was imparted to the Ionians; it brings them to Athens and through the Attic philosophers enables them to share in these esoteric doctrines.[140]

Proclus thus draws a noological map of ancient Greek philosophy. Athens is the point where higher knowledge is revealed. Athens' role on the metaphysical map of ancient Greek philosophy is also underscored by Proclus in his commentary on the *Timaeus*. Moreover, in his analysis of the geography of the *Republic*, Proclus takes note of the symbolism of the town in which the dialogue takes place, Piraeus: "it is clear I suppose to those who have listened attentively to Plato that places near the sea must be full of tumultuous and variegated life, but that cities further from the sea are pure of those evils."[141]

---

140 Proclus, *Commentary on Plato's Parmenides*, 28
141 Proclus, *Commentary on Plato's Republic - Vol. I*, 65.

Athens is the city of wisdom and order. Piraeus, a port city, symbolizes the domain of constant change and becoming. Proclus compares the sea and the humidity typical of Piraeus to the disorder of the lower manifestations of being, their instability, chaos, and lack of hierarchy. This geographical contrast between Athens (which is close to the One and is the City of Wise Men and the Mind) and Piraeus (the seaside port, a town of multiplicity and becoming) brings into relief a very important ontological signification. Aleksei Losev has drawn attention to the special role of Pallas Athena in Proclus' life: Marinus compared Athena to a midwife at work in Proclus' appearance in the world (it was she who sent Proclus' parents from Lycia to Byzantium), and in his childhood years Athena appeared to him and turned him towards philosophy. Upon returning to Lycia, Proclus stayed in Xanthos, where the Apollonian cult occupied a special place. Athena repeatedly appeared to him and called on him to return to the city. Losev writes:

> On the way from Piraeus to Athens, at the shrine to Socrates, the tired Proclus drank water from a local spring, which was a blessed sign of his forthcoming philosophical work in the Platonic Academy. The watchman who was supposed to lock the gate to the Acropolis miraculously did not do so for the young man who then arrived, Proclus, even though he knew nothing about him. When ideological turmoil arose in Athenian society, Proclus had to leave for a year to Lydia, and he returned to Athens again at the behest of Athena.[142]

Myles Burnyeat's studies have brought into relief the significance of the prologue to the *Republic*, where we note that Athens was always considered an aristocratic city, while Piraeus was an economic, commercial, democratic *polis*.[143] In fragment 327, Socrates uses a first person form of the past tense to refer to their movement from Athens to Piraeus: κατέβην, from the verb καταβαίνω, which is translated as "I went down, descended."

---

142 A. Losev, *Istoria antichnoi estetiki. Poslednie veka.* [http://www.gumer.info/bibliotek_Buks/Culture/los_7/87.php]

143 Myles F. Burnyeat, *Culture and Society in Plato's Republic*, Harvard Tanner Lectures on Human Values (1997).

This subtlety is not conveyed[144] in the Russian translation (which is usually translated as *khodil*, "went"), yet this verb has a symbolic importance: the "going down" from Athens to Piraeus is likened to a descent from the estate of rulers and guardians to the lower, agricultural estate, or a descent from the sphere of the intellect into the realm of the soul (if we consider this movement in the sphere of the soul, then it is like a passage from the domination of the higher principle of the intellect to the lower states of the soul, the furious, inspirited, and lustful parts). It is of interest that Socrates "descends" to Piraeus during the festival in honor of Bendis (a Thracian Moon goddess who in Greece was identified with Artemis). In Proclus' opinion, this choice of timing for the dialogue was no accident: Plato aimed to show that Piraeus was a city of farmers (Athens also celebrated the Bendidia, but Bendis' temple was located in Piraeus), and Socrates acts as a kind of "demiurge" in his unfolding of the doctrine of the ideal state. Before weddings, the goddess was offered expiatory sacrifices (which makes her similar to the ancient chthonic mother goddesses like Cybele and Ishtar). The cult of Artemis also included orgiastic elements. The goddess was identified with birth, i.e., becoming. Thus, even the choice of the dialogue's location has a dimension of ontological symbolism.

Proclus highlights the place of Greek thought in philosophy in his analysis of the speech by the priest of Sais, Pateneit, who says that the Greeks are "always children." The Greeks are therefore contrasted to the Egyptians: the Egyptians are the elders who have preserved true knowledge, while the Greeks have only partial and mutable knowledge. On the metaphysical level, Proclus identifies the Egyptians with the causes of the constancy of rational principles, while the Greeks are taken to be the world causes of becoming, i.e., a people of a younger demiurgy. The sign of the Greeks' metaphysical "childhood" is their frequent forgetfulness of the One.

---

144 In French, some editions translate the verb as *"j'ai descendu"*, while most translations render it as *"hier j'etais au Pirée."*

If in his commentaries on the *Republic* we can see an outline of Proclus' political philosophy applied to domestic politics, then the first book of his commentary on the *Timaeus* presents an outline of a philosophy of foreign policy, or more precisely "geopolitics," which is described not only as a paradigm of relations between "friend" and "enemy" or "better" and "worse" in the case of the relations between the Athenians and the mythical people of Atlantis, but also as a paradigm of clash between two types of qualitative space.

In Proclus' account, the war between Athens and Atlantis is of a decidedly metaphysical character; it is a clash between different ontological hypostases and eidetic series. From the point of view of this Neoplatonist, it is not just states, peoples, political regimes, and *poleis* that clash in war, but qualitatively different spaces, places, and topoi which are seen as divine lots endowed with "different powers and certain symbols of the various orders among the gods": "For this space is suspended immediately after her [the World Soul], and functions as her connate instrument. So she, being a rational and psychical cosmos, brings this too to be a perfect cosmos of space and life through the divine tokens."[145] This eidetic theory of space at the core of Proclus' philosophical geography is grounded not in material extension, nor in Plato's *khora*, but in the vertical eidetic chain that penetrates space from top to bottom and thereby constitutes symbolic axes and platforms. Proclus cites "the divine Iamblichus," who he says "did not identify the place with any corporeal part of extended space, but the immaterial cause, passing right through the earth, which supports bodies in its life and embraces all space within it."[146]

In the second part of his commentary on the *Timaeus*, in his analysis of the legend of Atlantis, Proclus defines ancient Athens as the embodiment of the ideal state. Proclus' Athenians are the best side of the cosmic dyad. Athenians' foremost

---
145 Proclus, *Commentary on Plato's Timaeus - Volume I, Book I*, 259.
146 Ibid., 263.

status is explained in particular by the fact that they are a land civilization, and therefore a symbol of stability and eternity. Moreover, the Athenians represent the lot of the goddess Pallas Athena, who embodies the best qualities of the Hellenic virtues: wisdom, courage, and purity. The Atlanteans are the exact opposite: they are the worse, or rather "less better" in Proclus' terms, side of the cosmic system. The Atlanteans came from the outskirts of the inhabited earth, that is from the West, from beyond the boundaries of the divinely organized cosmos, and are therefore compared to the Titans who encroach on the power of the Olympian Gods. Proclus' cites Plato's testimony of the story of Athena's war with the giants that was recited at Athenian festivals:

> So, through the parallel between humans and things divine, he [Plato] teaches us even of this war before the origin of the cosmos, adopting the Athenians to represent Athena and the Olympian gods and the people of Atlantis to represent the Titans and Giants… For presumably, among the Titanic gods, the very great Atlas is also one. In fact the theologians too say that after the dismemberment of Dionysus, who shows the divisible procession into the All from the indivisible creation, the other Titans were given a different allotment by Zeus, whereas Atlas was stationed in the western regions holding up the heaven.[147]

For Proclus, Atlantis is a territory arranged in accordance with bodily, material laws, with the principle of becoming, and its location in the West, beyond the Pillars of Hercules, signifies an intracorporeal zone, the border between being and non-being, the threshold of the descent into Hades (which the Greeks believed to be in the West), and a symbol of remoteness from the One. Proclus writes:

> That is why he said that the Atlantines set out 'from outside' insofar as they are further from the one and closer to matter, and that they inhabit an island bigger than Libya and Asia, insofar as they proceed towards mass and extension. For everything that proceeds further from the One gains in quantity as it loses in power, just as those that

---

147 Ibid., 272.

are compressed closer in quantity have a remarkable power, so that size here signifies subordination, and procession and extension over all.[148]

Here Proclus is accentuating the connection between quantity, mass, gigantic volume, and ontological insufficiency, eidetic weakness, and remoteness from the One. In Greek culture, size, enormity, and quantity were seen as characteristic of titanic, chthonic entities and cultures doomed to defeat and death in the wars with the gods.

By contrast, Proclus takes Athens to be a city (a lot, κλῆρος) that is ontologically close to the One. The worse character of the Atlanteans is associated with the notions of descending emanation (πρόοδες), division (διάκρισις), and hubris (ὕβρις). By invading the Mediterranean, the territory of the Olympic Gods, the Atlanteans committed what in Proclus' view was the typically titanic sin of hubris. Proclus explains this and other titanic sins of the Atlanteans in terms of Atlantis' connection with the element of sea, with its mutability, instability, becoming, as well as its fabulous wealth, which obviously belongs to the third demiurgy.

The war between Athens and Atlantis has a sacred character: it is not simply an historical episode, but rather, behind the scenes of this political and military clash, it is the unfolding of the paradigmatic conflict between metaphysical opposites, opposing eidetic representations, cosmic and azonal gods, angels, demons, heroes, and men who are dependent upon the eidetic structure of their place, their territory, their state. This clash is a sacred war of hierarchical verticals: dyads are in the intellect, in the Gods, in souls, and in bodies. In warring with each other, opposites constitute the ordered cosmos.[149] This is none other than a battle of the One, the Intellect, the constant and the eternal with the domain of becoming, change,

---

148 Ibid., 278.

149 Cf. Heraclitus fragment 53: Πόλεμος πάντων μὲν πατήρ ἐστι, πάντων δὲ βασιλεύς, καὶ τοὺς μὲν θεοὺς ἔδειξε τοὺς δὲ ἀνθρώπους, τοὺς μὲν δούλους ἐποίησε τοὺς δὲ ἐλευθέρους.

and multiplicity. This war is inscribed into the very structure of spaces — the space of Land, guarded by Athena, and the space of Sea, Atlantis, whose patron is Poseidon — and it is reflected in politics, in the *politeia* of two different states.

Proclus tells the myth of the origin of the first human in Athens. Hephaestus, the creator of the forms of the material world, loved the goddess of wisdom and war, Pallas Athena. Contemplating her form, he planted a seed into the Earth from which the first man, Erichthonius, was born. This myth allegorically reproduces the Platonic theme and topology: upon contemplating the ideas, the demiurge creates their corporeal copies. The Athenians, thus, have the divinity, form, and materiality of Land. Pallas Athena's main qualities are wisdom and war, and she is the patroness of philosophers and warriors. The city of Athens is the best eidetic series: it is located around the divine Olympus, it is the inner space, the embodiment of limit and order. Atlantis, on the other hand, is located beyond the Pillars of Hercules (on which was written "*Nec plus ultra*," "no further"). This state represents the "less better" series. It is the secondary *politeia*, a titanic one, just as the founder of Atlantis, Atlas, was a titan. The metaphysical principle that dominates Atlantis is the "limitless," the ἄπειρον. Atlantis' greatness is purely material, and it is inversely proportional to the state's spiritual poverty. Athens, according to Proclus, is being and eternity. It corresponds to identity, peace, mind, and form. In Atlantis, becoming, otherness, motion, irrationality, and matter dominate. Athens dwells under the sign of the One, wisdom, valor, honor, fidelity, and beauty, while Atlantis stands on material strength, mobility, innovation, material prosperity, and mass. In strengthening its power, Atlantis violates boundaries, enters the inner regions, the domain of Land, and manifests hubris and the principle of boundlessness.

In the war between Athens and Atlantis, Proclus shows us the models of two cities, two continents: the sacred city, *theopolis*, the city of the gods, ideas, the spirit, eternity, and solar reason, and *titanopolis*, the city of demons, of rebellious materiality, multiplicity, and brute force. The world of Atlantis, like everything in the Platonic cosmos, necessarily has its own vertical hierarchy, but one that is directed downwards, towards the lower limit of the material cosmos. The Atlantean hierarchy of angels, daemons, souls, and cosmic gods makes it much more than mere matter; it is its own soul and life, but inverted and reversed. In Plato's *Laws*, one passage speaks of the "evil soul of the world." Perhaps Proclus would not object if we allowed ourselves to draw a connection between the "good soul of the world" and Athens and the "evil soul" and Atlantis, which thereby becomes not merely matter, but a certain order of things. Proclus writes:

> The aggression [ὕβρις] relates to their procession, their division through subordination, and their bordering on matter. For that is what true limitlessness and ugliness is, for which reason they say that it works aggression upon what borders upon it and upon what is somehow in it. The theologian reveals their paradigm in the following terms: The ill-planning Titans, with over-violent heart. The advance from outside relates to their secession to a dwelling-place far from the gods and from the diviner things in the All. For this from outside does not signify an encircling of forces, but the kind of being that has passed beyond all that is stable, immaterial, pure, and unified. The Atlantic Ocean relates to matter itself, whether it is as an 'abyss' that you care to describe it, or as a 'sea of dissimilarity', or whatever. For matter receives the names of the inferior column of opposites, being called 'limitlessness', 'darkness', 'irrationality', 'measurelessness', 'principle of otherness', and 'dyad' – just as the Atlantic Ocean gets its name from Atlantis. In this way, by understanding the analogies in order, we shall declare that all the inferior column of opposites, both the more universal races with it and the more partial, is characterized by procession, division, and a move towards matter. In this way it pervades everything, being reflected in each kind in the way proper to it and appearing in a corresponding manner in each nature –divine, intellective, psychical and bodily.[150]

Thus, Proclus' symbolic interpretation of the geographical patterns described in the *Timaeus* should be seen as part of

---

150 Proclus, *Commentary on Plato's Timaeus - Volume I, Book I*, 275.

his political philosophy and as based on extended chains of analogies and homologies. Politics is a field of change, where there is always something better in which i the eternal, the higher, and, ultimately, the One and the Good is embodied, but there is also the worse, which represents removal from the supreme One and the Good, that is, the lower material and, ultimately, chaotic domain.

In this view, space in and of itself is not neutral, but is organized like a system of lots (κλῆροι) which reflect the structure of the ideal cosmos and are embodied in the distribution of countries, cities, and peoples. Encounters between one or another city or place, as well as wars between peoples of land and peoples of sea, are seen by Proclus as expressions of universal laws which in almost all cases take on a pronounced political character.

In Proclus' political geography, the best place is occupied by those who are the best in their spiritual qualities, i.e., the Greeks. Among the Greeks, the best are either the inhabitants of Italy (Magna Graecia) or the Athenians (in a different symmetrical structure). The best should rule over the worst, and it therefore follows that Proclus' political geography is Helleno-centric: at the center of the ecumene is Hellas itself, and in the periphery are peoples of worse series who at times rise up against the Greeks and wage war against them (like the Atlanteans). For Proclus, war is not merely war between peoples, but a war of places, a war of lots, and the roles in war are distributed in accordance with the more general chains of homologies and correspondences.

Even the finale of the war between the Atlanteans and Athenians is symbolic: the Atlatneans perish in a flood, the Greeks in an earthquake. Proclus sees the tragedy of the Athenians as a metaphysical continuation of the politics of war:

> For in order that the last things should be arranged and should enjoy divine providence, it was necessary that both the better column and

the inferior one should extend its own power from above right down to the foundation of the cosmos, each of the two in its own proper manner, the one by being shaken [by an earthquake] and sinking beneath the earth, which is the equivalent of 'advancing steadily and with solidity', and the other by vanishing, which would be the equivalent of becoming enmattered and without order or form. For beneath the earth is a symbol of an enduring and stable nature, while beneath the sea symbolizes what is easily changed, disorderly, and in flux.[151]

Here Proclus is speaking of an eschatological political scenario. In order for the universal order to be restored, he argues that the eidetic series must extend their martial presence to the very bottom of the cosmos. At the same time, the gods spread their "troops" through the earth by will, and then begin their ascent, their rise, while the titans, who are extremely divided, disintegrating, and turn the sea into an "impassable un-navigable" swamp, descend into the hypochthonic space, into the dark silt, the βόρβορος.

Athens' political victory entails the reduction of its political opponents to the lower ontological limit of the silt (βόρβορος), the last limit of dense bodies, the limit of dissolution into pure quantity. This can be conceived of as the Titans' return to their essential state of being. In war, the gods descend downwards, but they remain gods and then begin their new ascent. Thus, Proclus' political philosophy of war once again exhibits an ontological and metaphysical homology.

Concluding his interpretation of the story of the war between Athens and Atlantis, Proclus shows that the philosophy of politics is built on the immutable logic of the eidetic correspondences and noetic series of the Platonic universe. The gods are eternal and their topoi are irrevocable. Every god is attached to their respective place in the sensible world, which is allotted to them for all eternity to be nurtured and cared for. Every topos, every place in space, is a point of presence of the

---

[151] Proclus, *Commentary on Plato's Timaeus - Volume I, Book I*, 288

emanation, procession, and ascent of eidetic series. The pathways of intellectual being in its eternal dimension converge within them. Each focal point is a node from which one can contemplate the entire universe. All political scenarios, the life of society, matters of war and peace, the forms of political structures and cultures, the scenarios of historical events, and their foresight, prediction, and fulfillment are akin to homologous scenarios of the eidetic chains ascending from sensible things to the World Soul, the Intellect, and further to the One as the Good and the One as the ineffable, the Apophatic, Non-Being.

Within space and alongside the gods, daemons, heroes, and other eidetic entities, the human being is one of the foremost actors of the eidetic, ontological, aesthetic, ethical, and political orders. Neoplatonic political philosophy envisions man as being called to think and act analogously to the gods, to dwell in contemplating the intelligible forms, to attentively peer into the trajectories of earthly events, and to compare them to heavenly scenarios. Proclus' political philosophy demands that man raise the degree of his own participation in being by considering each point of his presence in the world as a node in which the intelligible series of all the best and all the worst orders of the Platonic cosmos arrive and meet, where war is waged and power is fought for — physical, mythological, eidetic, material, metaphysical, and political power. The Earth and its regions, the realms of Land and Sea, are living territories with a sacred topology, all with their own eidetic path through the ages. The human being's task, the human being's political task, is to participate in the Platonic noetic universe on the side of the forces of the higher eidetic series.

Conclusion

We have undertaken to demonstrate that the philosopher and scholarch of the Athenian school of late Neoplatonism, Proclus, had a system of political philosophy which was rooted in and developed from Plato's political ideas as well as the whole Platonic tradition. In this thesis, we have drawn upon Proclus' commentaries on the *Republic* and *Timaeus*. Our method was to identify analogies and homologies between the various domains of Neoplatonic philosophy, which are interconnected by the common Platonic approach to the primordial, ontological status of paradigms, ideas, and noetic objects of contemplation which figure as the sources of the eidetic series that constitute various phenomenon, i.e., different ontologies, cosmologies, souls, and states. The Political is one of these domains in which the emanation of ideas and the symbolic chains tied to them reveal their structures. Therefore, for the Neoplatonists, any domain of knowledge — from cosmology to gnoseology to theology — necessarily harbors a political dimension.

Proclus saw the social and political hierarchies in Plato's *Republic* as a special case of the universal law of the hierarchies of gods, intelligible principles, and states of the soul. In the *Timaeus*, Proclus politically interpreted spatial symbolism and transformed the symbolically interpreted legend of the Atlantean-Athenian war into a treatise on foreign policy, one which in many respects anticipated the geopolitics of the 20th century.

At the same time, our analysis of the political and historical situation in which the late Neoplatonists lived explains why this school's political philosophy did not take on systematic exposition. The Neoplatonists were pagans living in a Christian society whose norms did not, in their eyes, belong to the best eidetic types in terms of social, religious, and ethical constitution. Therefore, their political philosophy was left in a curtailed (and implicit) state. Nevertheless, it is not difficult to reconstruct this political philosophy out of numerous fragments and direct indications, as O'Meara and Ciorvanes have undertaken to do in their work. The fact that this topic has not been further developed is, in our opinion, linked to the fact that Neoplatonic studies have not yet reached a stage at which the attention of historians of philosophy has been drawn to not only what the Neoplatonists said and wrote openly, but also to what they hinted at and what they implied. I submit that the Neoplatonists, and in this case Proclus, did indeed have a political philosophy, and that we are still awaiting a more detailed and fully-fledged study of this political philosophy.

***

The Political Platonism of Emperor Julian

Introduction[152]

Historians of late Platonism often adhere to an approach which holds that the political plane is not part of Neoplatonism's sphere of interest, which is instead supposedly oriented exclusively towards intellectual contemplation and focused on the apophatic One ("Ἑν), the hierarchy of emanations, and theurgic practices. The German historian of Platonism Ehrhardt in particular adhered to this point of view.[153] This position, which is subject to repeated critique throughout Dominic O'Meara's work, *Platonopolis: Platonic Political Philosophy in Late Antiquity*[154], can be called into doubt, and one of the decisive arguments on this question might very well be the case of Emperor Julian (331/332-363), who not only put forth a developed Neoplatonic political theory, but also accomplished a number of decisive steps towards its political application in the governance of the Empire.

Julian the Philosopher-King

Emperor Flavius Claudius Julian, a representative of the Pergamon school of Neoplatonism, was a model Platonist who not only reflected on the philosopher's need to engage in politics (i.e., to be a ruler), but also, for a very short but also very lively period, was Emperor of the Roman Empire, he was also an Emperor who embodied the political project of the Platonic ideal state. Such a combination of reverence for contemplative life and political service was rare — there have been few philosopher-

---

152 Originally published in Russian in the journal *Context and Reflection: Philosophy of the World and Human Being* 7:2A (2018), 32-38.

153 A. Ehrhardt, "The Political Philosophy of Neo-Platonism" in *Studi in onore di Vincenzo Arangio-Ruiz nel XLV anno del suo insegnamento*, vol. 1, ed. M. Lauria (Naples, 1953), 457-82.

154 Dominic J. O'Meara, *Platonopolis: Platonic Political Philosophy in Late Antiquity* (Oxford: Clarendon Press, 2003).

rulers in history, but one such ruler, Marcus Aurelius, inspired Julian in many respects. "Dreamers of this style are rare among princes: that is why we ought to respect him [Emperor Julian]," remarked the French historian Victor Duruy.[155] What strikingly distinguished Julian from his predecessors was his genuine obsession with philosophy, the highest manifestation of which in his eyes was Neoplatonic doctrine. The young emperor was especially fascinated by Iamblichus (245/280-325/330) of the Syrian school of Neoplatonism. The Pergamon school at which Julian studied was essentially a branch of the Syrian school, and Iamblichus was regarded as an indisputable authority.

Iamblichus was Julian's model of "the mystical and the perfect," and in his writings Julian found "the most perfect wisdom that a man is capable of discovering." Yet, as Julian's biographer, Jacques Benoist-Méchin, has noted, Julian did not simply heed and reproduce Iamblichus' teachings, but added to and developed them, elaborating the doctrine of the middle element (the "middle world"), the Sun King (in three hypostases), and in so doing detailed the metaphysical landscape of Neoplatonic philosophy.[156]

Three Suns

The highest hypostasis of the Sun was the apophatic sun, identical to Plotinus' One ("Ev). The middle sun was the metaphysical Light connecting the intelligible (noetic) worlds with the cosmos. Finally, the third hypostasis was the sun of the visible, corporeal world, which represented the lower limit of the emanations of the absolute principle.

For Julian, the question of the connection between the intelligible and material world (the problem of the "middle sun") was fundamental. He sought an answer on both the ontological

---

155 V. Duruy, "Annuaire de l'Association pour l'encouragement des études grecques en France" in *Revue des Études Grecques* 17 (Paris: Revue des Études Grecques, 1883), 177.

156 Jacques Benoist-Méchin, *L'Empereur Julien ou le rêve calciné (331-363)* (Paris: Perrin, 1997).

and political planes. For Julian, as for any Platonist, the political and ontological planes are interconnected and homologous. The mediator, which for Julian was Helios, is at once a metaphysical and political figure: he is King in relation to everything below him as well as a representative of the metaphysically higher First Principle. To describe this sun, Julian uses the nouns βασιλεύς, "king," κύριος, "lord," and the verbs ἐπιτροπεύω, "to be a guardian" or "one who manages" and ἡγέομαι, "to govern," "to guide," "to lead," to "go ahead." The parallels between Helios and the figure of the ruler permeate the whole of his "Hymn to the King Helios." For example: "the planets dance about him as their king, in certain intervals, fixed in relation to him, and revolve in a circle with perfect accord."[157] Just as Helios, the Sun God, acts as the transmitter of ideas into the sensual world, the Philosopher-Emperor is the Sun-King's companion. "Companion" (ὀπᾱδός) is what Julian calls himself in the beginning of the hymn. Every ruler, Julian remarked, is fit to be a "servant" and "seer" of the "King of the Gods [Helios]." So too does the Sun King grant wisdom, knowledge, and being to the patron goddess of the *polis* and states, Athena — her wisdom, which flows from Helios, "is the foundation of political communion."

Julian's Helios also turns out to be the founder of Rome, proof of which Julian cites from a legend holding that Romulus' spirit descended to earth from the sun: "the close conjunction of Helios and Selene, who share the empire over the visible world, even as it had caused his soul to descend to earth, in like manner caused to mount upwards him whom it received back from the earth, after blotting out with fire from a thunderbolt the mortal part of his body." The unity of the metaphysically understood Light symbolizing Helios permeates the entire system of Julian's philosophy. According to the Neoplatonic conception, the One is always apophatic, inexpressible and transcends being. It can only be reached tangentially. The highest form of unity is accessible through ἕνας, or co-participation in the One. Hence,

---

157 Julian, "Hymn to King Helios, dedicated to Sallust" in Julian, *Complete Works* (Delphi Classics, 2017).

the cosmos seems to gather and gravitate towards the One without ever reaching it.

Likewise, Julian's highest hypostasis of the Sun-King is apophatic. The nature of Light originates in the apophatic darkness of the invisible sun and from there permeates all other levels of the cosmos. The state, understood as the Empire, is the gathering of many peoples toward this unity, which is to say that it is a henad. This is not oneness and Light itself, but a will towards it, movement towards it. Just as the soul or essence of the king descends from the higher spheres, so too does the kingdom itself strive towards the king as its source, which imparts politics with henadic grace.

Julian set before himself the virtually impossible task of implementing the Platonic ideal of the Philosopher-King in the actual context of the 4th-century Roman Empire, of becoming the "companion" of the sun and guarantor of justice (δικαιοσύνη) in the conditions of the growing strength and influence of Christianity. "His main driving force was a sense of responsibility as strong as that of the enthroned philosopher Marcus Aurelius, whom the philosopher idolized."[158]

During the year and a half of his imperial reign (and before then for several years as Caesar in Gaul), guided by the principles of the Platonic state (as Walter Hyde rightly noted, "Julian put Platonic theory into practice"[159]), Julian attempted to harmonize the political system with the philosophical ideal set down in the Platonic philosophical tradition, and he partially succeeded.[160] A successful statesman, he showed himself to be a gifted commander (winning remarkable victories over the Germanics in Gaul and effectively commanding the army until his death, until the last battle with the Persians in which the Emperor was killed) and as a radical reformer of the pagan faith

---

158 F.F. Zelinskii, *Rimskaia Respublika* (Saint Petersburg: Aleteia, 2016), 419.

159 W. Hyde, "Emperor Julian", *The Classical Weekly* 37:3 (Baltimore: Johns Hopkins University Press, 1843).

160 Polymnia Athanassiadi-Fowden, *Julian and Hellenism: An Intellectual Biography* (Oxford: Clarendon Press, 1981).

which had lost its force due to the advent of the new Christian religion which, although still blurred in its contours, already fragmented into countless persuasions in violent polemics with one another.

Julian was no mere secular ruler; he tried to embody the ideal image of the Philosopher-King in its ontological — pan-cosmic — understanding in strict accordance with the symbolic patterns of Neoplatonism. The religious tolerance that Julian decreed was also based on deep philosophical convictions. His decree was no mere rejection of the Christianization of the Empire in favor of secularism, nor was it a substitution of one religion for another. According to Julian's thought, faith, religion, and authority — the domain of opinion (δόξα) — ought to be subordinated to the higher principle of the King of the Universe, "the one around Whom everything exists." But this submission could not be formal, since the entire hierarchical structure of the ruling principle, the Sun-King, was open from above, i.e., henadic. In the structure of Neoplatonic philosophy, one can be certain only of moving towards the One, not certain about the One itself, which is unattainable. As follows, Julian's political model represented the principle of the "open Empire," in which the imperative was the pursuit of wisdom, but not wisdom itself, for, in the final analysis, wisdom cannot be embodied in any set of dogmas — whether Christian or pagan. Yet, the conclusion of this openness was the opposite of the secular tendencies of the New Age. Sacrality and the principle of Light are the imperatives of Julian's political philosophy, but this governance cannot be fixed in immutable laws. The meaning of Light is that it is alive. And so, too, should the open Empire and its ruler be. Here, the very concept of philosophy is restored to its deep meaning. Philosophy is the love of wisdom and movement towards it. It is the search for the Light, service to the Sun-King, accompanying him. But, if we impart this wisdom with a formalized character, then we are dealing not with philosophy, but with sophism. This, apparently, is what repulsed Julian in Christianity: closing unto strict dogmas, the henadic character of the open Empire was replaced by an estranged codex, and thus the Empire was closed to the above and lost its total sacrality in favor of only one possible version of religion. The domain of opinions (δόξα) is the sphere of the relative, the contingent. It must be oriented towards the Sun, in which case opinion becomes orthodoxy, ορθο-δοξία, meaning "right opinion," but it is still only opinion.

What is interesting about Julian's fate is the fact that he did not have any particular aspiration to gain power, as he primarily occupied himself with philosophy and was fascinated by theurgic rituals. Julian was first and foremost a philosopher, and only by the force of inevitability, fate, premonition, and the path chosen for him by Helios did he become a ruler. In his "Funeral Oration upon the Emperor Julian," Libanius remarked that he "strove not towards for dominance, but for the prosperity of cities," and the rhetorician noted that if in Julian's time any other candidate for the throne could have revived Hellenism, Julian would have "persistently avoided power."[161] Julian was a philosopher sentenced by Providence to descend, to emanate, and thus his mission bore a demiurgic and soteriological character. He was doomed to become a ruler, a companion of the Sun, by virtue of his philosophical nature.

The Sun of the Absolute Center

The "middleness" of the Sun of which we wrote above and its guiding leadership correspond to the Philosopher-King's position in the ideal state. Like Helios in his demiurgic activity that generates or adorns many *eidoi* ("For some forms he perfects, others he makes, or adorns, or wakes to life, and there is no single thing which, apart from the creative power derived from Helios, can come to light and to birth."[162]), the philosopher-ruler imparts the estates with their proper contours. He is the "middling one," the conductor of genuine knowledge about the secret nature of things and the builder of order based on this

---

161 [Russian edition:] Libanii, *Rechi*, vol. 1 (Saint Petersburg: Kvadrivium, 2014), 522.

162 Julian, "Hymn to King Helios."

genuine knowledge. Julian associated Helios with Apollo, the one who establishes oracles all over the earth to give people divinely-inspired truth.[163] Helios-Apollo is supposed to be the Emperor as well as the progenitor of the Roman people, which adds to Julian's political doctrine the thesis that the Romans were "chosen by God."

Helios-Zeus also acts as the bearer of the royal principle. Even the god of the nocturnal mysteries, Dionysus, who in Julian's thought becomes another embodiment of the Sun, Helios-Dionysus, is treated as a continuation of the same principle of authority within the depths of the corporeal worlds. Zeus, Apollo, and Dionysus are, according to Julian, the three points of the political demiurgy of the perfect ruler. Like Zeus, he governs the world. Like Apollo, he writes laws and monitors the observance of the sacred vertical oriented towards the solar Empire. Like Dionysus, he is the patron of religions, cults, and the arts, and also oversees the mysteries and liturgies.

There is some evidence that the figure of the sun mediator impressed the Emperor so much that in his reform of the army he replaced the Christian inscription on the imperial banner from "*In hoc signo vinci*" ("In this sign thou shalt conquer") to the Mithraic dedication "*Sol Invictus*" ("the Invincible Sun"). Obviously, the figure of Mithras is taken here as a philosophical metaphor, not as a sign that Mithraism inspired Julian's religious and political reforms. Sol Invictus is the very same King Helios in his general, primordial nature. He could act as the common denominator of various religious figures in the spirit of Neoplatonic synthesis or what the Neoplatonist Proclus later called "Platonic theology."

---

163 Apollo also occupies a central place in Plato's *Republic*: in the fourth book, he is recognized to be the only true lawgiver. In Socrates' opinion, the laws of the ideal state should be established not on the basis of previously held customs and habits, nor on any one person's singular will, but on the transcendental, divine principle. Thus, the state's laws can be understood like the Delphic prophecies, the monopoly on interpreting which is held by the ideal state's philosopher-king.

In the case of this replacement of *"In hoc signo vinci"* with *"Sol Invictus,"* which is sometimes interpreted as the most striking case of a "pagan restoration," we might also see something different: not a replacement of one cult by another, but an appeal to the philosophical source common to different religions and faiths. Just as the Empire gathers together peoples and kingdoms, so does fully-fledged imperial sacrality take all particular forms back to their henadic source. In the end, the cross is also a solar symbol, and its display on the imperial banner was closely associated with Rome's military victory and political heyday under Constantine.

An Attempt to Restore Platonopolis

Julian's era witnessed an attempt to build a universal Platonopolis-Empire. As a true Platonist, Julian tried to cover and reform all domains — the religious sphere (introducing the rite of repentance, charity, giving formal pagan cults an ethical character, the edict on religious tolerance)[164], the sphere of palace life (rationalizing court staff, inviting noble philosophers, orators, and priests to court, restoring the Senate's former status and power), and the financial sphere (restoring urban self-government, transferring to municipalities the right to collect taxes in favor of cities). But the course of history was already predetermined. Christianity, absorbing certain elements of Hellenism (in particular, assimilating the doctrine of the Platonic kingdom and the best elements of Neoplatonic mysticism and theology), irreversibly overthrew the dilapidated edifice of antiquity.

---

[164] In the 4th century, pagan religion was in a substantially weakened state. In his work *The Roman Empire*, Zelinsky notes that in Julian's time "The sight of the foremost temple in the ancient world, the temple of Apollo at Delphi, caused despondency. And Julian, wishing to hear the voice of the Delphic oracles, sent his theurgists there. The last Pythia proved to be worthy of her predecessors. The sad answer was:
Take this message to the lord: of the temple are left ruins,
Phoebus is not the householder of this shrine and has lost the laurel of the prophets,
The spring of inspiration has dried up and the Castalian streams have ceased." —
F.F. Zelinskii, *Rimskaia Imperiia* (Saint Petersburg: Aleteia, 2020), 425.

The historian W.R. Inge remarked that Julian was "a conservative when there was nothing left to preserve."[165] Julian's hour struck and a new ruler came into the world. Henceforth, imperial sacrality and the metaphysical mission of the Emperor would be interpreted in a narrowly Christian context as the figure of the Katechon (κατέχων), the "withholder," whose meaning was defined by the structure of Christian eschatology, in which the orthodox Emperor was, as in John Chrysostom's interpretation, held to be the main obstacle to the coming of the Antichrist. But even in this concept of the "Katechon," we can see a distant echo of the political ontology of the Sun-King, as Empire continued to be seen as a metaphysical phenomenon and therefore assumed a philosophical character in Byzantinism. At this point, however, we are dealing with a significantly reduced version of political Platonism, one that was narrower and more dogmatically delimited than the universal scope of Julian's political philosophy.

***

---

165 W.R. Inge, "The Permanent Influence of Neoplatonism upon Christianity", *The American Journal of Theology* 4:2 (Chicago: University of Chicago Press, 1900), 333.

Julianism

Plato's Ideal State as a Political Project

In the lecture course *Introduction to the Study of Plato's Dialogues* delivered at the University of Basil in 1871-1872, Friedrich Nietzsche noted that Plato's political doctrine was a turning point, a total transformation of the classical Greek perception of the polis and the citizen.[166] For Nietzsche, what was especially important and innovative in Plato's teaching was the object of the philosopher-king's contemplation being put above the plane of religiosity and faith (πίστις), the disclosure of a new horizon of contemplation over the "divided line," and the introduction of the Good as transcending everything, even being itself. The introduction of such an additional perspective into the polis along with the appearance of a new supra-political actor — a super-being — can be deemed to have been Platonism's truly revolutionary revelation. The Platonic political project is for an Empire of the Good, the ineffable ruler of which is a Superbeing (and it is this realm that the Neoplatonists would undertake to meticulously study).

One important kernel of Plato's political doctrine was manifest in the scenario of the obligatory "descent" back into the cave after the philosopher's liberation and exit from it (the realm of ignorance and becoming). As Socrates said: "We mustn't allow them to do what they're allowed to do today...To stay there and refuse to go down again to the prisoners in the cave and share their labors and honors, whether they are of less worth or of greater."[167] Plato put the well-being of the whole state, the whole *polis* as the union of three parts, above the individual. The philosopher's sacrificial and perhaps tragic descent (the tragic aspect of which is emphasized by Plato himself in the *Republic*)

---

166 Friedrich Nietzsche, *Introduction à la lecture des dialogues de Platon* (Paris: Éditions de l'Éclat, 1991).

167 Plato, *Republic* 519d.

is in the ideal *polis* an obligatory condition for the Good of the whole state. As the scholar of Platonism Georgia Mouroutsou notes in her article "The Allegory of the Cave: The Necessity Of The Philosopher's Descent," the philosopher's return to the cave as described in the seventh book of the *Republic* has an exoteric meaning (the philosopher is obliged to create justice within the state) as well as an esoteric meaning (the philosopher's descent is akin to the demiurge's gaze turning downwards, like the emanations of the world intellect).¹⁶⁸ In Plato's hands, the philosopher, like the Good, emits the light of the Intellect down into the world (κάθοδος, "descent"), and through this process of the establishment of justice the philosopher creates justice both in his soul and in the state.

Plato's *Republic's* introduction of a homology between the soul and political order was truly revolutionary. The state and the soul are acknowledged to be different dimensions or different letters of one and the same text. The tripartite soul becomes identical with the tripartite state.

The Byzantine Deep State

The most vivid experience of the implementation of Platonic political philosophy was, without a doubt, Julian the Apostate's Empire. In the span of a three-year reign, Julian, guided by the principles of the Platonic state, attempted to harmonize the political structure of the empire with the philosophical ideal set forth in the Platonic philosophical tradition.¹⁶⁹

Despite the fact that Julian's reforms were quickly overturned (Emperor Flavius Claudius Jovian canceled all of his religious decrees and restored the Christian religion's former privileges), and despite the fact that Platonic political doctrine passed into the shadows, the latter did not disappear, but began to coexist

---

168 Georgia Mouroutsou, "The Allegory of the Cave: The Necessity of the Philosopher's Descent", *Plato: The Internet Journal of the International Plato Society* 11 (2011).

169 Polymnia Athanassiadi-Fowden, *Julian and Hellenism: An Intellectual Biography* (Oxford: Clarendon Press, 1981).

alongside the official Roman political code, which took on Christian grounds.

The conventional point of view in the history of philosophy (of which the historian of philosophy Ehrhardt is the most prominent representative[170]) holds that late Neoplatonism lacked any political philosophy. Dominic O'Meara fundamentally disagrees with this point of view; he writes of the indelible presence of a political doctrine among the Neoplatonists and notes that the late Platonists had many political figures among their students.[171] In addition, this scholar recalls that the Neoplatonists included practicing political consultants, such as Hypatia, an advisor to Prefect Orestes of Alexandria, who fell victim to political intrigues (over the question of dividing influence in the city between "pagan" and "Christian" blocs).

Political Platonism became a secret doctrine of Empire, a kind of "deep state," and the very core of Neoplatonic political philosophy was taken over by Christianity in a certain interpretation. Paradoxically, Plato's teaching on the state and his idea of a homology between the political, psychic, and cosmic levels, in many respects especially skillfully developed by the scholarch of the Athenian school of Neoplatonism, Proclus Diadochus, came to lie at the heart of the teachings of such Christian theologians as John Chrysostom, Augustine, and Dionysius the Areopagite.

After Emperor Julian's death, the religious policy of the Roman Empire was for some time distinguished by a certain tolerance for pagans, as Julian's reforms enjoyed support among all segments of the population, and the emperors following Julian realized the need for a balanced religious policy. By the beginning of Theodosius Augustus' reign, no less than half of the whole empire's population were adherents of pagan religion.

---

170 A. Ehrhardt, "The Political Philosophy of Neo-Platonism" in *Studi in onore di Vincenzo Arangio-Ruiz nel XLV anno del suo insegnamento*, vol. 1, ed. M. Lauria (Naples, 1953), 457-82.

171 Dominic J. O'Meara, *Platonopolis: Platonic Political Philosophy in Late Antiquity* (Oxford: Clarendon Press, 2003).

Pagans were especially numerous in aristocratic circles close to the emperor. At the same time, the Christian Church was shaken by internal dogmatic disputes: the Arians retained a certain degree of influence, and their clash with orthodox officials took on the character of a real religious war.

In 380, Theodosius issued the famous edict *Cunctos populos*, which upheld the Nicene interpretation of the nature of Christ. This date can be called a turning point, a "bifurcation point," a rift in the harmonious coexistence of paganism and Christianity. With it began a wave of persecution of Arian heretics and pagans. At the same time, Christian theologians began to develop a political philosophy that they saw as rooted in the Apostle Paul's Second Epistle to the Thessalonians, in which the figure of the "withholder" stands in the way of the onset of the reign of the Antichrist. This "withholder" or "restrainer" (ὁ κατέχων) came to be interpreted by Christian theologians as the political figure of the Emperor. Christianity thus began to develop a political philosophy. Paradoxically, Christian political philosophy based its understanding of politics largely on the political teachings of Platonism. Even the doctrine of the "withholder" (ὁ κατέχων) in Christian political teaching might have been borrowed from Plato. Panagiotis Christias, a scholar of Platonism, writes of this in his work *Plato and Paul on the Brink of the Abyss: Towards a Katechontic Politics*, in which he notes that Plato had directly declared philosophers to be the bearers of a certain katechontic (restraining) principle: "The law is none other than the katechon of the many; the force of the law restrains the many."[172]

Thus, the Platonic "deep state" and its central concepts became the basis for the Christian political doctrine that endured in the world arena for more than 1500 years.

---

[172] Panagiotis Christias, *Platon et Paul au bord de l'abîme: pour une politique katéchontique* (Paris: VRIN, 2014), 155.

Proclus Diadochus: Implicit Political Philosophy or a Secret 5th-Century Julianism?

In the fifth century, the "Christian" and "pagan" proportions of the political plane shifted significantly, as Christianity became not only an alternative, monotheistic philosophy, but also developed its own political perspective in which there was increasingly less room for the former Hellenistic world.[173] Christianity began the process of developing the dogmatic contours of its own doctrine in which balance and "religious tolerance" were replaced with the principle of recognizing Christianity to be the one and only religion and treating all other points of view as heretical. Hellenism and its most striking expression, Neoplatonism, passed into the sphere of the "deep state," becoming a parallel political project that gradually began to decay and then finally left the European world in 529 when the Athenian Academy was closed at the behest of Emperor Julian. However, by that time, the basic principles of Neoplatonic metaphysics had already been firmly planted in Christianity, adapted to and becoming an indelible part of its monotheistic axis (vivid examples of this are the works of Eusebius of Caesarea, the Cappadocian Fathers, St. Augustine, Dionysius the Areopagite[174], Maximus the Confessor, John Philoponus, and many others of the Church Fathers).

One of the brightest representatives of late Platonism was Proclus Diadochus, the scholarch of the Athenian school. A fundamental Neoplatonic political philosophy was developed

---

173 It bears noting that the division between "Christian" and "pagan" is rather obscure, as these two phenomena did not exist independently of one another, but rather were tightly interwoven in their foundations. Plato's philosophy, for instance, formed the core of Christian metaphysics. It is also of interest to us that Plato and Aristotle with scrolls in hand were depicted on the parvise of the Cathedral of the Annunciation in the Kremlin built in the 15th century

174 As one of the most important Christian works, the *Corpus Areopagiticum* is a Christian recasting of the works of Proclus Diadochus. As George Florovsky wrote: "This is self-evident even before the Areopagiticum's dependence — both ideologically and literary — on the Neo-Platonic teacher Proclus (410-485) had been unquestionably established." — George Florovsky, *The Byzantine Ascetic and Spiritual Fathers*, trans. Raymond Miller, Anne-Marie Döllinger-Labriolle, and Helmut Wilhelm Schmiedel (Büchervertriebsanstalt, 1987).

in his commentaries on the *Republic* and the *Timaeus*. Proclus paid special attention to the question of homology between the political, the psychic, and the cosmic. Common to all of these planes is the presence of a triune hypostatic hierarchy (estates in the state, principles in the soul, and gods in the cosmos). Just as the Sun-King ruler (Helios) occupies the "middle," demiurgic position in Julian's thought, so is the philosopher a moderator of true hierarchy in the state system and the guide of justice and due correlation of the soul, castes, and parts of the world in Proclus' thought. In his commentaries on Plato's political works, Proclus noticeably focuses more on the psychic, religious, and contemplative than the direct expression of hierarchy in state format; however, such a prioritization might be linked to the political context of Athens at the time. As is testified by numerous historico-philosophical works (Prechter[175], Rosan[176], Beutler[177], Saffrey[178], Westerink[179]), Proclus was rather widely known in the circles of those in power (τοῖς τὰς ἐνίας ἔχουσι), and his student Marinus noted in his treatise *The Life Of Proclus, or Concerning Happiness*:

> He acquired political virtues, which he derived from Aristotle's political writings, and Plato's *Laws* and *Republic*. He was in this dilemma, that he could not mingle with politics, because his thoughts took a higher flight; and yet he did not wish people to believe that his knowledge was verbal only, and that he made no practical application thereof. So he encouraged Archiadas to devote himself to them, instructing him, explaining to him the political virtues and methods, acting like the coaches who pace runners, exhorting him to direct the affairs of his whole town, and at the same time to render services to individuals, in all kinds of virtues, but especially in justice.[180]

---

175 Karl Prechter (ed.), *Die Philosophie des Altertums* (Leipzig, 1926).

176 Laurence Jay Rosan, *The Philosophy of Proclus: The Final Phase of Ancient Thought* (New York: Cosmos, 1949).

177 R. Beutler, "Proklos der Neuplatoniker", *RE, Hlbbd* 45 (1957): 186-247.

178 H.D. Saffrey, *Recherches sur le Néoplatonisme après Plotin* (Paris: Brin, 1990).

179 L.G. Westerink, *Texts and Studies in Neoplatonism and Byzantine Literature* (Amsterdam: Hakkert, 1980).

180 Marinus of Samaria, *The Life of Proclus, or Concerning Happiness*, trans. Kenneth S. Guthrie (Phanes Press, 1986).

On the basis of this triadic model (the psychic, the cosmic, and the metaphysical), Proclus also put forth an ethnological systematization: Thracians harbored a violent element, Phoenicians were more inclined to commerce, and the Greeks, as Proclus rather predictably said, are the foremost people of the Mediterranean embodying the intellect (κὕβερνήτης - the charioteer).

Also of importance in Proclus' political philosophy was his designation of a correspondence between the three types of governance and the three gods Zeus, Dionysus, and Adonis. In his opinion, every king reproduces a certain demiurgy:

> For every statesman (*politikos*) wishes to imitate some Demiurge: the statesman who establishes all property in common wishes to imitate the Demiurge of the universe (*ta hola*), the one who apportions and divides wishes to imitate the Demiurge who divides parts from wholes, and the one who sets right the twisted form [of government] wishes to imitate the Demiurge who weaves anew what comes into being and perishes.[181]

Proclus attributed the creation of the state to the demiurgic Zeus, upholding justice being one of his main duties. Dionysus became responsible for upholding the integrity of the state (which is to say that he preserves the state and defends it from enemies with a furious, violent principle). Adonis and his demiurgy are the principle of well-being (resonating with the third caste). For Proclus, the best ruler is undoubtedly one who reproduces the demiurgic matrix of Zeus, for Zeus is the one who creates order, law, and norms. In the view of this scholarch of the Athenian school, the "degeneration of the *polis*" is a process that manifests itself as a gradual change of demiurgies: the reign of Zeus passes to the reign of Dionysus and the latter, in turn, passes to the reign of Adonis. For Proclus, the degeneration of regimes is a necessary and due transformation of ontological and cosmological states; it is not a catastrophe, but rather represents the continuous emanation of the One down into the lower

---

[181] Proclus, *Commentary on Plato's Timaeus - Volume I, Book I: Proclus on the Socratic State and Atlantis*, trans. Harold Tarrant (Cambridge: Cambridge University Press, 2007), 210.

layers of the universe. Proclus saw changes in political regime (from monarchy to tyranny through timocracy, oligarchy, and democracy) as a logically inevitable process. It is quite possible that Proclus encountered "tyranny" in his own lifetime in the Christian Empire which, from the optic of Platonism, as brilliantly noted by Professor Hofmann in his article "Proclus' Anti-Christian Grievance: Theological Ignorance," appeared to the Neoplatonists to be an "empire of the uneducated crowd."[182] The repressive measures of such a tyrannical regime would have been manifest in the new Christian elites' treatment of the old school as they came to replace the Hellenistic world.

Marinus wrote of Proclus;

> For he managed to save his life in the midst of the greatest perils, when he had to weather terrible tempests, when all the unleashed typhoons were shaking his so well regulated life, without letting himself be frightened or discouraged. One day, indeed, when he found himself the object of the suspicions and vexations of a sort of vultures that surrounded him, obeying that [divine] Power which starts revolutions in this world, he left Athens and made a journey to Asia, where his residence became most profitable to him.[183]

The great Neoplatonist thus "yielded to the course of affairs" that inevitably led to the end of the great Neoplatonic tradition. Henceforth, this tradition seeped into Christian philosophy and mysticism and would soon enough rekindle in the Areopagitic corpus, wherefrom it would later echo in the mystical theology of the Byzantine Empire.

***

---

[182] Philippe Hoffmann, "*Un grief antichrétien chez Proclus: l'ignorance en théologie*" in Arnaud Perrot (ed.), *Les chrétiens et l'hellénisme: identités religieuses et culture grecque dans l'Antiquité tardive* (Paris: Rue d'Ulm, Presses de l'École normale supérieure, 2012), 162.

[183] Marinus, *The Life of Proclus*.

Emperor Julian, Empire, and Neoplatonism

Greetings! I welcome all the participants of this seminar. May Christ save us for the presentations and topics raised today![184]

In my dissertation work, I'm dealing with the question of political philosophy in Neoplatonism or late Platonism. We're talking about the 5th-6th centuries AD. I'm working on Proclus Diadochus. But today I've been intrigued by the attempt to answer the question: Has the Platonic idea and political project been implemented in history? We can see the realization of this project in the Platonic Academy or in Plotinus' construction of a Platonopolis in Campania, but here we are talking about the construction of a Platonic or Neoplatonic school. Everything is clear on that matter. When it comes to various thinkers' attempts to live and realize Platonism in their soul, we find historical confirmation and evidence for this. But when it comes to the topic of a real political Empire being a direct expression of political Platonism, an application of Platonic principles, the fascinating dialectical hierarchy of the One and the Many, the One Intellect and the Soul, everything is much more difficult and complex. In fact, there are very few such cases. But there is one that is particularly interesting.

It bears noting that, in general, political Platonism and especially the political philosophy of Neoplatonism are not granted any attention in the historical-philosophical tradition. The classical point of view, represented in Germany by Ehrhardt,[185] is that there was no political project in Neoplatonism, that the Neoplatonists were oriented only

---

184 The present text is based on a presentation at the seventh session of the online Plato Seminar organized by Alexander Dugin and Paideuma TV, "Platonism and Empire," on 4 June 2020.

185 A. Ehrhardt, "The Political Philosophy of Neo-Platonism" in *Studi in onore di Vincenzo Arangio-Ruiz nel XLV anno del suo insegnamento*, vol. 1, ed. M. Lauria (Naples, 1953), 457-82.

towards the inner world, towards ascending along the hierarchy to the One within the individual soul.

This position was criticized in the 20th century by the scholar Dominic O'Meara, who says that there is in fact an historical case of the implementation of political Platonism.[186] This manifestation was in Julian's Empire. Julian himself was a very interesting representative of the Pergamon school of Neoplatonism. If we look at him from the point of view of the Platonic ideal, he is likely truly a ruler who deserved to rule. He did not want to rule and he did not aspire to become a ruler. Ever since childhood, he tried to get away from the menacing threat of gaining power that hung over him. He avoided political action, hid from it, and instead preferred, as Libanius writes, to remain in his inner work, to turn his gaze into himself. His rule, although very short (he ruled only from 361 to 363) became a grand example of the realization of political Platonism. In fact, it is interesting that when the historian Victor Duruy spoke of Julian, he remarked that "dreamers of such a style are rarely to be encountered among princes."[187] This is why we ought to respect Emperor Julian.

The Sun-King

We should direct our attention to the figure of the Sun-King in Julian's political philosophy. In his metaphysics, in his political philosophy, this is de facto the central figure. He elects the Sun-King to be the central metaphysical element, the greatest of the gods. He says that the Sun-King is the leader of the gods, while all the other gods are in symphonic accordance with Helios. For Julian, the sun is a metaphysical phenomenon. At the same time, it also acquires a political dimension. The central position of the Sun, its leading course, corresponds to the position of the Sun-King in the ideal state. In his demiurgic

---

186 Dominic J. O'Meara, *Platonopolis: Platonic Political Philosophy in Late Antiquity* (Oxford: Clarendon Press, 2003).

187 V. Duruy, "Annuaire de l'Association pour l'encouragement des études grecques en France" in *Revue des Études Grecques* 17 (Paris: Revue des Études Grecques, 1883), 177.

activity, the philosopher-ruler is akin to Helios. It is he who gives the rest of the estates their form, their due contours. Just as the sun gives shape to everything and puts everything in its place when it rises, so is the central philosopher-ruler the conduit for true knowledge of the secret nature of things who acts on the basis of this true knowledge.

A connection between Helios and the figure of Apollo can be traced throughout Julian's optic. Let me remind you that Apollo also occupies a central place in Plato's *Republic*. In the fourth book of the *Republic*, Apollo is acknowledged to be the only true legislator. You might recall that, in Socrates' opinion, the laws of the ideal state should be established not on the basis of "previously existing customs" or by some individual will, but on the basis of a transcendent, divine principle. Therefore, in the Platonic state, laws are given like the Delphic prophecies which in fact still need to be deciphered. Only the philosopher-king has a monopoly on this deciphering.

Therefore, the image of the Sun mediator, which in Platonic philosophy corresponds to the figure of the guardian, impressed Emperor Julian so much that in his reform of the army he replaced the motto "In this sign thou shalt conquer" on banners with the dedication "To the invincible sun." A clear testament.

Accordingly, the vivid two years of Julian's reign might be characterized as an attempt at building a universal Platonopolis-Empire. As a true Platonist, he tried to embrace and reform all domains, including the religious. Let us recall that Julian pursued an altogether original religious policy. Unlike other pagans, he issued an edict on religious tolerance. To some extent, this edict was akin to a recognition of some kind of multipolarity, where every part of the Empire has the right to its own faith. This is a modern interpretation, of course, I would even say "wishful thinking" dear to me personally. Historians, without a doubt, interpret Julian to have been a rather strict pagan, but, nevertheless, paganism itself underwent significant reforms under him. This was not simply an attempt to return to the past, but an aspiration to capture eternity itself in becoming, to refresh and renew it.

The question of faith was very important to Julian. In his work *The Roman Empire*, Faddey Zelinsky notes that Julian invested a great deal of effort to reform Hellenistic religion, because, at that time, in Zelinsky's words:

> The sight of the foremost temple in the ancient world, the temple of Apollo at Delphi, caused despondency. And Julian, wishing to hear the voice of the Delphic oracles, sent his theurgists there. The last Pythia proved to be worthy of her predecessors. The sad answer was:
>
>> *Take this message to the lord: of the temple are left ruins,*
>> *Phoebus is not the householder of this shrine and has lost the laurel of the prophets,*
>> *The spring of inspiration has dried up and the Castalian streams have ceased.*[188]

Julian indeed lived in the era of paganism's degeneration, but he nevertheless tried to somehow bring it back to a more authentic form. Indeed, he was not a Christian, but at the same time he was religiously tolerant, which is very important and in principle corresponds to the Platonic optic.

Without a doubt, Julian was a deeply tragic figure. He stood at the edge of a turn of ages. Unfortunately, he did not leave much work behind, because he was constantly drawn into politics, compelled to wage wars, to participate in campaigns, and so on. Nevertheless, he is a very important figure. Although his reign was short-lived, these two years were a visible testimony to the fact that Platonic philosophy can manifest itself in Empire. Although this experience was a tragic one, it is nonetheless important that it took place at all.

Thank you! I hope that this brief outline of the Middle-King Julian was of interest to someone and might prove to be useful in our common Platonic seeking.

***

---

188 F.F. Zelinskii, *Rimskaia Imperiia* (Saint Petersburg: Aleteia, 2020), 425.

The Apophatic Moment

Apophaticism in the Neoplatonic Tradition[189]

The Neoplatonic philosopher Damascius said that the domain of discourse on the inexpressible is the sphere of "hyper-ignorance," ὑπεράγνοια. Simply talking about apophatic theology and the apophatic instance is dangerous. It contains many traps and requires many reservations and digressions. I will try to guide us through these traps. If at some point you and I still fall into a trap, I propose to try to get out of it together.

In order to comprehensively consider the question of the apophatic principle and changes in its interpretation from late Neoplatonism to Christian theology, it is undoubtedly necessary to look at the source of apophatic theology. Here we come to Plato's main dialogue, *Parmenides*, in the first hypothesis of which the One is described as having no parts, not being a whole, having neither beginning nor end, being neither like nor unlike itself or another. Then come characteristics associated with time: the One does not exist in any time. Another important characteristic of interest to us in the context of today's presentation is how the One in no way partakes in being and is therefore somehow non-existent.

In the continued description of this apophatic One, which is ἐπέκεινα τῆς οὐσίας, "beyond being," above everything, a thesis appears that is of importance to the development of apophatic theology: the One has no name, there is no word for it, and there is no possibility of knowing or having an opinion about it, nor is there a possibility of sensibly perceiving it. If we literally quote Plato, we see the following phrasing: "Therefore, no name belongs to it, nor is there an account or any knowledge or perception or opinion of it."[190] Plotinus developed this theme and defined the apophatic One in the following manner:

---

189 The present text is an edited version of a presentation on apophatic theology at a conference of the Platonic Philosophical Society.

190 Plato, *Parmenides* 142a.

Since the nature of the One is what generates all things, it isn't itself one of them. It isn't anything, nor is it of any quality or size, nor is it either Intellect or Soul. It is neither moving nor standing still, nor in place nor period, but it is 'itself by itself, of only one form,' or rather of no form at all, being before all form, before motion, before rest. These things are part of being, and are what makes being many.[191]

This aspect is what interests us. The first hypothesis of Plato's *Parmenides* will be taken as one of the starting points in the development of apophatic theology in Platonism, first by Plato, then by Proclus, Damascius, and all the others.

Yuri Shichalin's Three Phases of Platonism

When Yuri Shichalin described the historical-philosophical process of ancient philosophy, he divided it into three periods. Using the prism of Neoplatonism, he distinguished:

1. The era of μονή (abiding)
2. The era of πρόοδος (descent, emanation, procession, for which Shichalin uses the term "fragmentation" in the sense of the partial reproduction of a model)
3. The era of ἐπιστροφή (return)

Abiding is Platonism proper. The descending emanation is the philosophy that began with Plato and continued up until the advent of the Neoplatonists. For a period of 300 years of πρόοδος, according to Shichalin, there were several divided schools, which corresponds to the fragmenting of the Platonic One into many. This is a brilliant intellectual find — the idea that 300 years after Plato, Greek philosophy was in a stage of fragmentation. This is a very successful application of the Neoplatonic triad to the historical-philosophical process.

Then follows the period of ἐπιστροφή, which Shichalin links with the period of late Platonism. This is the return to the source. Here he singles out Plotinus as the man and philosopher who made a radical turn towards the One. A radical turn to

---

[191] Plotinus, *Ennead* VI.9, trans. Stephen R.L. Clark (Las Vegas: Parmenides Publishing, 2020), 43.

return. Neoplatonic philosophy and the apophatic theology that constitutes the center of all Neoplatonic philosophy began to actively develop with Plotinus. Plotinus' famous *Ennead* VI.9, "On the Good or the One," describes the incomprehensibility of the One thusly:

> The puzzle arises because there's no understanding of the One by demonstrative science, nor by intuition, as with other objects of thought, but through a presence that is more powerful than demonstrative knowledge... So we must run up above such knowledge, in and in no way depart from being one, but rather we must stand aside from knowledge and from what is known, and from every other vision, even a beautiful vision. For every beauty comes after the One, and derives from it, just as the light of day is from the sun.[192]

I will quote the first part in Greek: Γίνεται δε η απορία μάλιστα, οτι μηδέ κατ" επιστημιψ η σύνεσις εκείνου μηδε κατά νόησιν, ώσπερ τα άλλα νοητά, αλλά κατά παρουσίαν επιστημης κρείττονα. Pay attention here to the term "παρουσία," that is the "presence" or "phenomenon" that is higher than "demonstrative knowledge" (or science). Neoplatonism is precisely an orientation towards the source that is above, to that which is before the emanation (πρόοδος), the principle and source of all that is at once nothing, as it is above and beyond our perception. Out of all of the Platonic tradition, Neoplatonism is oriented towards returning to the One (ἐπιστροφή). Therefore, it is precisely in Neoplatonism that apophatic theology is most clearly articulated. Apophatic theology is already fully present in Plato, albeit implicitly, as a possibility. Its disclosure, that is the very path of theoretical and supra-theoretical return, begins with the Neoplatonists. They are the ones who begin the process of ἐπιστροφή in the context of the Platonic tradition.

Proclus and the Systematization of the One

The pinnacle of the development of the apophatic method in Neoplatonism is undoubtedly Proclus. Here I am talking about his *Commentary on the Parmenides*, a genius work

---
192 Ibid., 44-45.

in which Proclus for the first time systematically expounded the apophatic method as the only possible way of reasoning, speaking, and thinking about the One.[193] He brings all previous versions of apophaticism into something whole and describes in detail the entire theoretical edifice of negative theology. First and foremost, he systematizes negation and reveals two versions of it: higher negation, which is what transcends affirmation, and lesser negation, which is below affirmation.

On Proclus' development of apophatic theology and his systematization of Plato and Plotinus' philosophies, Dodds wrote that Proclus overcame the yawning abyss that Plotinus had left behind.[194] In Proclus, apophatic theology begins with the distinction between negations and continues through identifying the different types of the One, of which Proclus recognizes three:

1. The One that is beyond being and stands above the whole world of beings. This One contains everything, including Plotinus' two hypostases, the Intellect and the Soul, from which the whole intelligible and corporeal cosmos is created.

2. The One that is adjacent to being. This is the Intellect, Plotinus' second hypostasis. Here it may be said that the One exists, but through such an affirmation the One ceases to be strictly the One and becomes the approximate One, i.e., the One is posited rhetorically, not logically.

3. The One that stands below being. This is the result of the partition of its integral wholeness into parts which ultimately lose their connection with the whole. This "one" corresponds to Democritus' (and the democratic) atom.

---

193 Proclus, *Commentary on Plato's Parmenides*, trans. Glenn R. Morrow and John M. Dillon (Princeton: Princeton University Press, 1987).

194 Proclus, *The Elements of Theology*, trans. E.R. Dodds (Oxford: Clarendon Press, 1964).

Thanks to this division, Proclus solves the paradox that had forced its way throughout the array of Platonic philosophy due to numerous referrals of the One to various meanings. If you read Plato, then each time the concept of the One is mentioned, it has its own context and is always very specific. When we talk about the One, if we want to be precise, we need to follow the Proclean method of distinguishing between the three types of the One. This is important.

The Apophatic Moment: The Beginning of the Point of Return

Now we pass directly to apophatic theology. Apophatic theology in Neoplatonism as well as in Christianity (I work primarily on Dionysius the Areopagite) begins whenever the thinker embarks on the path of ἐπιστροφή, when the philosopher turns away from "this world" into which he is thrown and turns his gaze towards the source of being, towards the spiritual source, the progenitor. If we take Christian theology, then naturally this source will be God. If we are looking at Neoplatonism, then we will encounter the concept of the One, the Supreme Principle.

Apart from the fact that it begins at this moment of return, the moment of ἐπιστροφή, apophatic theology is also co-present with this ascent. It is very important to take note of the spontaneity and suddenness of the apophatic leap. It is not as if everything is the same as when we first pass through the realm of cataphaticism, sorting out the best qualities of the world, and then we suddenly make some kind of leap, breaking with this world and moving into an apophatic experience. If we describe this process linearly, then perhaps such an experience takes place. But already in the philosopher's very pulse, in his directional intentionality and reorientation towards the One or God, the apophatic moment is already primordially there, like a rupture of levels, a sharp passage from one level to another — starting with the level of the cosmos and moving to the level of the Soul, and further from the level of the Soul to the hypostasis of the Intellect. This experience itself harbors an apophatic element.

It is a mystical experience, an experience of a rupture, a crack, a break.

Look, for instance, at how we can perceive beauty. The classical Platonic model is a consistent ascent from beauty within a single person to the beauty of knowledge, further to the unfolding of beauty up to the beauty of the Soul and the Intellect, and then beauty as an idea, that is beauty in and of itself. But in the very notion of beauty, there is something inexplicable, inexpressible, eluding any definitions, and this means that beauty's roots lie in the realm of the ineffable, in the realm of Hyper-Ignorance.

My main thesis which I would like to express today more as a hypothesis than as the final result of a fully-fledged philosophical study, is that apophaticism is co-present with and within a person already in the moment they begin the path of turning to return (ἐπιστροφή). Apophaticism begins in the moment of ἐπιστροφή. It seems to me that it is very important to understand apophaticism precisely as a moment, as something sudden, as an instant that is co-present with the very process of return. This is the first thesis.

Apophaticism and Mysticism

The second thesis is the link between apophaticism and mysticism. In Christian theology, the experience of mystically understanding God is woven into the Orthodox dogmas themselves. Exploring my own experience of living Orthodoxy as a spiritual tradition, I've come to the conclusion that the presence of the apophatic, ineffable principle that is beyond the control of the mind is clearly manifested at all stages of the Christian life, from its very beginnings. This was probably also the case in Catholicism, at least up until the eras when it was affected by rationalism, modern deism, and the emasculated philosophy of Modernity.

Apophatic theology is connected with mystical experience. It is an encounter with the mysterious, hidden, piercing presence that happens through a rupture of level, "*la rottura del livello*," as Julius Evola called it, a break with the everyday and ordinary. The etymology of the word μυστικός means hidden, secret. It comes from the verb μυέω, meaning "I close my eyes." This implies turning one's gaze from the exterior to the inner space. Mystical experience is the main methodology of apophatic theology. It is presented both in Christianity and in the tradition of apophatic theology developed within Neoplatonism. In his article "Mysticism and Doctrine in Plotinus," published in 1948, Émile Bréhier wrote that the word "mysticism" is most suitable for Plotinus.[195] Plotinus was a mystic. Bréhier defines mysticism as an immediate, direct, sudden, unexpected experience of the divine. Itself rare, it is often a brief, instantaneous experience of presence that does not fit into the framework of normal, everyday experience, and for this reason is accompanied by a deep shock of consciousness, a feeling of oneness, of unifying and merging with higher reality that erases all self-consciousness. This is an experience of real rupture with habitual given experience towards something other, something beyond, something that is absolutely not given and is mysterious and enigmatic.

At Saint Petersburg University, there was a special course entitled "Mysticism in Christianity." In one of the lectures, our colleague (who has been present at these Plato seminars) Karl Jaspers' metaphor was applied. This metaphor is quite simple, but vividly shows the experience of mystical rupture and can be taken to refer to what happens to a person when they pass into the apophatic realm. Jaspers talks about two concepts borrowed from Martin Heidegger: "we-being" and "not-we-being." These are two spheres. One is open to us, the other is completely remote from us. The mystical experience is precisely an experience of crossing this border. To some extent, it is similar to what the post-structuralists call "transgressive experience," meaning a gesture directed towards a boundary, at overcoming a boundary. Accordingly, what is inevitably

---

195 Émile Bréhier, *The Philosophy of Plotinus*, trans. Joseph Thomas (Chicago: University of Chicago Press, 1958).

present in apophatic theology is this mystical experience and the experience of passage, of building an axis that is absolutely transcendent in relation to what is given. This is an experience of absolute loneliness, an experience of a pure exit and taking leave. I'll reemphasize that the Evolian term *"la rottura del livello"* perhaps comes as close as possible to describing this.

To sum up my propositions in two theses:

1. The experience of apophaticism begins in the moment of man's return, it is co-present with man's turn, with his pivot in the Platonic cave, when the prisoner is freed from his shackles and turns towards the source of light. At first, he sees vague outlines, then his eyes get used to distinguishing more contrasting figures, and then begins the course of ascent.

2. The whole sphere of apophaticism is connected with mysticism, with turning to the secret side of things. This is manifest both in the Neoplatonic tradition and in Christianity. The most striking and extreme case of such an experience is the vision of the inexpressible Light of Tabor beyond creation.

***

Apophatic Tradition in the Theology of Dionysius the Areopagite

Christian Platonism

The oeuvre of the renowned Christian theologian and mystic whose works have become part of Christian tradition under the name "Dionysius the Areopagite" represents a unique phenomenon in the history of philosophical and religious thought. These works exerted an immense influence on the philosophy of Christianity, both Eastern and Western, as well as the philosophical thought of Modernity that in one way or another dates back to the Middle Ages, when the Areopagitic works played an important role.

Virtually all scholars of the Areopagitic corpus concur that we are dealing with Platonism in Christian form. As follows, we ought to situate it within the general context of Platonic philosophy in order to understand its place and examine its peculiarities.

The Areopagitic works have been reliably known since the 5th century AD. This means that they are separated from Plato himself and his Academy by approximately 10 centuries. Over this span of time, Platonism underwent a series of fundamental metamorphoses, institutionalizations, and interpretive shifts which need to be outlined in the most general terms in order to understand the historical-philosophical process that unfolded between Plato (6th-5th centuries BC) and the Areopagite (5th century AD). This period can be divided into three phases:

1. The Academy after Plato (Speusippus, Xenocrates, etc.), of which we have rather few reliable facts. Accurately determining the philosophical specificities of this school is problematic today by virtue of the presence of extremely scarce evidence.

2. Middle Platonism (Posidonius, Plutarch of Chaeronea, Apuleius, Philo)
3. Neoplatonism, which arose in Alexandria and right at the outset was divided into two schools: the pagan (Plotinus, Porphyry, etc.) and the Christian (Clement of Alexandria, Origen, etc.)

Neoplatonic Paideia

The Areopagitic corpus is closely adjacent to Neoplatonism, the peculiarity of this relation consists in the fact that we encounter the influence of both Neoplatonic tendencies at the same time: the Origenist (which indirectly even predetermined the dogmatic foundations of Christianity) and the pagan (embodied in the 5th century in the monumental philosophical and theological system of Proclus Diadochus, who devoted unprecedented effort to systematizing Platonism as a whole).

In the most general approximation, we can see the first stage as the continuation of Plato's *paideia* in the direction set by Plato himself: the improvement of philosophical discourse and hermeneutic practices in the general vein of the Platonic approach — i.e., without highlighting priorities and convincing attempts at systematizing Plato's own teaching. At the second stage began a systematization that led to the identification of key points in Plato's teaching, including a grappling with contradictions, problematic segments, and conflicting interpretations.

What is extremely important for us here is that Plato's teaching was for the first time being subjected to correlation with theological knowledge, which is to say that it was theologized. This can be seen first and foremost in the work of Philo of Alexandria, who attempted to correlate the Platonic philosophy and cosmology of the *Timaeus* with the religion of the Old Testament and its dogmatic postulates, such as the Creator God, monotheism, etc. Here, for the first time, the problem was posed of how the Platonic ideas and the Platonic demiurge relate to each other, and how they can be connected with the personal God of Judaic monotheism. Philo later exerted an immense influence on the formulation of Christian dogma. Accordingly, his philosophy's correlation of Platonism and theology was of key importance to everything that followed.

After Philo, the Christian Gnostics (first and foremost Basilides) formed an important link in the development of Platonism. As Plotinus conveys in detail in *Ennead* II.9, many of the latter were decisively influenced by Plato. However, the Gnostics read Plato through the prism of Middle Platonism, particularly the works of Philo, as well as in the context of early Christianity's heightened conceptualizing of how the New Testament and the era of grace relate to the Old Testament and the era of law. Among the Gnostics, this relation took on an antagonistic expression that led to dualism. What is important for us is that this dualism was formalized with the help of Platonic philosophy. Therefore, we can say that Christian Gnosticism represented a peculiar, dualistic version of Platonism.

Non-Dual Platonism

The schools of Plotinus and Origen, which is to say Neoplatonism, the third phase in the formation of the current that led directly to the author of the Areopagitic works, were the result of the development of Middle Platonism and, to a significant extent, a response to the dualistic Platonism of the Gnostics. Polemics were waged with the Gnostics not only by Clement of Alexandria and Origen, but also Plotinus. The rejection of Gnosticism pushed them to develop a dialectical and systematized Platonism that could take on the challenge of the theologization and duality that were characteristic of the Middle Platonists and Gnostics in order to give them a decidedly non-dual response. If we may borrow a term from Hindu philosophy, we could call Neoplatonism "Advaita-Platonism."

Areopagitic mystical theology fully fits into this context and is a vivid model of such a non-dual Platonism, although it is less systematized and developed than Origin or Proclus' systems. At the same time, the 5th century saw an attenuation of the dogmatic impulse that had enlivened the previous centuries' Greco-Roman patristics, and thereby anticipated the ensuing era of the Christian Middle Ages. The style and conceptual apparatus of the Areopagitic corpus could not have better fit such a transitional period. It crowned the era of Neoplatonism on the one hand and Greco-Roman patristics on the other, but at the same time constituted one of the most important influences and vectors for the future development of Christian thought, including Western European Scholasticism from John Scotus Eriugena to Thomas Aquinas.

In the Areopagitic corpus, we see a transition from the developed Neoplatonism of its peak to a Christian tradition that was picking up the most valuable vectors of Platonism and combining them with its foremost dogmatic premises. The Platonists' "unknown god" was revealed to be the God of Christianity, in his essence remaining unknowable, unattainable, and apophatic. If by "being" we understand the being with which we are dealing in creation, then God is radically above such being and has no common measure with it. Any movement by the human soul towards God means turning to the unknown and ineffable. Only in this way, by preserving the inaccessibility of the Divine nature, its mystery, and concealment, could theology be saved from the profanation and rationalization that destroy its true proportions.

The same goes for the Neoplatonic "return" (ἐπιστροφή). St. Maximus the confessor, the most famous commentator on the Areopagitic corpus, employs a similar term, μεταστροφή, that is "conversion," "turning," which is close in meaning to μετάνοια, that is literally "turning the mind," "converting the mind," which in Russian is commonly translated as *pokaianie* ("repentance"). Maximus the Confessor says that all forms are dispensed over the process of the mind coming to knowledge up above, which becomes ἄμορφος, "formless," and ἀσχημάτιστος, "shapeless," which is to say "apophatic" and therefore in the likeness of God himself.

The Christian is called on their religious path to "turn," to "convert," to change their orientation, to move in the direction of heaven instead of being exclusively concerned with earthly things. This is the "return of the prodigal son." Neoplatonism is extremely helpful for describing the stages of this return in detail. But, from the very outset, such a description will only be effective if we humbly realize that we will not achieve anything on this path without God's help. We draw near to Him only once He gracefully descends to draw near to us. Yet, this moment is incomprehensible and miraculous.

***

PART IV:
PHILOSOPHICAL FRAGMENTS AND THE INVOLUTION OF MODERNITY

The Voluptuous Universe of Lucretius Carus

Anticipating Modernity[196]

Titus Lucretius Carus (c. 99-55 BC) was heir to the philosophical current of Epicureanism, which was rather widespread and popular in the era of Greco-Roman antiquity. The beauty of his poetic style, his convincing existential illustrations of basic philosophical positions, his appeal to death and fighting against the fear that death instills, and the dialectical character of his description of the dynamics of cosmic processes — all of this lends Lucretius' ideas and texts a special force of attraction that compelled many generations of ancient intellectuals to study his works.

In the modern era (New Time), Lucretius' atomism and Epicureanism became so popular that they formed the basis for the modern scientific "world picture" through Galileo and Gassendi. Thus, it is completely legitimate to consider Lucretius Carus one of the main architects of Modernity.

Immanentism

Like Epicurus, Lucretius' philosophy was based on hedonism, on the idea of the primacy of personal well-being, pleasure, and happiness acquired over the course of a life spent whirling around in the world of sensual things, feelings, and images. Lucretius' universe is self-sufficient, wonderful, and therefore harmonious. Being harmonious, it is eternal. In contrast to Plato's problematic topology, Lucretius rejected the "second world," the world of ideas, the world of necessity, the noetic universe that lies "elsewhere." There is only this world, and no other. Such a recognition is the starting axiom of the poem *On the Nature of Things* (*De Rerum Natura*) and defines the whole structure of its fully-fledged, complete immanentism.

---

196 The present text was an essay written for one of Daria Platonova Dugina's courses at the Faculty of Philosophy of Moscow State University.

It is noteworthy that if Plato and the Platonists two thousand years ago created an essentially complete picture of philosophical dualism with a double topology (as Martin Heidegger wrote), i.e., classical ontology, which few subsequent philosophers managed to radically change — unless, of course, they disagreed with idealism and noocentrism — then Lucretius' world picture anticipated the main features of the physics of Modernity which has remained unchanged in its philosophical premises ever since the time of Lucretius' elegant poetic argumentation.

Removing the Problem of the Nothing

It is telling that the poem begins with a hymn to Venus, the progenitor of Aeneas and, as follows, of all Romans[197]:

Aeneadum genetrix, hominum divomque voluptas,	Mother of Romans, joy of gods and men,
alma Venus, caeli subter labentia signa	Venus, life-giver, who under planet and star
quae mare navigerum, quae terras frugiferentis	visits the ship-clad sea, the grain-clothed land
concelebras, per te quoniam genus omne animantum	always, for through you all that's born and breathes
concipitur visitque exortum lumina solis.	is gotten, created, brought forth to see the sun

The goddess of voluptuousness, bodily joys, and pleasures is not chosen here by chance: it is these qualities that constitute the philosophical norm of Epicurean ethics, that of *homo voluptas*. The anthropology of this "voluptuous human" constitutes the corresponding world in which this human would be comfortable. This world stands on the following postulates described in elegant detail throughout the poem:

---

197 [The following English translations are from Lucretius, *The Nature of Things*, trans. Frank O. Copley (New York: W.W. Norton & Company, 1977). For alternative renderings, see Lucretius, *On the Nature of Things*, trans. Martin Ferguson Smith (Indianapolis: Hackett Publishing Company, 2001) — Trans.]

Principium cuius hinc nobis exordia sumet,	[...by the face of nature and her laws]
nullam rem e nihilo gigni divinitus umquam.	And this is her first, from which we take our start:
	nothing was ever by miracle made from nothing

The problem of nothing is thus removed once and for all. The world is given to us immediately as an actual infinitude that dynamically moves by and within itself. Pleasure is this "in and of itself." Any eschatology or theology no longer has a place. The absence of the nothing is the philosophical guarantee of Epicurean happiness.

Huc accedit uti quicque in sua corpora rursum	And now add this: nature breaks up all things
dissoluat natura neque ad nihilum interemat res.	into their atoms; no thing dies off to nothing.

Since nothing is created out of nothing, nothing disappears. This inspires Lucretius with a fundamental optimism. Lucretius argues for the absence of irreversible death with a faith in the goodness of nature:

nam siquid mortale e cunctis partibus esset,	For if a thing were mortal in all its parts,
ex oculis res quaeque repente erepta periret;	it would be whisked away, just drop from sight,
nulla vi foret usus enim, quae partibus eius	since there would be no need of force to wrench
discidium parere et nexus exsolvere posset.	one part from another, or to dissolve their bonds.
quod nunc, aeterno quia constant semine quaeque,	But things are made of atoms; they are stable.

donec vis obiit, quae res diverberet ictu	Until some force comes, hits them hard, and splits them,
aut intus penetret per inania dissoluatque,	or seeps to their inner parts and makes them burst,
nullius exitium patitur natura videri.	nature brings no destruction to our sight.

Further comes another interesting referent to Venus, the mother of voluptuousness identified with "nature":

Praeterea quae cumque vetustate amovet aetas,	Besides, take things that time removes through aging:
si penitus peremit consumens materiem omnem,	if when they died their matter were all consumed,
unde animale genus generatim in lumina vitae	whence does Venus bring animals forth to life
redducit Venus, aut redductum daedala tellus	kind after kind, and earth, the magic-maker,
unde alit atque auget generatim pabula praebens?	nourish, increase, and feed them, kind by kind?
unde mare ingenuei fontes externaque longe	Whence could native fountains and far-flung rivers
flumina suppeditant? unde aether sidera pascit?	supply the sea? Whence ether feed the stars?
omnia enim debet, mortali corpore quae sunt,	For everything of mortal mass long since
infinita aetas consumpse ante acta diesque.	had been used up as boundless time passed by.
quod si in eo spatio atque ante acta aetate fuere	But if the stuff of which this sum of things
e quibus haec rerum consistit summa refecta,	is built has lasted down through empty ages,
inmortali sunt natura praedita certe.	surely it is endowed with deathless nature;
haud igitur possunt ad nilum quaeque reverti.	no thing, therefore, can be reduced to nothing.

Physics under the Sign of Venus: *Homo Voluptas*

In Lucretius' universe, voluptuousness is the law, and this magical materialism is built on the total predominance of the laws of Venus permeating all cosmology. These laws of the "eternalization" of matter in the dominion of Venus-Nature require the presence of something hidden which would be the deep foundation of the voluptuous order of things. This hidden principle is the structure of the invisible pair of atoms and void:

Nunc age, res quoniam docui non posse creari	Come, now: I've shown that things cannot be made
de nihilo neque item genitas ad nil revocari,	from nothing nor, once made, be brought to nothing
ne qua forte tamen coeptes diffidere dictis,	Still, lest you happen to mistrust my words
quod nequeunt oculis rerum primordia cerni,	because the eye cannot perceive prime bodies,
accipe praeterea quae corpora tute necessest	hear now of particles you must admit
confiteare esse in rebus nec posse videri.	exist in the world and yet cannot be seen.

Atoms and emptiness are essentially the blueprint of the voluptuous world picture, one which consists of indestructible and indecomposable singularities (necessary for eternity) and a void between them. Singularities love each other, yearn for each other, entangle and disengage from one another only to reattach. This lasts for eternity. Everything in such a world both changes and remains the same.

The secret of happiness was thus found by Lucretius Carus. And all other philosophers, as he expressively argues in his rhythmic and refined lines, have been mistaken.

Lucretius' philosophy was received in the Renaissance in both of its hypostases: as an atomic-scientific philosophy and as an ecstatic-Hermetic philosophy. Gassendi, in fact, used

Lucretius to substantiate the reality of alchemical transmutation of lead into gold (*pan-chrysium*), and we encounter the theory of entanglements developed in the ecstatic theology of the Platonist Bruno.

However, after Descartes and Newton, the voluptuousness of the universe of Venus left the domain of modern science and passed into the realm of art. The tension subsided and Epicurean atomism lost its poetic quality. In liberalism and liberal libertarianism ("li-li"), the last flashes of Lucretius' gallant materialism ultimately degenerated into pan-sexism.

***

Wolffian Theology and Gogol's Insight into Decay

The Philosophy of Modernity and its Refraction in Russia[198]

Western philosophy came to Russia in rather strange ways. There was no logic or consistent sequence. We took some things from the West, often by coincidence, such as whatever was popular there, while neglecting other more important things. Hence the quirkiness of Russian-Western philosophical dialogue. At times, these fragments have been reconciled with each other in absolutely exotic ways. Logic was taken and turned into morality, and dry rational philosophy inspired writers and poets to completely unanticipated conclusions and images.

Despite the fact that Russian thinkers and writers have at times interpreted Western philosophy in completely arbitrary, even distorted ways, they have grasped some of its aspects so penetratingly that it even began to seem to the West that Russians had discovered something new and unexpected that had eluded them.

On the whole, the correlation between Western European thought and its reading in Russia in the 18th-19th centuries is a separate topic. Proceeding from the chaotic nature of this reception, we can draw any number of parallels and compare both obvious sources of influence and less apparent ones.

Yet, the most profound and the most original Russian authors understood what is foremost in the Western culture of Modernity. Vladimir Solovyov referred to this as the atomization of culture, individualistic disintegration into fragments, and he saw in this the fate of European Modernity. In the very beginning of his programmatic article "Three Forces," Solovyov spoke of a culture of forced unity which he identified with the

---

[198] The present text was an essay written for one of Daria Platonova Dugina's courses at the Faculty of Philosophy of Moscow State University.

East and a second, opposing force, that of the modern West. Solovyov wrote of the Western cultural force:

> It strives to break the stronghold of dead unity, to everywhere give freedom to individual forms of life, freedom to the individual and his activity; under its influence, individual elements of mankind become the starting points for life, act exclusively from and for themselves, and the common loses the significance of real, essential being, and turns into something abstract, empty, into a formal law, and finally is completely deprived of any meaning. Universal egoism and anarchy, a multitude of individual units lacking any inner connection — this is the extreme expression of this force. If it were to attain sole dominance, then mankind would disintegrate into components, the connection of life would be torn asunder, and history would end in a war of all against all with the self-destruction of mankind.[199]

Indeed, the European civilization of Modernity led to this "universal egoism and anarchy" and "multitude of individuals lacking any inner connection." Despite the fact that it all began with a completely unifying, universalist rationalism — Descartes and even more so Leibniz and his followers — the West moved towards none other than gradual disintegration and the decomposition of society into atoms. Russians saw this process in its full scale and posed the question: Who will stop this from developing to dismember the human being as such? After all, the unleashed force of civilization exceeds the capacities of the individual. This means that, starting from the universal monad and its teleology, we arrive not only at the individual, but to even more advanced phases in the breaking up of the human being into individual parts.

These considerations have led me to pose for comparison two completely heterogenous figures: the neat and pedantic German philosopher Christian Wolff, a follower of Leibniz, and the genius Russian writer Nikolai Gogol.

From Leibniz to Wolff

Christian Wolff was one of those thinkers who laid the foundations of the philosophy of New Time (Modernity).

---
199 V. Solov'ev, "*Tri sily*" (1877) [https://www.vehi.net/soloviev/trisily.html].

God the Mathematician and the Hierarchy of Monads

For Wolff, the world was created by God the mathematician. This world is strictly determined by mathematical laws and consists of mechanisms in which all things have the end of serving man. To some extent, Wolff's concept of theology is a development of Leibniz's hierarchy of monads that ranges from lower (sleeping) monads to animals and finally to man. Human monads (souls) praise God and build the Heavenly City. Wolff shares Leibniz's conclusion that "the totality of all spirits must compose the City of God, that is to say, the most perfect State that is possible, under the most perfect of Monarchs."[203] God, according to Leibniz, is the "Architect of the mechanism of the universe" and the "Monarch of the divine City of spirits."[204]

The body becomes the state of monads, and the soul becomes the "ideal ruler." In Leibniz, this hierarchy is established by mathematical laws and is a state of permanent, pre-established harmony. Wolff appends the teleology of the lower monads to the higher ones, which is to say that the lower has its purpose in serving the higher. Thus, matter finds itself in the position of being a servant of the spirit.

This intersects with Wolff's political philosophy, in which he appears to be an advocate of the Platonic state of philosophers.[205] The monad's end has the character of a gradual climb up the ladder: the blind monads serve animal monads ("food chains" per Wolff), and animals serve humans. The telos is taken outwards to another level. Wolff argues that animals, of whatever kind they may be, whether the largest quadrupeds or the smallest insect, have neither meaning nor reason nor will nor freedom, and therefore are incapable of knowing God. Therefore, they are insufficient, for God cannot realize his main

---

203 Leibniz, *Monadology* §86.

204 Ibid., §87.

205 Christian Wolff, *De rege philosophante et Philosopho regnante* (Marburg: Renger, 1730).

aim for which he created the world through them.[206] As follows, the animal's telos is to serve man, who is the bearer of higher rationality. Only man is capable of knowing the world.

Reason and Miracle

In this strict system of co-subordinated monads — a kind of special caste state of monads — the question arises: Where are we to put miracles? What practical benefits do they offer a person? Let us recall that miracles will be vehemently criticized in the Enlightenment. Max Weber described this process as the "disenchantment of the world," *Entzauberung der Welt*, and associated it with Protestantism. Wolff does not argue against miracles like Hume does in his *Enquiry Concerning Human Understanding*[207], but rather seeks to interpret them in a rational way. Miracles become natural phenomena acquiring symbolic meaning from God. Thus, the philosopher interprets Genesis 9:13: "I have set my rainbow in the clouds, and it will be the sign of the covenant between me and the earth." The rainbow existed before the flood, but it receives the status of a sign (that is, a miracle) at a particular moment. Its purpose is to serve as a sign of reconciliation, of the Covenant, laid down during creation, but it manifests itself in a moment of time strictly allotted by God. Wolff wrote:

> "You can establish its origin as much as you like, observe its colors and other properties in the most accurate way, and still never reach the conclusion that God did not want to punish people with a flood ever again, i.e., in this way he established the course of nature, which made a universal flood no longer possible by any natural means, and no miracle is required to produce it. Only God can work miracles, but God prefers the natural course of things to sudden miracles that disrupt it. Divine wisdom creates the course of things founded on laws, and the miracle is a manifestation of power, of the omnipotence of the Divine."[208]

---

206 Christian Wolff, *Vernünfige Gedancken von Gott, der Welt und der Seele des Menschen* (Halle: Renger, 1720).

207 David Hume, *An Enquiry Concerning Human Understanding*, ed. Tom L. Beauchamp (Oxford: Oxford University Press, 1999).

208 Morozov, "M.V. Lomonosov i teleologiia Khristiana Wol'fa."

For Wolff, thus, a miracle is something completely rational. Miracle is not the pinnacle of teleology, but only a rich affirmation of the rationality of the world. Moreover, with respect to Leibniz's identity of monads, Wolff shifts the center of the subject towards the individual and the surrounding world arranged by God the mathematician. This is a partial step towards Newton, but not yet a decisive one.

Gogol and the Philosophy of Miracle

When you begin to analyze Gogol's works, it might seem that his ideas are extremely remote from the strict philosophical theses of Christian Wolff. In his time, however, the educated class in Russian society was well acquainted with European philosophy, and the fact that Lomonosov himself translated Wolff's works gave this German thinker special significance. Gogol knew the German language very well from gymnasium and he very well could have become acquainted with Wolff's works in their original tongue.

Through Wolff, Russian society became acquainted with the Western philosophy of Modernity as a whole. Surely, Russians were impressed by the integrality of Leibniz's theory and its rational piety. But the most attentive Russian minds probably noticed the downside of hyper-rationalization. Monads fragmented and miracles disappeared. As if in response to this, Russian writers created their own literary and poetic ontologies, their own worlds, in which the West collided with Russia in an at times dramatic and combative manner. In Gogol and Dostoevsky, this clash gave rise to a painful contrast.

In utter contrast to the growing pan-rationalism and *Entzauberung* of Europe, the world of Gogol's works features endless miracles: the moon is abducted by the devil, deals are made with witches, drowned women are resurrected, a nose walks down the capital's boulevards, etc. These episodes look like Christmas season carols accompanied by the release of dark forces, of demons, mythological entities, omens, and symbols from dreams.

Let us recall Wolff's teleology of the Northern Lights, which are interpreted to be like nighttime lighting for the city. Does Gogol's moon serve to light the way for man? No, the moon is stolen by the devil who is trying to take revenge on the blacksmith Vakula for depicting him on icons in an inappropriate guise. In *Evenings on a Farm near Dikanka*, we behold a mythological, "un-unenchanted" world of pure tradition and sacrality in which there is no strict division between good and evil and where the sacred lives in all of its diversity and fullness.

There is no strict rationalism here, no teleology and scientific categorization of signs. It is also impossible to distinguish any utilitarian teleology in Gogol's works on landlords, such as *Dead Souls, The Inspector General*, etc. The aim of Chichikov's rational, albeit not entirely legal operations is ultimately absurd. He tries to pave the way to the heights of society in accordance with a formally rational system, relying on lacunae in the legislation he notices which allow, according to the documents, him to consider dead peasants to be "alive." Chichikov has a teleology, but in Russian conditions it does not lead him anywhere. Not only are the machinations discovered after his ephemeral triumph, but the very aim gradually dissolves amidst the swelling labyrinth of the absurdity of Russian life.

Gogol's world is irrational, nothing adds up in it. Hierarchies are broken and goals are grotesquely displaced. The dead souls (blind monads?) become a means for realizing the immoral aim of acquiring unrighteous income. This is a kind of ironic critique of utilitarian teleology. Through the dead souls that become Chichikov's tool for generating income, Gogol highlights the immoral essence of the utilitarian approach. Perceiving the lower monads as mechanisms, man loses his organic connection with the miraculous structure of the world.

In *The Inspector General*, Gogol ironically describes Khlestakov as the eschatological figure of the Antichrist, as the one who comes before Christ or instead of Christ (*anti-Christus* or *ante-Christus*). Once again, the rational strategy on the part of the bureaucracy of a small Russian county town faces the yawning abyss of parody. They bow to the wrong one. The aims implode.

The Loss of Meaning: Mr. Nose

In the *Petersburg Tales*, everything that exists completely loses its meaning. We find a nose strolling along the avenues of the moonlit city. Is this the body without organs, a systems failure in the ruling monad's governance over the corporeal state?[209] Why and for what does this lonely nose, sniffling with a cold, exist?

The nose embodies the disintegration of the optimistic "pre-established harmony" which neither Wolff nor his teacher Leibniz doubted. Being a small monad within the constitution of the generalizing monad of the whole organism, the nose is supposed to unquestioningly fulfill its functions and be in its "natural" place. But in Gogol, it rises up in the form of a black miracle and in so doing challenges the "pre-established harmony." The world of European rationalism begins to disintegrate in the midst of Gogol's Russian reality, and the secondary monads rise up against higher logic.

The nose manically pursues the goal of becoming an independent master. Thus, the state of organs enters the era of democracy, where every part is for itself and the hierarchy of the monads has been abolished. This frightened Gogol — this could not possibly be the aim of enlightening society. Therefore, Gogol called for correlating progress with God and Christian ethics.[210] His anti-heroes, from the nose to the devil,

---

[209] Antonin Artaud's concept of the "body without organs" became one of the most important elements in the Postmodernist philosophy of Gilles Deleuze.

[210] "For a Christian there is no graduation: he is eternally a pupil, a pupil until the grave... He who already has intelligence and reason cannot receive wisdom otherwise than by praying for it day and night, asking God for it day and night, raising his soul to the mildness of the dove and gathering into his very inner self all possible purity in order to admit that celestial guest who shies away from dwellings to which a moral order and an absolute harmony in all things has not come." — Nikolai Gogol, *Selected Passages from Correspondence With Friends*, trans. Jesse Zeldin (Nashville: Vanderbilt University Press, 1969), 68, 70.

demonstrate the danger harbored in Russian society's uncritical acceptance of the Western European rules and standpoints of Modernity.

The Christian Order of the Universe

Gogol critiqued European Modernity and its rationality and called to return to the foundations of the Christian and folk perception of the world. Then the place of black irrationality is taken by other structures — the structures of Premodernity. In one of his letters, Gogol wrote:

> "To enlighten" does not mean to teach, or to edify, or to educate, or even to illuminate, but to illuminate a man through and through in all his faculties and not in his intelligence alone, to take all his nature through a purifying fire. This word is borrowed from our Church, which has pronounced it for almost a thousand years, in spite of all the darkness and ignorant gloom surrounding it on every side, and it knows why it pronounces it. It is not for nothing that the bishop, in the celebration of the service, raising with one hand the three-branched candelabrum, which signifies the Holy Trinity, and with the other the two-branched candelabrum, which signifies the descent to earth of the Word in its double nature, divine and human, by them clarifies everything, pronouncing, "May the light of Christ enlighten all!" It is not for nothing either that at another moment of the service there loudly thunders forth, as though from Heaven, the words: "Lord of enlightenment!" and nothing more is added.[211]

The Light of Christ is not the dry, deistic rationality of the German Enlightenment. It is the secret, mysterious voice of being that transforms the world and makes it miraculous.

Theoretically, of course, Russian philosophy and Russian culture, upon being confronted with the Western Enlightenment, could have chosen a consistent strategy, such as reinterpreting Leibniz in a genuinely Christian, Orthodox key. But herein lies the peculiarity of our psychology: we piercingly see substitution, we feel falsehood, and we anticipate catastrophe. If it reaches our heart, then we turn to our tradition. But we can't manage to consistently correlate one with the other and untie the Gordian

---

211 Ibid., 95.

Knot of European Modernity. Hence, we have the *Petersburg Tales*, the degenerate nobility, the rise of the darkest forces on the one hand, and the troika of Rus' and the Light of Christ on the other. There is nothing between them.

Modernity is Mr. Nose. But how can the nose be put back onto the body, and the body into the soul, and the soul into the Church, and the Church into the Heavenly Kingdom — we surely do not know. In this lies our tragedy: we see that we are rushing into the abyss, we harbor no illusions, and we know what we have lost (in this lies the secret of Russian nostalgia), but how can we turn back? We will not find a clear answer to this in Russian culture, even less so in rudimentary Russian philosophy. Perhaps this is what our founding fathers have left for us.

***

Bergson and Popper's "Open Society": A Traditionalist View

Freedom for the Particular

The concept of the "open society" figures constantly in contemporary political philosophy. On the whole, the "open society" is contrasted to traditional society on the one hand, and contemporary forms of dictatorship and totalitarianism on the other. Today, this concept has practically become the sacred cow of liberalism, and anyone who tries to objectively and detachedly analyze, not to mention directly critique, the "open society" will find themselves blacklisted.

Of course, the open society is the complete and direct antithesis of hierarchy and integrality. It is an expression of the force that Vladimir Solovyov called the desire to "give freedom to individual forms of life" and it expresses the essence of the modern West. The deification of this concept reveals to us the "religious essence" of democracy, which, as it turns out, has its own dogmas, creeds, symbols of faith, and untouchable principles.

However, here I will break these taboos and try to consider the emergence of the concept of the "open society." I will do so on the basis of the two authors who were the first to formulate it: Henri Bergson and Karl Popper.

The Idea of Evolution as Co-Evolution and Divergent Lines

The first to use the expression "open society" was the French philosopher Henri Bergson, who is known as a theorist of evolution and the "vital impulse" (*l'élan vital*). He was led to this concept by applying his philosophical views to social structures. Therefore, a few words should be said about his understanding of evolution.

One of Bergon's central works, *Creative Evolution* (*L'Évolution créatrice*), published in 1907, put forth the idea that the world is a product of evolutionary development. Evolution is understood firstly in its philosophical aspect: as the gradual co-evolution of one single vital impulse (*l'élan vital*), the creative driving force of all living things. Bergson compared this creative force, the "vital impulse," life itself, and consciousness to a rocket that takes off and leaves behind all of its creations: "Consciousness, of supra-consciousness, is the name for the rocket whose extinguished fragments fall back as matter; consciousness, again, is the name for that which subsists of the rocket itself, passing through the fragments and lighten them up into organisms."[212]

This might be interpreted as a version of phenomenology, but this is not the case. Bergon was working to resolve the task of explaining how the linear time of the material world — which as an axiom of Newtonian mechanics and therefore the cornerstone of modern physics, and, moreover, the whole scientific worldview of Modernity — can be correlated with the theory of social progress which, starting in the 18th century, became a dogma in the humanitarian disciplines of European society. In Newton, linearity is strictly neutral, it is the mechanical determination of a process unfolding in the sphere of material bodies and phenomena. There is no progress here. In the public sphere, by contrast, under the influence of the Enlightenment, progress was conceived as the main law of societal development. In order to reconcile these two models — both linear, but arranged in completely different ways — Darwin created the theory of evolution, where there is a transition from inanimate matter to forms of life which, in accordance with the principle of natural selection and the struggle for survival, develop up to man. Thus, progress in society is a kind of continuation of the process of the evolution of species. The founder of Social Darwinism, the English liberal philosopher Herbert Spencer, directly continued Darwin's train

---

[212] Henri Bergson, *Creative Evolution*, trans. Arthur Mitchell (Lanham: Henry Holt and Company, University Press of America, 1911), 261.

of thought and proposed to consider the development of society and its stages as a continuation of the struggle for survival. Thus, a conceptual connection was established between the linearity of material time and social progress.

Bergson critiqued the idea of understanding of the evolutionary process as something which ran from simple to complex as was widely accepted in his time. According to his version, evolution does not occur in a single direction, but consists of parallel developments (and here Bergson is directly polemicizing with Spencer's "evolutionary philosophy"[213]). Bergson critiques mechanicism and teleology, noting in the second chapter of his *Creative Evolution* that the character of evolution absolutely differs from a series of adaptations to circumstances (man, for instance, who is considered to be the pinnacle of evolution, is the least adapted to external circumstances). Mechanistic concepts cannot explain creativity by assuming different combinations of the same elements over the course of evolution. Such concepts do not explain the emergence of anything qualitatively new, first and foremost qualitatively new states of living matter. Mechanistic conceptions offer us only combinations of originally present elements. In addition, the weakness of mechanicism is that it lacks any driving force of evolution. Without this force, according to the second law of thermodynamics, entropy would take over the system of all living things and the state of an organism would become primitive and, ultimately, die. The unified force which Bergson proposes is the vital impulse (*l'élan vital*) or life itself, which mechanistic doctrines completely ignore. Bergson also argues against teleological conceptions which, much like mechanistic ones, are incapable of explaining the emergence of anything new (every new thing already exists in advance either in an ideal space or as some kind of function of the vital impulse that neo-vitalism puts at the heart of the theory of life).

---

213 See Herbert Spencer, *Social Statics, or The Conditions essential to Happiness specified, and the First of them Developed* (London: John Chapman, 1851).

Hence, Bergson appeals to such a category as "consciousness" or "supra-consciousness," in which one can see echoes of Leibniz's monad or Wolff's teleology.

L'élan vital

Bergson gradually creates his own original concept of evolution. Its driving force is the vital impulse, *"l'élan vital,"* which is creative, creating, moving life itself. Life and the "vital impulse" strive forward, i.e., bear a tendency towards creation, towards passion, a force that creates increasingly complex forms in unpredictable designs. The vital impulse is the movement of non-linear rationality as it grows out of the intense movement of living matter.

Matter as such is understood to be the cooling down of this burning activity, like the flakes that have fallen off a rocket during takeoff, like an aspiration for peace. Both matter and life are interpreted to be two aspects of a single rocket flight (the vital impulse). After take off, the parts that break off constitute different forms: immobile plants void of consciousness, animals, and man. Insofar as the hallmark of consciousness is movement, insects are "a-conscious," animals have a weak degree of consciousness, and the human being has the maximum expression of consciousness.[214]

All of these gradations are parts of the singular process of creative evolution. Bergson distinguishes three types of cognitive abilities in creative evolution: instinct, intellect, and intuition. Unlike classical evolutionary theories, these abilities are non-linear and are strictly non-hierarchical: instinct is closer to life than intellect, but it cannot pose the question of the essence of life, as it lives life too intensely and has no distance from it.[215]

---

[214] The notion that animals are "deprived of consciousness" can be found later in the thought of Martin Heidegger, who described animals as "*weltarm*," or "world-poor." See Stuart Elden, "Heidegger's animals," *Continental Philosophy Review* 39 (2006), 273-291.

[215] For Bergson, instinct and intellect represent two divergent developments of one and the same element: in one case, this element is turned inwards, toward the self, while in the other it goes outwards, and everything is consumed by the utilization of inanimate matter.

When intellect becomes itself, it gives rise to a special dimension, this time static and detached from the very element of the vital impulse. It gives rise to the main dialectic of subject and object that is the backbone of philosophy.

Instinct / Intellect / Intuition

In the second chapter of *Creative Evolution*, upon defining the evolutionary movement, Bergson resorts to the image of an artillery shell that explodes into pieces:

> The evolution movement would be a simple one, and we should soon have been able to determine its direction, if life had described a single course, like that of a solid ball shot from a cannon. But it proceeds rather like a shell, which suddenly bursts into fragments, which fragments, being themselves shells, burst in their turn into fragments destined to burst again, and so on for a time incommensurably long. We perceive only what is nearest to us, namely, the scattered movements of the pulverized explosions. From them we have to go back, stage by stage, to the original movement.[216]

The intellect thinks in images of motionless bodies, which is a kind of evolutionary adaptation to working with solid bodies. In the intellect, movement (life) is replaced with immobility, hence all becoming is conceived as a series of states and creativity is discarded. The intellect clearly imagines only the discontinuous, the stopped, the immobile. It strictly dismembers the object of its attention and can reassemble it into any system and establish its relations. The function of the intellect is to find the means of getting out of difficulties under any circumstances. The intellect can be both lower ("predatory") and higher (aspiring to creativity, the intuitive intellect that borders on intuition), but the intellect possesses one serious defect: it is incapable of comprehending life, movement. Bergson formulates the difference between instinct and intellect thusly: "There are things that intelligence alone is able to seek, but which, by itself, it will never find. These things instinct alone could find; but

---

216 Bergson, *Creative Evolution*, 98.

it will never seek them."[217] Further, Bergson deems the intellect to be "characterized by a natural inability to comprehend life."[218]

Unlike intellect, instinct is directed towards life, not dead matter. Bergon's understanding of instinct is peculiar: he uses the notion of sympathy to characterize instinct. The object in instinct, being living and moving, is "grasped" internally, directly, and irrationally. Instinct is a form of sympathy. It is developed to an even greater extent in the world of insects. Instinct knows life from within, without dismembering the world, and its knowing is ceaseless. However, it also has a significant disadvantage compared to the intellect: instinct is incapable of taking any distance in relation to life in order to ask about it. Instinct is incapable of posing the question of the nature of life.

Bergson also puts forth a third kind of cognitive capacity: intuition. The intellect is capable of posing the question of the nature of life, but it is not able to answer it, since it is absolutely distant from life. But the intellect can overcome itself and become intuition. Intuition is the comprehension of life. Unlike instinct, intuition is capable of being conscious of itself, questioning the nature of life, and reflecting on its own object and expanding it into infinity. Bergson points out: "But it is to the very inwardness of life that intuition leads us — by intuition I mean instinct that has become disinterested, self-conscious, capable of reflecting upon its object and of enlarging it indefinitely."[219] It is in intuition that we know life and the vital impulse.

Intuitive Society

Bergson critiqued classical metaphysics and put forth a new model of philosophizing that came to be called "intuitionism." In this French philosopher's opinion, classical metaphysics

---

217 Ibid., 151.

218 Ibid., 165.

219 Ibid., 194.

based itself on the intellect, which does not deal with life itself. Remaining distanced from life, metaphysics tried to present life discontinuously and thereby left it "dead." According to Bergson, it is necessary to build a new type of metaphysics founded on intuition. With such a means of cognition, we can grasp the continuity of life and its diversity.

Bergson's significance in the history of philosophy is grand: as a critic of classical metaphysics, he influenced Martin Heidegger as well as the Postmodernist tradition.[220] However, Bergson's new metaphysics nonetheless remains ambiguous. On the one hand, it continues evolutionary thought, which is to say the Darwinist theory of the evolution of species, bringing it to the stages of human history and thereby combining it with progress. On the other hand, contrary to the evolutionists, and above all the Social Darwinists (like Herbert Spencer), Bergson denied that progress can be interpreted linearly and that the rationality of Modernity can be considered its culmination.

It is no coincidence that Bergson was the first to propose the theory of the "open society," one which differs substantially from the later version put forth by the liberal theorist Karl Popper. Bergson's "open society" is not programmed. Rationality is not the last word in social organization due to the inherent limitations of reason. Therefore, the next stage in evolution is supposed to be the mode of the "intuitive society," in which the life impulse can find the freest and most creative expression. This means rejecting any dogmas, including liberal ones. It is no coincidence, therefore, that Bergson's ideas have drawn such interest from left-oriented philosophers. To the dry analysis of Marx, he added the explosive energies of emancipated vitality.

---

220 Deleuze paid special attention to interpreting three of the main concepts of Bergson's philosophy: duration, memory, and the vital impulse. Proceeding from the standpoint of Deleuzeian philosophy, Bergson's duration is to be interpreted as virtual multiplicity (rhizomatic co-existence), memory as the co-existence of all the levels of differences within this multiplicity, and the vital impulse as the actualization of virtuality in accordance with the differential lines of these levels. See Gilles Deleuze, *Bergsonism*, trans. Hugh Tomlinson and Barbara Habberjam (New York: Zone Books, 1991).

Bergson's Open Society as Determined by the Flow of Life Alone

The application of Bergson's basic principles to social life yields an altogether peculiar interpretation of the openness of the society that Bergson postulates. The non-linearity of evolution that was of such fundamental importance for him requires choosing intuition rather than intellect as the main source of knowledge, and this always leaves room for the most unexpected turns in the history of civilization. Such a society is truly as unpredictable as life itself. Life, faced with cooling down and freezing in matter as well as intellect, tries to reignite itself. Therefore, from time to time, living history explodes any and all ideological dogmas — not only in traditional society, but also in democracy and liberalism. As soon as democracy, which for Bergson is progressive compared to caste society, becomes more static and intellectual, it turns into a dogma, social life will explode and open up new horizons.

Hence why Bergson's ideas have been seized upon by so many on the left — Bergson was one of the main sources of inspiration for the Postmodernist Gilles Deleuze. Bourgeois democracy is more in sync with life than medieval hierarchy, but even democracy is capable of degenerating, after which it will be necessary to carry out a new — this time anti-bourgeois — revolution. In order for society to be open, from time to time it needs to be changed beyond recognition and observe the multi-linear nature of creative evolution. As follows, the "open society" should never be locked into one ideology. Sooner or later, life itself and its impulse will destroy liberalism and its dogmas. This is demanded by openness, according to Bergson. Understood in this way, the history of evolution can have no end — like life itself.

Bergson's "Open Society" Viewed from the Right

For Traditionalists, of course, Bergson is a thoroughly modern author, and despite his appeal to "consciousness" and even "supra-consciousness," his ideas and his peculiar, horizontal Platonism (which inspired one of the greatest historians of philosopher, Étienne Gilson, who attended Bergson's course on Plato) exclude the dimension of eternity and are completely bound to becoming. Hence Bergson's typical interpretation of the Middle Ages and his belief in progress, which he justifies with the concept of "creative evolution."

However, if we interpret the "open society" in Bergson's spirit, then why not propose that the unpredictability of the vital impulse might lead mankind to realizing that the dogma of liberalism and the "open society" in the interpretations of Popper or Fukuyama (with the completely anti-Bergsonian "end of history") might in turn be overcome? Life might very well spill over into something illiberal, and there is nothing that forbids us from turning towards a conservative revolution instead of mere conservatism (as something purely intellectual, to apply the terminology of Bergson's position). If liberalism becomes an obstacle to life and elevates its postulates into untouchable dogmas, then it shall be overcome.

Thus, the theory of the "open society" which Bergson introduced and interpreted might very well be applied, albeit with caveats and adjustments, and even somewhat outside of its original context, to the anti-liberal non-conformism of the right. This brings us to the topic of "Postmodernity viewed from the right" which is in and of itself very interesting and which I am preparing to explore more fundamentally. After all, who claims that liberals are more intuitive and closer to the primal element of life than anti-liberals?! Everything is always different, and many organicist philosophers have adhered to conservative views — after all, life also needs to be preserved. This means that the fight against Social Darwinism, an ideology most fully represented by none other than liberal circles today, is a matter of preserving life. Thus, we arrive at the interesting thesis of a true "open society" against the dogmatic, pseudo-open society.

Karl Popper

We encounter an altogether different interpretation of the "open society" in the works of the Austrian-British philosopher Karl Popper. Unlike Bergson, who sympathized with the left, Popper was a convinced and consistent liberal, and a dogmatic one at that. Popper was a follower of another theorist of neoliberalism, the Austrian philosopher Friedrich von Hayek. But Hayek himself was still more cautious about making liberalism something universally obligatory, and instead he focused his criticism on totalitarian ideologies. He retained a certain respect for existing traditions, although he did not attach any decisive importance to them.

For Popper, however, social progress achieves its culmination in bourgeois democracy and its further development — after overcoming traditional society and the end of the Middle Ages — takes place in the struggle against anti-democratic versions of the ideologies of Modernity, first and foremost communism and fascism. Popper considers "fascism" and "communism" to be totalitarian regimes that close society and establish dictatorship instead of democracy. Therefore, the "open society" is only and exclusively liberalism, that is the absolutization of individualism and the "individual parts of life" of which Solovyov spoke.

This is a completely different "open society" than Bergson's. It becomes dogmatic and ideologically intolerant of anyone who calls into doubt its axioms, postulates, and laws. Hence, Popper titled his book *The Open Society and Its Enemies*, because whoever dares to disagree with Popper automatically becomes an enemy who is slated to be destroyed — at the very least morally. There is no more multi-linearity, and that means no more openness in development: liberalism is the only line along which the progress of civilization unfolds. The latter statement of Popper's alone looks absolutely peremptory and totalitarian. In order to understand Popper and his interpretation of the "open society," let us take a more attentive look at his philosophy.

Falsificationism and the Critique of Logical Positivism

The first half of the 20th century was a time of rethinking the meaning and role of metaphysics. Positivist attacks on metaphysics made it necessary to clarify the relationship and proportions between metaphysics and science. The Vienna Circle and the positivists in general accused metaphysics of being incapable of posing real problems, and they characterized its principles and notions as meaningless.

But Karl Popper constructed his doctrine in polemic with the logical positivists as well.[221] First of all, Popper does not agree with the positivist principle of verification as the main criterion for the scientific or non-scientific quality of a theory. On the contrary, according to Popper, the scientific quality of a theory is determined by its refutability through experience. Knowledge is scientific if and only if it is potentially refutable. Philosophy and science are closely intertwined, and determining the boundaries between them necessitates close attention to analyzing the falsifiability of knowledge.

Scientific theory ought to be structured in such a way that it prohibits certain kinds of events. In such a case, the detection of such events falsifies a theory. A scientific text ought to be built on three kinds of judgements:

1. Singular existential statements or fixations of fact;
2. Purely existential statements;
3. Universal statements or scientific laws (the peculiarity of which lies in that they are formulated as prohibitions on certain empirical facts).

Purely existential statements are ruled out of science. On the whole, these principles of Popper's do not yet contradict Bergson, because Popper still insists on denying the reducibility of the whole diversity of scientific facts to criteria other than the strict intellect of the positivists. Popper's falsificationism

---

[221] Karl Popper, *Objective Knowledge: An Evolutionary Approach* (Oxford: Clarendon Press, 1979).

and that of Imre Lakatos following him expand the concept of scientificness. Now, in order for a hypothesis to be scientific, it must be accessible to rational criticism. Notions like God, Good, Will, etc., on which metaphysics is built, can neither be confirmed nor refuted, and hence are not scientific.

The Critique of Historicism

Karl Popper gives a critical evaluation of "historicism" in his works *The Poverty of Historicism* and *The Open Society and Its Enemies*. Popper reasons thusly: The historicist approach to analyzing history presumes that history is treated like a process under the influence of natural or supernatural laws which are independent of and not subject to man, which allows for one to speak of a certain logic of history, to divide it into phases, periods, formations, and isolate paradigms which can be studied, predicted, and used to project the future. Popper deemed St. Augustine, Marx, Spengler, Toynbee, and other philosophers of various epochs to have been adepts of "historicism."

Historicism can be based on economic or theistic principles determining history, yet what is common to all of them is faith in "historical necessity" and the identification of "tendencies" or "laws" of development within history. In his critique of historicism, Popper naturally has a negative attitude towards historicist predictions of the future, which are inappropriate and resemble the unsuccessful past attempts at prophecy.

Replacing "Laws" with "Tendencies"

Popper writes:

> The hope, more especially, that we may someday find the 'laws of motion in society', just as Newton found the laws of motion of physical bodies, is nothing but the result of these misunderstandings. Since there is no motion of society in any sense similar or analogous to the motion of physical bodies, there can be no such laws.[222]

---

[222] Karl R. Popper, *The Poverty of Historicism* (New York: Harper&Row, 1964), 115.

And further:

> In order to avoid misunderstandings, I wish to make it clear that I believe that both Comte and Mill have made great contributions to the philosophy and methodology of science: I am thinking, especially, of Comte's emphasis on laws and scientific prediction, of his criticism of an essentialist theory of causality; and of his and Mill's doctrine of the unity of scientific method. Yet their doctrine of historical laws of succession is, I believe, little better than a collection of misapplied metaphors.[223]

Thus, Popper believes that the delusion of historicism's advocates is taking "tendencies" to be universal "law." Tendencies are important, but they are only material for further study and they can be seen as singular "existential" ascertainments, but not universal laws.

From Popper to Shigalev

In the critique of historicism and scientism in Popper's understanding of society, we can see a call for the very same openness that we found in Bergson. In this lies the identity of both philosophers' theses on the "open society." But there is an important difference here.

In his approach to science, Popper defends something quite analogous to the "life impulse," and he rejects prescriptive dogma. On this count, he is consistent. But by transferring this principle onto society and formulating liberal ideology, he runs into a paradox: the refusal to prescribe any ban or restrictions on certain views, of which the essence of classical liberalism consists, imperceptibly turns with Popper into prohibitive measures against those whom he classifies as "enemies of the open society."[224] It turns out that only he who agrees with the basic principles of liberalism, that is, with its very definite interpretation of freedom, can be free. Whoever thinks otherwise is deliberately placed into the category of those deprived of any

---
223 Ibid. 119.

224 Karl Popper, *The Open Society and Its Enemies* (Princeton: Princeton University Press, 2020).

rights. Thus, protest against any prescriptiveness and any historicism ends in the harsh directive to follow the norms of liberal ideology, for the latter is seen as the crown of historical progress and development.

Later, this paradox of the totalitarian nature of the "open society" will become even more exacerbated, and in the case of Popper's student, George Soros, it will acquire a genuinely extremist character. The prophecy of Dostoevsky's *Devils*, where one of the heroes, the utopian Shigalev, reasons that "coming out of unlimited freedom, I end with unlimited despotism," comes true, this time in the liberal environment.

The Paradox of Liberalism

In Popper, this important paradox of liberalism reaches its apogee. The openness originally postulated by Popper and Bergson was oriented towards not creating artificial obstacles in the way of the "flow of life," especially by not allowing for the absolutization of rational, purely intellectual knowledge or projects. In his ideas on the philosophy of science and the criteria for science, Popper continued to follow this interpretation of 'openness'. At this point, there is no sharp contradiction between these two philosophers.

But as soon as Popper moves onto society and projects onto it the laws he defended with regards to the openness of the scientific method (falsificationism significantly expands the scope of science compared to verificationism), the whole picture changes. Bergson generally refrained from granting any normativity to his ideal of the "intuitive society" as the apogee of openness. Life can take one turn or another. Fragmentation into individuals (civil society) might not necessarily be the crowning peak of social progress. Just as the many in the sixth hypothesis of Plato's *Parmenides* dialogue can form a new whole out of the particular, so too can society switch from a bourgeois democracy into a holistic system, such as to socialism or, theoretically, nationalism. The movement of life is not subordinate to rationality, and division might be one phase before the next round of integration.

Popper, however, following his teacher Hayek's critique of the very idea of a "project," rejects any holism as an artificial, violent, and thus "totalitarian" project. He turns out to be a convinced supporter of the seventh hypothesis of Plato's *Parmenides*, which rejects the formation of one out of many and leaves the many as simply the many in order to avoid the totalitarian holism of the one.[225] This is where Popper departs from his own views on science and his demand for the freedom of scientific hypotheses and even contradicts his own ban on projects in the social domain: if we believe liberal democracy to be the only possible, normative type of society, then an insurmountable barrier is already placed in the way of the evolution of life. Hayek understood this difficulty, and therefore his liberalism was evolutionary. Sure, he opposed other projects — both right and left —, but he did not directly defend the liberal project. Popper goes exactly down this road and declares anyone who does not agree with his interpretation of the open society to be an enemy. Liberalism itself becomes totalitarian, and the openness of such a society is not only dubious, but non-existent, illusory. Therefore, we have a model liberal concentration camp in which everyone is free to be a liberal, but no one is free to be anything else.

Thus, if Bergson's "open society" is still somehow compatible with Traditionalism — even though for Traditionalism Being is within the boundaries of the One, i.e., within the five first hypotheses of Plato's *Parmenides* — then Traditionalism

---

[225] This is addressed in the nine hypotheses in Plato's *Parmenides*. The first five hypotheses are based on acknowledging the One as preceding everything else. They are formulated thusly: 1. The One, 2. The One-Many, 3. The One and Many, 4. Many and the One, 5. Many. Next follow four hypotheses which derive from the Many and negate the preceding One: 6. From Many follows the One, 7. From Many the One does not follow, 8. From Many follows Many, 9. the Many does not follow from the Many.

is decidedly incompatible with Popper's "open society," or, in other words, with liberal totalitarianism.

These are the conclusions I've reached over the course of comparing Bergson and Popper's ideas of the "open society." But, in the spirit of old democracy, I do not insist on them, and I am ready to discuss other points of view.

***

Dark Deleuze:
A Postmodern Reading of Leibniz's Monadology

Enlightenment and Post-Enlightenment: Light or Dark?

The dialogue between Postmodernism and classical philosophy is as exotic and strange as Postmodernity itself. At the core of Postmodern philosophy lies a bizarre and complex strategy: it is necessary to completely dismantle Modernity, leaving no stone unturned, but at the same time it is necessary to go even further away from the Tradition that Modernity opposed, and to continue the cause of progress. The aspiration to become even more progressive than the thinkers of Modernity is generally what most catches the eye. It is as if Postmodernists simply shift Modernity into the place of Tradition and find themselves in the position of being the true vanguard. This approach is taken by the so-called "left accelerationists" (Mark Fischer, Nick Srnicek, etc.). For them, the classics of Postmodern philosophy, and first and foremost Gilles Deleuze, are something "luminous," "liberating," and "revolutionary." But there are also the "right accelerationists" (Nick Land, Reza Negarestani, etc.) who understand all the ambiguity of Postmodernism and do not look away from its dark sides — after all, by crushing Modernity, the Postmodernists are also kicking away the stool from under their own feet at the gallows, as progressivism and faith in a brighter future no longer have any grounds. This also affects their reading of Deleuze, in which "right accelerationists" begin to distinguish completely dark sides. Thus is born the figure of "dark Deleuze," whose overtly destructive work to dismantle the illusions of New Time (Modernity) appears in a rather infernal optic. Welcome to "Dark Enlightenment."

In any case, Postmodernists of both left and right do not turn to Tradition, but their reading of Postmodernity itself is polar. Accordingly, the Postmodernists' attitude towards the founders of the philosophy of New Time (Modernity) looks completely different. I will try to examine the relationship between two such iconic figures of philosophy: Leibniz and Deleuze. One belongs to the beginning of Modernity, the other summated its outcomes and marked the blossoming of Postmodernism. I will not issue a final judgment on how Deleuze is correctly understood, whether as dark or as light. I will simply try to trace what Deleuze's system turns "monadology" into.

Monads

In his *Monadology*, Leibniz begins his philosophical study with an examination of complex objects in which monads are the simple substances, the "atoms" (spiritual atoms or units of being).[226] Every complex substance is defined as an aggregate (a collection) of simple substances. Leibniz gives a detailed description of monads: they come into being through creation (by God) and they die by destruction (both processes occur instantly and immediately as a *tout d'un coup*, which is to say that they are not put into any slice of time).

Monads differ from one another — there are no identical monads, just as there are no internally identical beings. Monads cannot be affected by substances or accidents from the outside — they "have no windows" through which something might enter or exit. Monads are identical (or semantically close to) the notion of entelechy. Leibniz writes: "All simple substances or created Monads might be called Entelechies, for they have in them a certain perfection (ἔχουσι τὸ ἐντελές); they have a certain self-sufficiency (αὐτάρκεια) which makes them the source of their own internal activities and, so to speak, incorporeal automata."[227]

All monads are created by God through the boundless radiations of His divinity. A monad is an imitation of the perfection of God, but it is only a copy, a reflection. Leibniz

---

[226] Gottfried Wilhelm Leibniz, *The Monadology*, trans. Robert Latta (1898) [http://home.datacomm.ch/kerguelen/monadology/].

[227] Ibid., §72.

divides all monads into simple and complex. It is in the analysis of complex monads that Leibniz introduces the concept of the soul, which he defines as a complex monad endowed with distinctive perception and accompanying memory. A complex monad such as the soul possesses a body and constitutes the living being.

Matter and Monad

I would like to examine the relation between the body and the soul as a relation between matter (corporeality) and the monad (the complex type). The soul (a complex monad) and the body (as the organic aggregate of a monad) are inseparable from each other. As Leibniz writes: "nor are there souls entirely separate [from bodies] nor unembodied spirits [genies sans corps]. God alone is completely without body."

Leibniz constructs a strict hierarchy of the subordination of the body to the soul similar to Plato's state. The body is the "state of monads," while the soul is the central monad, the ruler of all other monads. The throne is a dark, windowless room towering above corporeality. At the same time, the ruling monad and the body-state are absolutely inseparable and indivisible (even with changes to the body). This point of view is the opposite of Malebranche's occasionalism, according to which there is no necessary connection and interaction between the body and the soul. The soul and the body might not interact directly (the soul only thinks the body, but has no direct influence on it, and the same goes for the body on the soul), but only through some intermediary, which for Malebranche is God.

The Hierarchy of Monads

The idealism of Leibniz's psycho-physical concept is manifest in the strict hierarchization of monads, in the setting up of a ruling spirit (a complex monad) over the domain of the corporeal and other micro-monads. Leibniz writes that "there are infinite levels of life among monads, some of which are more or less dominant over others."[228] Here we are dealing with a vertical topology wherein the highest is God, who creates monads which are strictly hierarchical (from blind monads to animals to human spirits). Monads are the spiritual principles of things, they are not material. The psycho-physical problem in Lebiniz's concept can be explained in the spirit of idealism. In the foreword to the French edition of *Monadology*, Michel Fichant defines Leibniz's idealism as a "monadic idealism" which holds that substances are spiritual and God has established harmony between them.[229]

On the whole, Leibniz's picture, albeit described in the language of modern philosophy that began to unfold with Descartes, continues the medieval concept of God, the soul, and hierarchy. "Monadic idealism" can be considered a philosophy of Tradition framed in the intellectual context of Modernity, of New Time. If we consider Leibniz's monadology from Leibniz's own standpoint, then it is a continuation of vertical thinking dressed in a new language. However, this already imparts his ideas with a certain strangeness. This brings us directly to the 'baroque' style, which literally means "strange," "irregularly-shaped."

Leibniz's Monadic Structures and Deleuze

This strangeness is precisely what the greatest philosopher of Postmodernism, Gilles Deleuze, took up. In his book *The Fold: Leibniz and the Baroque*, Deleuze proposes to view Leibniz's psycho-physical topology through the lens of baroque style and therefore considers Leibniz's doctrine on the interaction of the soul and body in the context of his era's architectural canons and style. For Deleuze, the main, philosophically significant characteristics of baroque are: (1) "two floors" and (2) "pleats" (the first floor being the pleats of matter) and "folds" (the

228 G.W. Leibniz, "Principles of Nature and Grace Based on Reason," trans./ed. Jonathan Bennett, *Early Modern Texts* (2017), 3 [https://www.earlymoderntexts.com/assets/pdfs/leibniz1714a.pdf].

229 G.W. Leibniz, *Discours de métaphysique suivi de Monadologie et autres textes*, trans./ed. Michel Fichant (Paris: Gallimard, 2004).

second floor being the folds of the soul). Deleuze applies these characteristics to Leibniz's psycho-physical model. The two floors communicate with each other. The upper floor (dark and without windows to the outside world) is the floor of rational souls, the higher monads, while the lower floor is that of matter, although souls — sensual ones as well as those of animals — might be present there. Deleuze writes:

> It is the upper floor that has no windows. It is a dark room or chamber decorated only with a stretched canvas diversified by folds, as if it were a living dermis. Placed on the opaque canvas, these folds, cords, or springs represent an innate form of knowledge, but when solicited by matter they move into action.[230]

The lower floor in baroque architecture contains the "reception rooms" or "common rooms." Deleuze characterizes this lower floor as containing "several small openings: the five senses (four windows and a door)."[231]

Both floors are "inextricably" linked to each other. Up top are the folds of the soul, down below are the pleats of matter. It is interesting that Deleuze applies the metaphor of a marble slab with stains to both floors. Deleuze thus projects innate ideas onto corporeality.

Monads Eluding Rule

In characterizing the relationship between the soul and the body in Leibniz, Deleuze speaks of their inseparable "floating" between two floors. But Deleuze's attention is mainly directed not to the second floor, but to the smaller monads. Deleuze examines the hierarchization of monads into higher, rational ones, and lesser, subordinate ones. The rational monad ("with a knot") takes into its environment an infinite number of micro-nomads (in the case of the body, such micro-monads would be the monad of the liver, the monad of the heart, etc.) as a "community" over which it rules. Monads are present in the

---

[230] Gilles Deleuze, *The Fold: Leibniz and the Baroque*, trans. Tom Conley (London: The Athlone Press, 1993), 4.

[231] Ibid., 5.

body through the projections that manifest as dominant at some point in the body.

Deleuze then shifts his study towards the ruling monad, the lower members in the hierarchical scheme, the subordinate monads subject to being ruled over. Gradually, the architectural metaphor becomes predominant in the interpretation of Leibniz, and his style — the new language of which I spoke — begins to overshadow and crowd out the content. The vertical collapses almost in slow motion, like the Leaning Tower of Pisa, although Deleuze never loses sight of Leibniz's hierarchy. This hierarchy merely seems to be slightly lopsided, like a rotten stem in a field propped up by wires.

From Monad to Nomad: Chess and Go

Here we are faced with the problem of power and rulership, the central notion subject to critique in Postmodernist philosophy. Can there be a situation in which the monads elude dominance? Deleuze's project is to discover in Leibniz's rigid system some kind of system failure whereby the monads might be unchained ("untied out of the knot") and no longer subordinated to the rule of the "dark room" on the second floor (the main ruling monad). Deleuze tries to find the possibility for a revolt of the micro-monads against the integrality of the central ruling monad. This is what Deleuze in his *Thousand Plateaus* calls the uprising of the "rhizome" (a tuber system) against the Tree (the root), a mutiny of thin roots in a disorderly branching against the trunk that is vertically directed upwards with a small number of branches.[232]

Is Deleuze's idea nothing other than an attempt at eliminating the idealism in Leibniz's psycho-physical model? At destroying the second floor and putting it in the "common rooms"? This attempt is Delueze's "anti-idealist" revision of Leibniz's psycho-physical concept. This revision and elevation of the first floor without the second (or reduction of the second to the first)

---

232 Gilles Deleuze and Felix Guattari, *A Thousand Plateaus: Capitalism and Schizophrenia*, trans. Brian Massumi (London: Continuum, 2003).

is carried out via the concept of the "body without organs" and the "nomad." The "nomad" is a rhizomatic, mobile instance of the spontaneous creation of unobliging, short narratives that take shape over the course of the erosion of structures. This is the basic concept of post-structuralism. The nomad is contrasted to the monad as the opposition of the mobile and nomadic to the strictly fixed and immobile.

Deleuze and Guattari put forth numerous examples to lucidly illustrate this opposition: for instance, the types and organization of games among settled and nomadic peoples. The game of chess is a settled game, and sedentary life, according to Deleuze and Guattari, is a sign of Western European philosophical culture. Chess has a strictly delineated playing field, coded space, "system of places," and strict rules for arranging the pieces on the board. This contrasts the nomadic game of Go, in which there is no strict delineation of the playing field and space is visually de-territorialized (with the scattering of elements, the throwing pebbles, giving a situational, vague uncertainty of space). In chess, there is a hierarchy in the titles and functions of the elements and figures, i.e., the king, queen, pawn, etc., which reproduce vertical power. In the game of Go, all of the figures and elements (the stones) are equal. Chess preserves the model of the two-floor topology: the laws, machines, and monads of control are transferred to corporeality and a hierarchy is established (the body, the chessboard, the king-monad's state, the bishop, rook, pawns, etc.) In Go, we have only one dimension, one floor, no strict laws, and only the situational transformation of space (the absence of any dominant monadic authority, for "the rhizome connects any point to any other point"[233]).

Applied to Leibniz's topology, this may be expressed as follows. The upper floor is always characterized by its creation of wholeness, while the lower floor yields the material for this creation. The top (the dark room) imposes mechanical laws and organs to structure an organism that is realized in the body

---
233 Deleuze and Guattari, *Thousand Plateaus*, 21.

(it is interesting that the light comes from the dark, that the bodily becomes luminous thanks to the dark monad).

In the concept of the "body without organs," Deleuze proposes to transfer the creative potential from the upper floor to the lower one, to make corporeality the creative structure. Following Antonin Artaud's definition of the "body without organs" ("The body is the body, it is all by itself, and has no need of organs"), Deleuze speaks of the inevitability of the body shedding (losing) its organs.[234] Instead of the two-story topology of Leibniz's interpretation of the relation between soul and body, we have only one corporeal floor that is closed unto itself and which, over the course of this self-closing, generates the simulacra of consciousness (the psyche). Deleuze's corporeality is not ordered as it is in Leibniz. "The BwO [body without organs] is not at all the opposite of the organs. The organs are not its enemies. The enemy is the organism."[235] The "body without organs" that escapes the control of the rational monad is a system of streams, points, and micro-monads that is formless, unstructured, ungenerated. The organism (the two-story building) is declared to be an instrument of suppression and a "dungeon of life" and is abolished as a factor of violence. In Leibniz's baroque building, the servants and residents of the cellar rise up in revolt.

The Elimination of Hierarchies: Desiring-Machines

Let us examine more closely the floor that remains after Deleuze's demolition of the Leibnizian model's building. The corporeal floor is distinguished by the abolition or elimination of hierarchies: for instance, the monad of the heart and the monad of the liver are absolutely equal and are not assembled into the hierarchical chain of an organism. Here we are dealing with democracy (in the network sense, a global network), equality, and biopolitics. Moreover, the very integrity of the

---

234 Gilles Deleuze, *The Logic of Sense*, trans. Mark Lester and Charles Stivale, ed. Constantin V. Boundas (New York: Columbia University Press, 1990).

235 Deleuze and Guattari, *Thousand Plateaus*, 158.

monads of individual organs is called into equation — they, too, after all, contain even smaller components. This comes close to Spinoza's model of the "liberated multitude," which is based on a fundamental pantheism, an identity of God and nature (*deus sive natura*). While preserving atomic entities to some extent, the monads/machines and their mechanical principles, we no longer have a whole (i.e., a community of micro-monads united under the authority of the ruling monad).

This condition is very precisely expressed by Deleuze and Guattari's concept of the "desiring-machine" (*machine désirante*). The desiring-machine is a hybrid lifeform project in which the mechanical is no longer opposed to the natural and spontaneous. The suppressive authority of consciousness is placed close to the classical object of suppression, i.e., desire (*libido*), in this post-Freudian topology.

Leibniz and Deleuze: The Beginning and End of Modernity

Deleuze's interpretation of Leibniz reveals two psychophysical models: the baroque (New Time, Modernity), and Postmodernity. If Postmodernity is oriented towards the concept of the "body without organs," then by analogy we could call the concept that constitutes the axis of Leibniz's monadological study the "organs without a body." In idealism, the rational dominates over the corporeal (the material) in the relation between the psychic and the physical, and the corporeal is therefore not assigned any independent ontological status. Leibniz's concept represents the idealist philosophy of Modernity's partial preservation of the medieval religious orientation and its partial, sometimes unconscious anticipation of the later ultimate "disenchantment of the world" (Max Weber). At the dawn of the New Time of Modernity, nature is declared to have been written by God in mathematical language. In later Modernity, the figure of God is subject to harsh critique, is taken out of the scope of considerations, and is subsequently eliminated altogether (in Nietzsche's nihilism). Matter, on the contrary, is ontologized through the recognition of gravity let into the first floor of the baroque structure.

Deleuze is at the other end of the philosophical cycle of New Time across from Leibniz, when Modernity's mission to liberate (from any ideal) was almost complete. Henceforth, strictly immanentist models of psychology in the likes of "schizoanalysis" begin to confidently dominate and eliminate, at least in theory, any vertical topologies such as those inherent in idealism.

Deleuze's encounter with Leibniz is an interesting dimension of the path from the open theistic idealism of the Middle Ages to the complete psycho-physical immanentism of poststructuralist and ultra-democratic notions of bodily consciousness which Postmodernists take out of everything even remotely resembling reason. If Leibniz (like his follower, Wolff) constructed an apologetics for power (the monad's priority over corporeality), then Deleuze's Postmodernism proclaims the slogan, "Do not fall in love with power!", and advocates the complete destruction of authority (the decomposition of structures into nomadic atoms). Taken in an ontological and metaphysical sense in Deleuze's thought, revolting against the totalitarian axis of the monad's power is supposed to lead to a sovereign democracy of nomads, the triumph of the rhizome, and the liberation of the body without organs from all restrictions.

What is of interest in Deleuze's *The Fold: Leibniz and the Baroque* is the dialogue between these polar opposite philosophical approaches, which takes place in the context of what is outwardly common to both thinkers, but which fundamentally differs in the foundational interpretation of the language of modern philosophy. The Postmodernist Deleuze's aim is to bring down Leibniz's already slightly rickety baroque philosophical structure. Alas, one could admit that he indeed managed to do so.

***

- AFTERWORD -

Daria Dugina: Philosophy as Destiny

Life as "Noetic Ascesis"

Life in the modern world presupposes and even demands of us enormous effort of mind — and not just in everyday affairs and external motions, but precisely inner, intellectual, mindful effort, "noetic ascesis" [*umnoe delanie*] as it was called in the monastic tradition of the "holy fathers." This praxis of the Mind, the Intellect, is necessary not only for the sake of "discriminating," or *diakresis*, as the Greek Platonists said, that is, for distinguishing one thing from another, the worthy from the worthless, good from evil, the accidental from the fateful, but also for the sake of something that is of much grander scale and significance. We live in a damaged, twisted world, in a broken civilization. Its very backbone, the idea of the vertical, the hierarchy of the supreme, is broken. Intellectual effort is needed in order to restore this world to its attuned, hierarchical proportions, the very model of which was established by Plato and Platonism.

The Imperative of Platonism

Daria Dugina chose the pseudonym "Platonova" in honor of the greatest philosopher of all time, and she devoted herself to studying Platonism and the works of the Platonist philosophers. In his time, the American philosopher Alfred Whitehead said that all of world philosophy is nothing other than a series of footnotes to Plato. By engaging Platonism, we find our way into the center of the typhoon, the heart of the problem of the generation of meaning, of the creation of the structures of thought, the mind, history, cultures, civilizations. Daria knew this and she deliberately chose this path.

The path of the Intellect is dangerous. People fear the Intellect like fire. The city authorities of Athens once executed the most intelligent thinker of Greece and all mankind, Socrates, and the inhabitants of Alexandria murdered the Neoplatonic philosopher Hypatia. Today, the Western global elites have a ferocious and totalitarian hatred for free thinking. They are killing and they intend to kill thinkers, philosophers, wisemen, prophets, and geniuses — anyone who thinks about the fates of mankind and is not in unison with the group of villains who have seized modern global discourse and are generally preparing to close the project of the Human Being, to turn man into a clown, a computer, information in the cloud. Daria Dugina knew that this rational obscurantism must be resisted first and foremost by the Intellect — with thought, idea, concept, design, and project. She chose Platonism as her reference point in this struggle. Why?

The Two-Floor Harmony of Platonism

Plato built a harmonious and coherent, two-floor world where ideas, models, and the forms of things and events of the world are on the upper floor, while on the lower dwells matter and things themselves exist by beholding the Logoi-Ideas and imitating them as celestial models. This is how the hierarchy of Heaven and earth was structured — a hierarchy of ideas at the head of which shines the Idea of the Good or the One, that which is inexpressible, ineffable, and transcends everything that can and even cannot be thought about it. Platonism described the intellectual structure of the world as open on the top, from above. In this structure, the human being is located in the middle of the vertical hierarchy as a kind of intermediary between worlds. Contemplating the ideas, man beheld how the world was built, how things are produced, and the repetition of the heavenly archetypes. This model of the world existed for millennia. Its structures, hierarchies, and ladders of ascent and descent are reflected in all the world religions. Within this model, man is the "ascending being" (ascending to the Spirit, the Good, Truth,

Beauty, Justice, the One) and at times the "returning being" (as in Plato's "Myth of the Cave") who then once again ascends up Jacob's ladder, the ladder of spiritual perfections. This ascent of Man, his perfection, his transubstantiation, and, finally, in the Orthodox tradition, his deification, is the aim of life.

Becoming and the Dark Side of Freedom

But the world decays with time, and man becomes dumber. In one way or another came Modernity, and after it Postmodernity, in which we partially dwell today. The 20th-century prophet of Postmodernity, the French philosopher Gilles Deleuze, falsified Plato in the margins of his works, fundamentally distorting the Platonic picture of the world. Deleuze argues that Platonism does not speak of a dualism of ideas and matter, but of a duality within matter itself, between that which heeds the ideas, copies, and that which eludes the influence of the ideas altogether, hides from them, and evades the influence of the intellectual model, the Logos. In the world, this philosopher says, there are things which slip away and avoid any form, any determination. He calls this "pure becoming," "limitlessness," the "shadow of the copy," the "copy without an original," or the "simulacrum." According to Deleuze, it is not the case that such undefinable things and essence which evade the idea, the Logos, have no measure at all, but rather that this measure is not above, but below them, in the underground of their existence. They dwell not in the shade of the One Creator and the highest heavenly meanings, but under the spells and hypnosis of the mindless, primal element, living in exile from the order that things in the Platonic universe acquire from the Logos, from the world of the Intellect and ideas.

Gilles Deleuze: Copies and Simulacra

Thus, Deleuze admits two worlds. One is administered by the World Intellect, which receives models and forms from the celestial sphere. This world is formed by reality, fixed determinacy, and therefore the world of "pauses" and "stops" in Deleuze's clumsy language, which seem to him to be dilapidated, unfree, undynamic, and even totalitarian. The second world is new and beautiful, it comes to the aid of the old, bringing with it slippery semantics, the flowing, light element of a stream, and "rebellious becoming" without any stops and pauses.

Through the immobility and inflexibility of the old hierarchical world of ideas and things (and here it is not difficult to intuit that Deleuze is dealing with the double *topos* of the Platonic world), Deleuze's second world emerges like an apparition — it is a realm of paradoxical becoming, where everything is mobile to such an extent that the meanings of the past and the future are identical, and "before" and "after," "more" and "less," cause and effect, excess and deficiency, crime and punishment all merge together in an inexplicable accord and glischroidic interconversion. We find ourselves in a world without limits to be transgressed, and therefore in a world of crime and lawlessness. This is a world of the mutual reversibility of events, a place where cause is problematized. Deleuze is fascinated by the thought that, in addition to formed things and beings, there exist indefinite events, on the surface of which even smaller events, which he calls "effects," frolic around. Effects are mobile, light, ungrounded, arbitrary, and spontaneous.

The Human as a "Little Event"

"What is a wound on the surface of a body?", Deleuze asks. Is it a dense thing with its own status? It is an effect, a small incident that "doesn't even exist, but only persists in its manifestation for some time," i.e., it is becoming, it possesses a minimum of being.

What, then, are we ourselves? Deleuze prompts us: "Is human life, including our I, our inner peak which we revere as the subject, our world, our dream, merely a blind stirring on the surface of some event? We are merely a light crackling on the surface of being, the rustle of a piece of paper, like fog wafting around the edges of things." Deleuze continues: "What is the redness of iron, the redness of a face? It is a mixture: red mixed in with green. We, too, are mixtures, mingling in sympathy or hatred with things and each other."

Deleuze's "world of events and effects" mixes, coagulates, and flows. Within it, we move about within the boundless aeon of becoming.

There is no Whole in the world, the master of French rhetoric says, and there is nothing of the sort that would order and be responsible for the metamorphoses of things and ourselves. There are no causes and no reason in the world. What is required of us is not being, but slipping and sliding.

The Overflows of Chaos

Deleuze's world is a journey into a Chaosmos, along which names are lost and everything that is constant, including knowledge, is denied (for "constancy needs peace and God, and we cannot provide you with this," Deleuze remarks). This is an ephemeral universe where there is no vertical, where the symbol of the tree as a vertical axis and hierarchy is replaced with the image of the "rhizome" — a tuber, like a potato root, which sprouts out in random, unknown directions, sideways, down, sometimes even up. It is a world of limitlessness, of apeiron, which the ancient Greeks especially hated in contrast to the limit, *peiros*, that crowns and fixes a thing.

Deleuzeian becoming presupposes the melting down of language, whereby nouns are swept up by verbs as more mobile agents, and everything dissolves and disappears in becoming. Deleuze's world of becoming is a world that decomposes and mutates over the course of the disintegration of language. Since denotation was abolished even before Deleuze's philosophy, in Ferdinand de Saussure's structuralism from which Deleuze pushed off, reality turns into a purely linguistic residuality in which the semantic fabric itself, the semantic field of being, dissolves and fades away, dragging Man as the former possessor and steward of language into extinguishing along with it. The post-language that is acquired in becoming turns into inexplicable mumbling, into a momentary flash of "effect" on the molten surface of matter tumbling into the infernal depths.

It must be said that Daria Dugina reflected on Deleuze's philosophy a lot, as if succumbing to the ambiguous charm of this master. An essay she devoted to him, "Dark Deleuze," appears in this book, and she often referenced his philosophy in her talks, presentations, and lectures. I remember that she liked Deleuze's idea that we have come into this world not in order to simplify it, but to leave it no less or even more complex than it was before.

Predatory Things and the "Leaky" Subject of Object-Oriented Ontology

Today, the dissolution of the Human Being and the destabilization and dissolution of the world itself are being worked out not only in Deleuze's extravagant and perverse programs, but also among the post-Deleuzian philosophical groups of the contemporary Western "hyper-materialist realists" or "object-oriented ontologists" like Reza Negarestani, Nick Land, Graham Harman, Raymond Brassirer, Quentin Meillassoux, and others. These philosophers insist that man unjustifiably appears in classical Western philosophy as too vertical, authoritarian, and arrogant. Compared to artificial intelligence, for instance, he is extremely imperfect and vulnerable. Hence, indulging in man and his illusions of being the organizer of the universe and the genius of social progress is senseless and dangerous. Man is too burdened by the Logos. Object-oriented ontologists ask: Why are we so certain that the Human is the measure of things, the main pole of correlation? There is Nothing and there is its cycle, which is called "becoming," and the world of that being which was hitherto called "human" is characterized by indeterminacy, blurriness, fluidity, "leakiness," chaotic randomness, and this applies not only to the events of man's life, but also the state of his flimsy and unstable I. Cosmic objects, ordinary things, the Earth and its core, clamped in the vice of the frozen earth's crust, are what is truly durable and reliable in the world. Objects, although they are phenomenologically unprovable, are practically reachable: it is enough to extinguish our human Dasein and they will reveal themselves to us fully, in completely unexpected light, and most likely in the form of monsters, according to the weird-realism of Graham Harman. As long as our human presence lingers on, noumena are inaccessible. They (noumena, things) live a radically external (infernal) life that is inaccessible to us and is rather predatory, all the while as we use them and naively posit ourselves to be their lords and masters. But the great uprising of things is coming! — says Bruno Latour. Man, with all his ephemeral claims, abilities, projects, and illusions, is insignificant. Objects ought to be liberated from man and given the freedom to create and to pursue their own cosmic trajectories. Man must be taken out of the picture, out of the way of the earth's core in order to release the nuclear demon inside the Earth, so that this furious, luminous entity might unite in a cosmic dance with the Sun — such is the dream of the American philosopher of Iranian origin, Reza Negarestani, following the English philosopher Nick Land.

Daria Dugina attentively studied the texts of contemporary object-oriented ontologists, and she polemicized with them in her articles and speeches. We can even recall one curious case. Daria once participated in an online presentation of the Russian translation of Reza Negarestani's book in Moscow. This episode became widely known after, in the middle of intellectual discussion, one of Dasha's admirers offered her his heart and asked for her hand. Daria politely promised to consider his proposal, but only after this suitor of conservative and Traditionalist views mastered the philosophy opposite to his own and learned Negarestani's *Cyclonopedia* by heart. This whole episode happened live in front of the astonished Iranian-American philosopher.

Surfaces on the Attack

As we can see, the theme of the insolvency and futility of the human being raised by the adepts of object-oriented ontology is synchronized with the dissolution of man in Deleuze, that subtle philosopher who proclaimed truth and true freedom not for the masses of things and huge cosmic bodies and objects, but for the weak and light effects on the surfaces of all substance. In the panorama of contemporary Western philosophy, we face a philosophical front attacking our spiritual tradition — Christian, Platonic, traditional — from different flanks. In contemporary Western philosophy's attack on us, we find no verticals, no hierarchies, no forms, no ideas, no values, no objects, no essences, no subjects, no causes, no qualities, no archetypes, no *telos*, no language, no depths, no heights, no freedom, no spirit, no God. Nor does it have any place for the Human Being, who is now ordered to not go too deep and to not look up and out into the distance, not to dream, not to project, not to think, but to slip and slide and dissolve, to stick to quiet rustling and not imagining too much about himself. We are prescribed, even ordered, to remain on the surface of things, to slip and slide along the plane of events, to follow trends, agendas, and rules.

The War of Minds

I've just written that "we are ordered"! Yes, exactly! Behind the light rustle of Deleuze's cheeky discourse, we, Traditionalists, hear the heavy tread of a totalitarian imperative. Doesn't this mean that there is someone in the world who understands what rules are being put forth to us and knows that in the world there are no orders of things in themselves, but rather orders of interpretations? Under the guise of an allegedly random philosophical game, demands are imposed upon things and ourselves — doesn't this mean that someone is sticking principles and rules to us for certain standards of perception and behavior? Yes, this is precisely the case. Our intellectual opponents in the West understand this. Just as the main law of geopolitics states that "He who controls Heartland

(Middle Earth, Eurasia) rules the world," here the formula is at work that "He who controls the discourse, who sets the metalanguage, dominates everything." Do some in the West know about paradigms, about the keys to worldviews, civilizations, and cultures, the codes of history and the future of mankind? Yes, without a doubt. But they are in no hurry to share this knowledge even with their "own," not to mention those who are obviously counted among the epistemological herd.

In Russia, our answer to this question is put forth by Russian Traditionalism, which is the choice of our entire family, starting with its head. Daria Dugina's father devoted his 24-volume cycle of works, *Noomakhia*, to the study of Logoi, civilizations, and paradigms in the history of mankind. Daria grew up on this, absorbing the taste for Tradition and vertical ontologies from early childhood. Born and raised in a family of philosophers, she was and remains an integral, organic part of it. She is the ever-rising star of Russian thought.

As strange as this may sound, to all the acute questions posed to us by toxic Modernity and Western Postmodernity in decline, we have been given the key answers by the West itself, in the face of the great Western Traditionalists of the 20th century — René Guénon, Julius Evola, Mircea Eliade, Ernst Jünger, Lucian Blaga, Emil Cioran, Louis Dumont, Georges Dumézil, Alain de Benoist, and dozens of other wonderful thinkers. These authors exposed the disease of the Western spirit and tried to find a way out. They were Daria Dugina's favorite authors. She studied and thought through them. She considered the Traditionalists to be the pioneers of the Intellect in 20th-century history, the ones who tried to understand the meaning of the shipwreck of mankind as a transition from the spiritual paradigm of Tradition (antiquity, the Middle Ages, the Renaissance) to the materialist, individualist, anti-hierarchical paradigm of New Time, Modernity, and then the paradigm of the "Newest Time," Postmodernity, which washes away everything.

The themes and topics of Daria's book are of different colors and shades, but they constantly echo one another.

These themes are the paradigms of Tradition, Modernity, and Postmodernity, metaphysics, transcendence, chaos, modern nihilism, the groundlessness of modern man, and taking a new look at Traditionalism and those personalities who dared to problematize Modernity in their intuitions (or we could say, each had their own "modernity"). Among them are: Mircea Eliade and Friedrich Nietzsche, Julius Evola and Ernst Jünger, Lucian Blaga and Emil Cioran, Georges Deleuze and Louis Dumont, Plato and Plotinus, Proclus Diadochus and Julian, Donna Haraway and Tatiana Goricheva, Bergson and Popper, Camus and Bataille, Leibniz and Wolff, Berdyaev and Shestov. Over them all, gathering together and dividing their names and judgements, the thought of Plato hovers, the wind of Dionysius the Areopagite blows, and the breath of Russian Orthodox tradition is heard.

All of these thinkers and topics deeply interested my daughter. She devoted her articles, presentations, texts, and parts of her unfinished dissertation to them. Daria Dugina followed her parents, themselves Traditionalists, who have devoted their entire lives to analyzing, translating, expounding, and teaching Traditionalist doctrines and their interpolations in various spheres of the humanities: philosophy, sociology, political science, the history of philosophy, science and the arts, international relations theory, etc.

My mention of two current intellectual trends, Deleuzeianism and object-oriented ontology, is not coincidental. As remarked above, the state of mankind today demands solid effort of the Intellect, not simply detached mental work on deciphering and updating the intellectual landscape of modernity, but decisive, deep, and, I would say, initiatic insight into the essence of the modern intellectual war. War, indeed — the total confrontation of Minds in the modern world, the real battle, the *Noomakhia* as Alexander Dugin has called it. What is most surprising and unexpected to the superficial onlooker is that this war is full of battles and clashes lost and won, intellectual intelligence and reconnaissance operations, deceptive maneuvers, brain recording, and intellectual disinformation. Today, in the rhetoric of official political science, this is called "mental wars," which are the very same "Wars of the Mind," Wars of the Spirit. Our enemies in this war of Intellect know the value and price of a thought, of an idea, of a project. We, too, should know it, as did Arthur Rimbaud when he said that "spiritual battle is just as fierce as the clash of armies."

The philosophers of Tradition, Traditionalist philosophers, those who have penetrated the modern world's strategy and recognized the paradigms of Modernity and Postmodernity as foreign to us, find themselves in this ferocious battle today. These paradigms have been imposed on us by modern Western civilization with its special paths in history, with its specific principles and values of liberalism, individualism, anti-hierarchy, materialism, and conformism. These principles are foreign to Russian civilization and are not harmless to the Russian mentality. When they penetrate us, they reformat our whole spiritual tradition, our way of life, our understanding of the world. Ultimately, they destroy man as a fully-fledged being and will lead to mankind being crossed out of the Book of Life.

Daria Dugina was certain that wars are won first on the territory of the Spirit, and only then on the battlefield. She fought in the territory of the Spirit — courageously, wholeheartedly, and unhesitatingly.

Carving a Perfect Statue

For Daria, the most important idea was the Awakening and Transformation of the Human Being, Metanoia. This did not mean awakening some abstract or distant human being, but first of all herself, her friends and comrades, those close to her and those who shared her conservative and revolutionary-conservative views. In recent years, she tried to convey knowledge of Tradition to everyone who would listen: she delivered lectures on philosophy and politics in youth clubs, participated in symposiums, conferences, live streams, and on TV. She proceeded from the fact that the traditional notions of God, hierarchy, and verticality are gradually disappearing from culture in the modern world, are fading away in man's consciousness, as man himself is in decline. Then comes, as Emil Cioran wrote, the special state of man's fall, or more precisely, his falling out of time, his sinking into the recycling of one and the same thing, into the meager indivisibility of tired, suffocating, dead timelessness, "into the inert, into the absolute stagnation where the Word itself bogs down, unable to rise to blasphemy or prayer."[236] Despite this, against all odds, man must awaken and "begin to grow, and not shrink," begin to move up the vertical and carve a perfect statue out of the block of their nature. Man is called to overcome his fall and move to spiritually transform his materiality, the carnal dimensions of his soul. Daria was certain that the higher orientations within a person need to be cultivated, even compelled, by exerting immense efforts to bring both oneself and the world into a state of accepting the imperatives of the Intellect and the Spirit.

Gentle and vulnerable, subtle and poetic, but strong in will and spirit, my daughter, Daria Dugina, was on the razor's edge of the war of the Minds, on the intellectual "frontier," as she liked to say, in the midst of clashes of paradigms and duels of ideas, in the heart of the global conceptual clash of civilizations. As it turned out, these battles are no longer only intellectual, but terroristic, criminal, vile, and diabolical, at least from the side of the enemy. This means that the alternative civilization confronting us has exhausted its intellectual resources, degenerated in substance, and become a hostile pole to us cynically proclaiming the bloody law of the liberal animal pack: "man is a wolf to man." This civilization is no longer able to wage war on the level of ideas, so it substitutes ideas with their TNT equivalent.

To the question, "Who killed Daria Dugina?", there is one final and true answer: "the enemy of humankind," the modern world, the dark spirit waging eternal struggle against the Light,

---

[236] Emil Cioran, *The Fall into Time*, trans. Richard Howard (Chicago: Quadrangle Books, 1970), 181.

against the Intellect, against the sublime and the noble. It can use anything as a tool — it is not for nothing that it is called the "prince of this world," and a prince's orders are not discussed with his subjects. Those who, like Daria, are citizens of the kingdom which is not of this world, those who through death go to immortality, to the resurrection of the dead, and to the Transformation of the world and man — they are another matter.

"*Abaissement du niveau mental*"

When you talk with people in the modern world, there sometimes arises this piercing feeling that any thought, statement, or remark, insofar as there is at least some conceptual clarity or minimal structuralization to it, falls into a whirlpool, into the darkness of Plato's Cave, no sooner than it is conveyed to a person. It sometimes seems as if modern man has been completely excommunicated from reason, from the Platonic harmony of ideas, and instead avoids any notion of hierarchy, shuns any conceptual apparatus, and remains selflessly devoted to the sudden outburst of emotions, to absurd, fleeting opinions expressed indiscriminately and over trifles. In psychology, this phenomenon is called "*abaissement du niveau mental*," "reduction of mental level," and is considered to be an eloquent sign of mental disorder.

Modern Western liberalism persistently proclaims to all peoples that thinking, projects, and logic are something totalitarian and therefore undesirable, and that freedom is disorder, fluidity, chaos. This hypnosis is taken at face value by the majority. Today, it seems as if one is constantly dealing with people who are fickle, unprincipled, lacking a structured psyche, and in a pure "floating" momentariness. Modern man *en masse* avoids recognizing any principles, hierarchies, decisions, does not accept and cannot make any choice, and slips away from these most important determinations of his fate. He hopes that he has gotten free. But not here. By indulging in mindless liberation, he comes under the shadow of the "dark freedom" of the swampy underbelly of being.

The Awakening of the Angel

Daria followed Emil Cioran's idea that, in his fall and in the conditions of the modern world, man must somehow face a choice similar to the one that the angels were once offered to make — to become warriors in the ranks of the Archangel Michael or to serve the Serpent, Satan. There is a Gnostic myth cited by Cioran which describes how the angels hesitated in their decision at the crucial moment and were thus cast down to earth, to be allowed to make their decision at a later time. These angels, having lost their memory of their immaculate past, walk the earth in the conditions of entropy and degradation, finding themselves in an increasingly confused state of mind. Nevertheless, they must make their "decision" without instructions, prompts, and hints, showing only pure will and radical voluntarism. Such a will has, as Russian Traditionalists call it, a post-sacral character, i.e., it does not guarantee any positive outcome in the end, but it suggests that at the very moment of its manifestation, in the moment of "decision-making," a metamorphosis happens to man — "*la rottura del livello,*" "the rupture of level," to use Evola's term — and then man becomes non-human, something other than himself, and he discovers within himself the dimension of the Angel. Or, if he is wrong, he will stumble and be cast down into the demonic ranks of the adversary. According to Cioran, man can and must — and this is his only chance — go beyond his limits and transgress his insufficient state, a state which the 20th-century utopian theorist Ernst Bloch called "*Noch Nicht Sein,*" or "not-yet-being," with reference to Martin Heidegger's concept of "eternally (self-)withholding Being."

Daria saw this transgression of the human being as a person's passage to their own/not-own higher inner Human, like a trail to the throne of their I, their altar, their secret room, the center of their "active intellect" that is the supra-individual instance along the vertical linking the human being with the higher hierarchies of the Spirit. The Rhineland mystics wrote about this, Alexander Dugin reflects on this in his *Noomakhia*, and Daria also thought about the human being in the same mode.

She understood that a transformed human being is one who affirms their point of support in the supreme, the fundamental, in that which transcends the rational and the human; she thought of the transformed person as a special type of human being who has transfigured their individual stock by mastering their highest properties, their creative intellectual potential, the fullness of their intellect and the strength of their will. This is the Radical Subject (in the spirit of the "new metaphysics" discussed by Russian Traditionalists) who understands his place among the metaphysical ruins without support and roots, where the only foundation that remains is his own awakened higher consciousness, illuminated by the transcendental axis present in his very core, in the light of which he becomes Dasein, genuine "here-being," aspiring towards the Other.

This human metamorphosis, Daria always emphasized in her texts and lectures, takes place in the modern world in toxic conditions: philosophers describe it through the mechanism of "turning poison into medicine," "plunging into the regions of chthonic chaos,""working in black" (in alchemical transcription), as a clash of two universal principles, the battle between the Apollonian and the Cybelean, etc., the meaning of which is a test of the heroic subject and the transformation of his inner being. Seen through this perspective, it becomes clear why Daria paid special attention to those forms of human existence that anticipate inner transformation, such as the "life in danger" (Friedrich Nietzsche), "being without shelter in the risk of all risks" (Martin Heidegger), "total mobilization" (Ernst Jünger), the "political soldier" or "theological soldier" (Ernst Jünger and Geydar Dzhemal) — in other words, that which anticipates everything capable of resisting the "naked life," that animal self-identity which, according to Giorgio Agamben, turns a person into an agent of his needs alone.

Guardians of the Vertical

Daria was very sensitive to the space that is opposite to the angelic perspective of the human being — to the landscape of the Eleusinian marshes, the dark Cybelean fabric of modern culture. She read her fill of gloomy Cioran, was fascinated with subversive Deleuze and the Ahrimanic Negarestani. But she always remains, and will remain enterally, a true knight of the Vertical, of Meaning. She was a real luminous "guardian-philosopher." This is what Plato called philosophers, for they defend the most high that a person has: their intellectual dignity, thought, intellect, the right to freely understand and choose to be Human. She guarded the right of the personality and the people to not surrender their positions in preserving their ethical pillars and intellectual principles, in defending the unique cultural code of their homeland, their civilization. After all, they keep the human dream of ascending the ladder of contemplating the higher principles, they provide access to what in Platonism is called Light, Truth, Justice, Beauty, and the Good.

The book before you, Daria Dugina's *Eschatological Optimism*, was assembled out of her philosophical and historical texts, articles, speeches, presentations, parts of her thesis and her unfinished dissertation. In this book, as well as in Daria's diary, *The Depths and Heights of My Heart* (*Topi i vysi moego serdtsa*), which has recently been released by the publishing house ACT, we become witnesses to how painfully the battle against the swamps of the illusory freedom of the Great Mother Cybele is ongoing in contemporary philosophy, in the minds of modern people, youth, and in the soul of a young girl. We become witnesses to how philosophical attunement is first born, how spiritual turmoil and disappointments come to a head, and how painfully philosophical bearings of support are acquired. We notice how the light wings of a debuting philosopher grow, how thought cuts through chaos with concepts, how thought suffocates and comes to life again in extreme ascent, inevitably colliding with Deleuze's "line where reason and madness, life and death play with one another."

— Natalia Melentyeva

***

www.ingramcontent.com/pod-product-compliance
Lightning Source LLC
Chambersburg PA
CBHW071954110526
44592CB00012B/1081